ARABIC ASTRONOMY BANK

ISATION CALCULUS CANAS

MMERCIAL CORRESPONDENCE

NG CRICKET DRAWING DR

ELECTRICITY IN THE HOUSE

ENGLISH RENASCENCE TO THE

ERYDAY FRENCH TO EXPRESS YOURSELF

BOOK GARDENING GAS IN THE HOUSE GEOGRAPHY OF

ARY GERMAN GRAMMAR GERMAN PHRASE BOOK GOLF

OOD FARM ACCOUNTING GOOD FARM CROPS GOOD FARMING

FARMING GOOD GRASSLAND GOOD AND HEALTHY ANIMALS

GOOD POULTRY KEEPING GOOD SHEEP FARMING GOOD SOIL

HINDUSTANI HISTORY: ABRAHAM LINCOLN ALEXANDER THE

CONSTANTINE COOK CRANMER ERASMUS GLADSTONE AND

TON PERICLES PETER THE GREAT PUSHKIN RALEIGH RICHELIEU

··· AND HE WILL BE
YET WISER *Proverbs 9.9*

ROW Y   EMENT
N   ETTER
GIN   ANICS
ERN   ORING
OSO   HYSICS
IMBI   PUBLIC
CKO   USSIAN
TS M   AND PURPOSE SOCCER SPANISH SPE   AND
SWA   SWEDISH TEACHING THINKING TRIGO METRY
BRIT H RAILWAYS FOR BOYS CAMPING FOR BOYS AND GIRLS
R GIRLS MODELMAKING FOR BOYS NEEDLEWORK FOR GIRLS
S AND GIRLS SAILING AND SMALL BOATS FOR BOYS AND GIRLS
K FOR BOYS ADVERTISING & PUBLICITY ALGEBRA AMATEUR
3 BIOLOGY BOOK-KEEPING BRICKWORK BRINGING UP
Y CHEMISTRY CHESS CHINESE COMMERCIAL ARITHMETIC
VELLING TO COMPOSE MUSIC CONSTRUCTIONAL DETAILS
DUTCH DUTTON SPEEDWORDS ECONOMIC GEOGRAPHY
EMBROIDERY ENGLISH GRAMMAR LITERARY APPRECIATION
L ROMANTIC REVIVAL VICTORIAN AGE CONTEMPORARY
SHING TO FLY FREELANCE WRITING FRENCH FRENCH
E GEOGRAPHY OF LIVING THINGS GEOLOGY GEOMETRY
BOOK GOLF GOOD CONTROL OF INSECT PESTS GOOD
RM CROPS GOOD FARMING GOOD FARMING BY MACHINE
GOOD AND HEALTHY ANIMALS GOOD MARKET GARDENING
GOOD SHEEP FARMING GOOD SOIL GOOD ENGLISH GREEK
Y: ABRAHAM LINCOLN ALEXANDER THE GREAT BOLIVAR BOTHA
NMER ERASMUS GLADSTONE AND LIBERALISM HENRY V JOAN OF
PUSHKIN RALEIGH RICHELIEU ROBESPIERRE THOMAS JEFFERSON
ME NURSING HORSE MANAGEMENT HOUSEHOLD DOCTOR
NALISM LATIN LAWN TENNIS LETTER WRITER MALAY
ENTS WORKSHOP PRACTICE MECHANICS MECHANICAL
MORE GERMAN MOTHERCRAFT MOTORING MOTOR CYCLING
Y PHYSICAL GEOGRAPHY PHYSICS PHYSIOLOGY PITMAN'S
E PSYCHOLOGY PUBLIC ADMINISTRATION PUBLIC SPEAKING

THE TEACH YOURSELF BOOKS
EDITED BY LEONARD CUTTS

SWAHILI

TEACH YOURSELF

SWAHILI

By

D. V. PERROTT

Reader in England for the Inter-Territorial Language
(Swahili) Committee
Member of the International Institute of African
Languages and Culture

THE ENGLISH UNIVERSITIES PRESS LTD
102 NEWGATE STREET
LONDON, E.C.1

First printed 1951
This impression 1957

Printed in Great Britain for the English Universities Press, Limited,
by Richard Clay and Company, Ltd., Bungay, Suffolk

CONTENTS

My thanks are due to the Rev. Canon Hellier for reading the MS. and for his helpful comments.   D. V. P.

FOREWORD

I HAVE been asked to write a foreword to this book, and I gladly take the opportunity of doing so. It covers the whole of the Swahili language, without being in any sense a formal grammar; in fact, anyone should be able to teach himself from this book, even if ignorant of the grammatical terms used in it. Such terms there must be, partly for the sake of brevity and partly for the convenience of the index, but they are few, and all are explained fully as they occur.

The book begins by explaining the construction of a Swahili sentence, using about a dozen of the commonest words, and then goes on to show the changes caused, first by the different classes of nouns, and then by the various verb tenses. All the time new words are introduced and a useful vocabulary is built up. After each leason there is a list of new words and an exercise. The Swahili is up to date, as the author has taken account of modern tendencies shown in recent books, manuscripts and vernacular magazines, as well as the rulings of the Inter-Territorial Language (Swahili) Committee.

Swahili is an easy language, its use is widespread, and it may be that there is no language more easy to learn; there are no real difficulties of pronunciation, and none of spelling. The present writer, like the author, can from personal experience assure the reader that it is possible, and easy, to TEACH YOURSELF SWAHILI.

A. B. HELLIER.
Canon and Chancellor of Zanzibar.

INTRODUCTION

THE ALPHABET

Vowels

SWAHILI uses the same letters for the vowels as English does: a, e, i, o and u; but the pronunciation is entirely different. I know of no better way of getting the right pronunciation than by comparing the English exclamation *Oho! I say!* with its Swahili transcription, **Ohou! Aisei!** which I came across in some Swahili writing a little while ago. Say slowly, **O-ho-u A-i-se-i,** with the same pronunciation as *Oho! I say!* slightly exaggerated, and note the value of each Swahili vowel.

You will find that:

A is something like the *a* in *father*, but not quite so deep.

E is like the *a* in *say*, without the final sound we give it in English by slightly closing the mouth.

I is like the *e* in *be*. When unstressed it is the same sound as we make at the end of the English words *say* or *I*.

O is like the *o* in *hoe* before we begin to close the mouth at the end; very much like the first *o* in *Oho!*

U is like the *oo* in *too*; it is never like the *u* in *use* unless preceded by *y*.

There is no difficulty in pronouncing the Swahili *i* or *u*, and if one does get the *a* a little too deep it does not greatly matter. But much good Swahili is spoilt by pronouncing the *e* and *o* in the English way, and it is worth taking a little trouble to get the right sound—that is, to avoid closing the mouth towards the end.

Note that the sound of the vowel is the same in an unstressed syllable as in a stressed one. Do not pronounce **baba,** father, as **barber,** or **paka,** cat, as **parker.** The second syllable is pronounced lightly, but it should have the *a* sound and not *er*.

If we say the Swahili vowels in order, a e i o u, we shall notice that the mouth position of *e* is intermediate between that of *a* and *i*. This enables us to understand why *a* and *i* sometimes combine to form *e*.

Except for a few instances of combining in this way which will be noticed when we come to them, when two Swahili vowels come together each keeps its own sound:

bei, price, pronounced as in English we pronounce *bay*;
tai, eagle, as the English *tie*;
au, or, as the *ow* of *cow*.

When the two vowels come together in the middle of the word where one takes the stress, the fact that they are pronounced separately is more easily noticed:

taúni, plague; **faída,** profit; etc.

As each vowel has its own sound, it forms a separate syllable, and the words can be divided **bé-i, tá-i, á-u, ta-ú-ni, fa-í-da.**

When two similar vowels come together they are pronounced as one long vowel. This is nearly always due to the loss of a consonant, usually *l*, between them, and there were originally two separate syllables: e.g. **kaa,** sit down; **juu,** above.

Consonants

All letters which are not vowels are called consonants. The same letters are used as in English, with the exception of *c*, *q* and *x*. *C* is replaced by *s* or *k*; *q* by *k* or *kw*; and *x* by *ks*.

Swahili, like other languages, has its dialects, and small variations in the pronunciation of some consonants occur, but they are ignored in Standard Swahili, and the reader need not trouble about them here. He can pronounce the consonants as he does in English, noting the following points:

F has always the sound of *f* in *fat*, never that of the *f* in *of*, for which *v* is used in Swahili.

G is always hard like the *g* in *got;* for the soft *g* in *gin* *j* is used.

S has always the sound of the *s* in *sin;* for its sound in *is z* is used. The speaker should be careful about this when *s* comes in the middle of the word, as in *visu*, knives, and avoid giving it the sound of *z* as in *visit*.

Sometimes, as in English, a sound is expressed by two consonants put together:

CH and SH have the same sounds as in English.
TH is used for the *th* sound in *thin*, *think*, *both*, etc.
DH replaces *th* when the sound is that in *this*, *then*, *with*, etc.

These two sounds, *th* and *dh*, come from the Arabic, and many Africans find them very difficult to pronounce, and use *s* or *z* instead. The reverse takes place, too, and a speaker in his desire to be correct will use *th* or *dh* where he should have used *s* or *z*.

The letter R causes similar difficulty. It has come into Swahili from the Arabic, the vernaculars of the mainland having only an *l* varying in sound between the English *l* and *r*. Consequently, up-country Africans tend to use *l* in place of *r*, and many coast-dwellers, imitating Arabic, use *r* where they should have used *l*.

The only sounds which give any difficulty to English speakers are the Arabic KH and G̱H and the nasal consonants M and N. We need not trouble much about the Arabic sounds. KH has been replaced in Swahili by a simple H, and is only found now in proper names and in Arabic greetings. It is something like the *ch* in the Scotch *loch*, but rather rougher; but you can always pronounce it as *h*. GH is found in a very few words, such as **lugha,** language, **ghali,** expensive. It is a guttural *g* almost resembling an *r* made in one's throat. Most people give it up and just say *g*.

But the M and N sounds are very important. It will be advisable to return to the paragraphs which follow after working through Lessons 3, 4 and 5.

M occurs very frequently as the prefix of nouns where originally it was **mu.** In this position it is pronounced as a distinct syllable, like the murmured *m* in *m-m-m*, with closed lips but with a slight *u* sound before it. Sometimes it bears the stress, as in **ḿ-tu, ḿ-ke, ḿ-le.** There is no *u* sound before the *m* when it is followed by *w*, as in **mwili,**

mwana, etc. This *m* occurs in all singular nouns of the **MITI** and **WATU** classes.

But sometimes the *m* is not a separate syllable, but arises from an *n* before *b* or *v*. In this case the *m* has no *u* sound and the *b* or *v* follows quickly. This *m* arising from *n* is found at the beginning of nouns of the N class, and in the middle of many nouns, e.g. **mamba,** crocodile; its sound is that of the *mb* in *amber*. Note that **mamba** would be divided into syllables **ma-mba,** and the pronunciation of its second syllable shows you the right pronunciation in words beginning with **mb**. It is a peculiarity of Swahili, however, that in one-syllable words, like **mbu**, mosquito, the *m* is made into a separate syllable, and the word is pronounced **ṁ-bu**.

N is pronounced as the English *n*. When it precedes a consonant in the middle of a word it is pronounced as in the English words *condone, canteen*, etc. To get the right pronunciation at the beginning of a word, we can isolate the particular syllable of the English word; e.g. **co-*nd*one,** *nd*ogo; be-*nzi*ne, *nzi*ge; a-*ngo*-la, *ngo*ma, etc.

Before a vowel, *n* is found as *ny*. Be careful to make it one syllable with the following vowel, e.g. **Nya-sa,** not **Ny-a-sa.**

The only difficult sound is that written **ng'**, which is the sound of *ng* in *singer*, **not** in *finger*. It causes difficulty to many people, especially when it comes at the beginning of a word, as in **ng'ombe, ng'ambo,** etc. The best way to achieve it is to divide the word **si-nger,** and then practise the sound of the second syllable with the Swahili vowels, **ng'a, ng'e, ng'i, ng'o, ng'u.** There must be no *g* sound in it. The sound of *ng* as in *finger* is written in Swahili **nga, nge,** etc.

Syllables

All Swahili syllables are " open "—that is, they end with a vowel. Notice how these words are divided: **pe-mbe-ni; a-ska-ri; se-nti; nya-ng'a-nya.** The stress always comes on the last syllable but one. There are one or two Arabic words, such as **lázima, thúmuni,** which are exceptions to this rule, but they can be, and often are, made to conform to it.

Intonation

There are two points which should be kept in mind, especially by women, in speaking Swahili.

1. Never try to put expression into speaking or reading. It cannot be done, and to try to do so will only make all that you say unintelligible. You cannot call attention to a word by emphasising it, or express surprise or excitement as is done in English.

2. Keep your voice level. Until you can speak with the native intonation you will be much more readily understood if you prevent your voice from going up and down. And when you have caught the native intonation you will find that, even with its rises and falls, it has none of the high tones and emphasis of English. Get some African child to imitate an English person speaking Swahili, and learn from his imitation what to avoid.

Dialects

Most of the languages spoken in East, Central and South Africa belong to a family to which the name Bantu has been given. The name comes from the word " people ", found in various forms—**bantu, wantu, watu,** etc.—in many of the languages of this family.

Swahili is a Bantu language, but it has been greatly modified by the intercourse of the inhabitants of the coast regions with the traders and settlers who came to East Africa from very early times. Its name is derived from an Arabic word meaning *coasts*, and originally it was the language of the coast. But it has now spread over most of East and Central Africa, and is said to be one of the twelve great languages of the world.

Swahili developed rather differently in different parts of the coast, and we still speak of " Zanzibar Swahili " and " Mombasa Swahili ". The three important dialects are **Kiunguja,** the Swahili of Zanzibar (Unguja) which has spread through Tanganyika; **Kimvita,** the Swahili of Mombasa and parts of Kenya; and **Kiamu,** spoken on the island of Lamu and the coast opposite to it. These dialects are now unified in Standard Swahili, but many variations still remain. Kiunguja was taken as the basis for Standard Swahili, so that the variations are most noticeable on the Kenya coast.

LESSON I

THE SWAHILI SENTENCE

THE foundation of the sentence is the noun which forms the subject of the sentence—that is, the name of the person or thing about which something is said.

In English we are accustomed to changes at the end of a noun, e.g. child, children, childish, childhood, etc., and the first thing we notice about Swahili is that the changes come at the beginning. Swahili nouns consist of a stem with a prefix attached, and they fall into different classes, according to their prefixes. For instance, from the stem **-toto** are formed: **Mtoto,** child; **WAtoto,** children; **KItoto,** childish; **Utoto,** childhood; etc.

Or, to take another stem, from **-tu** we get: **Mtu,** man; **WAtu,** men; **KItu,** thing; **VItu,** things; **Utu,** manhood; **JItu,** a huge man; **MAJItu,** huge men.

It is convenient in Swahili to count **mtu** and **watu** as one class with different forms for the singular and plural, i.e. for one thing or many. So also **kitu** and **vitu** form one class, and **jitu** and **majitu** another. **Utu** makes a fourth class, but has no plural.

The second thing we have to notice is that any adjective describing the thing denoted by the noun, or any verb showing its action, has to agree with the noun. To illustrate this, we will take four nouns of the **kitu** class:

kitu	thing	vitu	things
kisu	knife	visu	knives
kiti	chair	viti	chairs
kitabu	book	vitabu	books

With these let us take five adjectives:

-kubwa, big; **-dogo,** small; **-refu,** long; **-zuri,** good; **-baya,** bad;

and five numbers:

-moja, one; **-wili,** two; **-tatu,** three; **-nne,** four; **-tano,** five.

To say *one little knife,* we begin with **kisu,** knife, and attach the same prefix **ki** to the adjective and number:

kisu kidogo kimoja.

To say, *two large books,* we begin with **vitabu,** books, and give the adjective and number the same prefix:

vitabu vikubwa viwili.

Similarly:

a small thing	**kitu kidogo**
the bad chairs	**viti vibaya**
some long knives	**visu virefu**
five books	**vitabu vitano**

NOTE:

1. The order of the words is the reverse of their order in English.

2. There is no word in Swahili for *a* or *the*; **kiti** can be *a* chair, or *the* chair; **viti,** chairs, *some* chairs, or *the* chairs; the sense must decide.

The verb has to have a similar prefix, together with another syllable to show the tense or time of the action. We will illustrate this by taking one verb, **tosha,** suffice, and three tense prefixes:

-li-	past
-na-	present
-ta-	future

Study these sentences:

One knife was sufficient.	**Kisu kimoja kilitosha.**
Three knives are enough.	**Visu vitatu vinatosha.**
The small knives will do.	**Visu vidogo vitatosha.**

In each of the verbs we see (a) a subject prefix agreeing with the noun; (b) a tense prefix, showing the time of the action, past, present or future; and (c) the stem of the verb, i.e. the unchangeable part. In dictionaries it is the stem of the verb which is given; e.g. **kilitosha** would be found under T.

A complete sentence can be expressed without the use of a noun at all; the subject prefix taking the place of the English " it " or " they ":

Kitatosha.	It will be enough. It will do.
Vilitosha.	They were enough.

In Swahili there is no change in the order of words when a question is asked:

Viti vinatosha.	There are enough chairs.
Viti vinatosha?	Are there enough chairs?

Sometimes attention is called to the question by the exclamation **je!**

Je! vilitosha?	Well, were they enough?

In spoken Swahili the difference is shown by the voice.

LESSON 2

NOUNS: THE KI VI CLASS

Nouns in this class are, with a very few exceptions, things without life: it may be called the **KITU** (thing) Class.

The noun prefixes are **ki**, singular, and **vi**, plural; and **the adjective prefixes** and **verb prefixes**, as we have seen, are the same. When the stem of the noun begins with *a*, *e*, *o* or *u*, the prefixes often become **ch** and **vy**, e.g. **chumba** (**ki-umba**), room; **vyumba** (**vi-umba**), rooms.

Many nouns beginning with **ki** are derived from Arabic words in which the **ki** is part of the word, and not a class prefix, but these words are treated as if they belonged to the **KITU** class and, unless they are names of people or animals, given the **ki** and **vi** concords. Only a few of the nouns beginning with **ch**, however, belong to the **KITU** class.

You are strongly advised, before you go any further:

(1) to *learn* the short vocabulary by heart;
(2) to *write* the exercise, not looking at the key till you have finished;
(3) to translate the exercise back into Swahili in writing.

Vocabulary

kichwa, head
kifua, chest
kidole, finger, toe
kidonda, sore
kiatu, shoe
kiazi, potato
kiko, pipe
kioo, glass, mirror
kijiko, spoon
kikapu, basket
kikombe, cup
kisima, well
kisiwa, island

kiwanja, plot of ground
kibanda, hut
kitanda, bed
kipande, piece
kitambaa, cloth
chakula, food
chombo, vessel of any kind
chumba, room
chuma, iron, piece of iron
chungu, earthen cooking pot
cheti, certificate, short note
cheo, rank, measure
choo, latrine, excrement

na, and
au, or

Exercise I

Write in English: kichwa kikubwa; kiko kibaya; kisima kirefu; kidonda kibaya; vyeti vizuri; viatu viwili; kitanda au kiti; visu na vitabu; viazi vidogo vitatu; kipande kikubwa kimoja; visiwa virefu viwili; vyombo vikubwa na vidogo; kiwanja kizuri; vibanda na vyoo; kikapu na chakula; vidole vitano; kibanda kimoja na vyumba vinne; kitanda kirefu na kiti kikubwa; vikombe vinne na vijiko; kisu kidogo kimoja; vyuma vikubwa. Kipande kimoja kitatosha. Vyungu vitatu vinatosha. Chakula kilitosha? Kilitosha. Viazi vitatu vitatosha? Viazi vikubwa vitatu au vidogo vitano. Vikombe vidogo vitatosha? Vitatosha. Kitambaa kidogo kitatosha.

LESSON 3

THE M MI CLASS

THE class we are now to consider is, like the **KITU** Class, a class of non-living things, but it includes also trees and other plants. It may be called the **MITI** (tree) Class.

The singular prefix is **m** (sometimes **mw** or **mu**), and the plural **mi**. Originally the singular prefix was **mu**, and the discarded **u** shows itself as a **w** when the noun stem begins with a vowel:

mwaka (mu-aka), year	miaka, years
mwili (mu-ili), body	miili, bodies

It often shows itself, too, before **h**, as in

muhindi, maize plant or cob; pl. mihindi
muhogo, cassava; pl. mihogo

and persists, also, in

muwa, sugar-cane; pl. miwa

The **w** usually found before a vowel has dropped out in some words whose stem begins with **o** or **u**, e.g.

moto, fire; pl. mioto
moyo, heart; pl. mioyo
moshi, smoke
mundu, cutlass; pl. miundu

For illustration we take the five nouns:

mti, tree, pole, wood; pl. miti
mji, town, village; pl. miji
mguu, leg, foot; pl. miguu
mkono, arm, hand; pl. mikono
mwezi, month, moon; pl. miezi

with the adjectives and numbers already learnt.

Adjectives, including numbers, are brought into agreement with nouns of the **MITI** class by prefixing **m** or **mi** (sometimes **mw** and **my** before a vowel):

a large village	mji mkubwa
four high trees	miti mirefu minne
one month	mwezi mmoja
two hands	mikono miwili

But **the subject prefixes of the verb** are different; they are **u** and **i**:

| One month will be enough. | **Mwezi mmoja utatosha.** |
| Five poles were enough. | **Miti mitano ilitosha.** |

The Verb HAS

" Has " is expressed in Swahili by **-na** with the appropriate verb prefixes; i.e. **ki, vi,** for the **KITU** class, and **u, i,** for the **MITI** class:

Kibanda kina vyumba vitatu.	The hut has three rooms.
Vyumba viwili vina vitanda.	Two rooms have beds.
Mwili una mikono na miguu.	A body has arms and legs.
Miji ina visima vizuri.	The villages have good wells.

NOTES:

1. Nouns beginning with **m** followed by a consonant may be taken as belonging to the **MITI** class unless they denote persons or animals, except nouns beginning with **mb** or **mv,** which may have a different origin.

2. Names of trees are in this class, but the names of their fruits take different prefixes and belong to other classes.

3. Words given in the Lesson are not repeated in the Vocabulary.

Vocabulary

mchungwa, orange tree	**mlango,** door
mgomba, banana plant	**mlima,** hill, mountain
mnazi, coconut palm	**mswaki,** toothbrush
mtende, date palm	**msitu,** forest
mwembe, mango tree	**msalaba,** cross
mpunga, rice	**mshahara,** wage
mchele, husked rice	**mto,** river
mtama, millet	**mzizi,** root
mfuko, bag	**mzigo,** load
mkate, bread, loaf	**mwiba,** thorn
mkeka, plaited mat	**mwiko,** large spoon
mkia, tail	**mwavuli,** umbrella

Exercise 2

Write in Swahili: a long tail; a good umbrella; a small river; a high mountain; a bad toothbrush; large loads; five loaves; good maize plants; a small cross; a big wage; mats and bags; three orange trees and four mango trees; tall coconuts and dates; one year and five months; (husked) rice and millet. The fire has smoke. The village has bananas and sugar-cane. The trees have thorns. The hut has two doors. Cassava has large roots. A body has hands and feet, a head, a chest, and a heart.

LESSON 4

THE M WA CLASS

Nouns beginning with **m** or **mw** denoting persons belong to another class, which may be called the **WATU** (people) class, and make their plural with the prefix **wa**:

mtu, man; pl. **watu**
mtoto, child; pl. **watoto**
mgeni, stranger; pl. **wageni**
mzee, old man; pl. **wazee**
Mwislamu, a Moslem; pl. **Waislamu**

The **w** usually found in the singular prefix before a vowel is omitted in the words

mume (pl. **waume**), husband, and **Mungu,** God.

Some small changes have occurred where the **a** of the plural prefix **wa** is followed by another vowel, and the following plurals should be noticed:

mwana, son, child; pl. **wana**
mwanafunzi, learner; pl. **wanafunzi**
mwanamke, woman; pl. **wanawake**
mwanamume, man; pl. **wanaume**
mwanadamu, human being; pl. **wanadamu**

mwali, maiden; pl. wali
mwalimu, teacher; pl. walimu *or* waalimu
mwenzi, companion; pl. wenzi
mwenyewe, owner; pl. wenyewe
mwenyeji, inhabitant; pl. wenyeji
mwivi, mwizi, thief; pl. wevi, wezi

NOTES:

1. **Mungu,** God, and **mtume,** prophet, have irregular plurals **miungu** and **mitume.**

2. **Mtu** denotes a person; **mwanamume,** a male person; **mwanamke,** a female person; and **mwanadamu** (i.e. **mwana wa Adamu,** Son of Adam) a human being.

Adjectives, including numbers, take the prefix **m** (or **mw** before a vowel) in the singular, and **wa** in the plural, with nouns of this class:

two tall men	**watu warefu wawili**
a little child	**mtoto mdogo**
nice guests	**wageni wazuri**
a bad old man	**mzee mbaya**

Some adjectives with these prefixes can be used alone as nouns; e.g. **mkubwa,** the elder one, the senior; **mdogo,** young brother; **wazee,** the village headmen; etc. **Mzee** is a title of respect, often used in speaking of parents or elders.

With **verbs, the subject prefix** in the plural is **wa,** but in the singular it is **a.**

They have two children.	**Wana watoto wawili.**
He has a book.	**Ana kitabu.**
One man will be enough.	**Mtu mmoja atatosha.**
Two boys will do.	**Watoto wawili watatosha.**

All words in this class denote human beings, except the two words **mnyama,** animal, and **mdudu,** insect. But note that most names of family relations are not in this class, although their adjectives and verbs take the prefixes of the **WATU** class. The same is true of the names of most animals. These words will be considered in a later lesson.

Vocabulary

mke, wife	**msimamizi,** overseer
mkwe, in-law	**mtumishi,** servant
mgonjwa, sick person	**mpishi,** cook
mganga, native doctor	**mtumwa,** slave
mchawi, wizard	**Mzungu,** European
mjane, widow	**Mwingereza,** Englishman *
mjinga, foolish person	**Mwarabu,** Arab
mlevi, drunkard	**Mhindi,** Indian
mfalme, king	**Mkristo,** a Christian

Exercise 3

Write in Swahili: One God; bad servants; two drunkards; three widows; a great fool; five people; sick men and doctors; kings and slaves; men and women; husband and wife; old men and children; the inhabitants and the strangers; teacher and pupils. The cook has rice and bread. The servant has a big wage. The women have millet and cassava. The old man has two wives and five children. One wife is enough. The European has large loads. The Englishman has an overseer and four servants. The town has Moslems and Christians. The thieves have big knives.

LESSON 5

THE N CLASS

THE trouble about this class is that the **N** is generally not there. The noun may have begun with an **N** which has been dropped or turned into another letter; or it may be a foreign word which has no prefix and will not fit into any other class.

In theory, **the noun prefix** is **n** in both singular and plural, and **the adjective prefix** is the same.

* Scots, Welsh and Irish included.

(1)

In order to understand the concords of this class, we will take first a few nouns which do begin with **N**:

ndege	bird(s)	**njaa**	hunger, famine
ndizi	banana(s)	**njia**	road(s), way
ngoma	drum(s)	**nyumba**	house(s)
nguo	cloth(es)	**nyoka**	snake(s)
ng'ombe	cow(s)	**nzige**	locust(s)

In Swahili **n** can stand before **d, g, j** and **z** only,* and, as **ny,** before a vowel.   So that, in our five adjectives, the **n** prefix can be used only with **dogo** and **zuri,** and it cannot be used with any of the five numbers.

a good drum	**ngoma nzuri**
a small path	**njia ndogo**
large houses	**nyumba kubwa**
three bananas	**ndizi tatu**

Note that names of animals and people take the prefixes of the **WATU** class:

pretty birds	**ndege wazuri**
a bad snake	**nyoka mbaya**
large cows	**ng'ombe wakubwa**

The subject prefixes of the verb with N class nouns are **i** in the singular and **zi** in the plural.

The house has two doors.	**Nyumba ina milango miwili.**
The paths have thorns.	**Njia zina miiba.**
There are enough bananas.	**Ndizi zinatosha.**
One garment will be enough.	**Nguo moja itatosha.**

But names of persons and animals take the verb prefixes **a, wa,** as if they belonged to the **WATU** class:

A snake has a small head.	**Nyoka ana kichwa kidogo.**
Birds have two legs.	**Ndege wana miguu miwili.**

(2)

If we try to pronounce **n** before **b** or **v,** we see how easily the sound changes to **m.**   This change has taken place in

* Unless the stem is a monosyllable.

many N class nouns, and **mb** and **mv** are found instead of **nb** and **nv**.

mbu	mosquito(s)	**mbwa**	dog(s)
mbegu	seed(s)	**mvua**	rain
mboga	vegetables	**mvi**	white hair(s)

There are many words beginning with **mb** in the **N** class, but **mvua, mvi,** and **mvinyo** (wine), are the only ones with **mv**.

Adjectives beginning with **b** prefix **m** instead of **n**; so does the number **-wili,** two, which with **N** class nouns becomes **mbili**:

	a bad road	njia mbaya
	two bananas	ndizi mbili
but	small mosquitos	mbu wadogo
	two dogs	mbwa wawili

Another change caused by **N**, which has to be remembered in connection with the adjective **-refu,** is that **nl** or **nr** becomes **nd**:

	a long road	njia ndefu
	long clothes	nguo ndefu
but	a long snake	nyoka mrefu

(3)

Before all other letters **N** just drops out, unless the stem is of one syllable only. Moreover, the foreign words with no prefix which are put into this class may begin with any letter, e.g. **akili,** common sense; **baridi,** cold; **dawa,*** medicine; **chai,** tea; **kazi,** work. Hence there is no uniformity among words of the **N** class.

Adjectives beginning with one of the letters before which **n** cannot stand take no prefix:

	heavy rain	mvua kubwa
	one banana	ndizi moja
	four seeds	mbegu nne
	five drums	ngoma tano
but	five big dogs	mbwa wakubwa watano

* **Dawa:** any preparation for treating persons or things, e.g. **dawa ya viatu,** shoe polish.

When the stem of the noun is a single syllable, the **n** is not discarded; on the contrary, it becomes a syllable and takes the stress, e.g. **nchi**, country; **nta**, wax.

The subject prefixes of the verb are always **i** in the singular and **zi** in the plural, unless the nouns denote living things.

Vocabulary

kahawa, coffee
sukari, sugar
chumvi, salt
nyama, meat
samaki, fish
asali, honey
siagi, butter
nazi, coconut
tende, date
siku, day
saa, hour, clock
taa, lamp
meza, table

fedha, money, silver
faida, profit
hasara, loss
hesabu, number, sums
furaha, joy
huzuni, sorrow
shida, trouble
nguvu, strength
habari, news
hatari, danger
ruhusa, permission, leave
kalamu, pencil, pen
chupa, bottle

Exercise 4

Write in Swahili: nice honey; small coconuts; a large clock; a bad lamp; good clothes; a great famine; a long table; one drum; five dates; two countries; three hours; four days; good news; small danger; joy and sorrow; profit or loss; meat, fish, bread and potatoes; bread and butter; tea or coffee; sugar or salt; two big lamps; two big dogs.

Write in English: Je, fedha itatosha? Itatosha. Nazi mbili zitatosha? Nazi kubwa mbili au nazi ndogo tatu. Mpishi ana chai? Ana chai na kahawa. Meza ina miguu minne. Saa ina mikono miwili. Mnazi una nazi nne. Mzee ana mvi. Nyumba ina baridi. Mwalimu ana ruhusa, mwezi mmoja na siku tatu.

LESSON 6

THE MA CLASS

WE name this class by its plural prefix, as there is usually no prefix in the singular. If, however, the noun stem is of only one syllable, or if it begins with a vowel, **ji** or **j** is prefixed in the singular.

Examples of nouns with no prefix:

> **shauri,** plan, advice; pl. **mashauri**
> **shamba,** cultivated field; pl. **mashamba**
> **jibu,** answer; pl. **majibu**
> **yai,** egg; pl. **mayai**
> **ua,** flower; pl. **maua**

Words with a **ji** or **j** prefix in the singular which is changed to **ma** in the plural:

> **jicho,** eye; pl. **macho**
> **jiwe,** stone; pl. **mawe**
> **jino,** tooth; pl. **meno (ma-ino)**
> **jiko,** fireplace; pl. **meko (ma-iko)**
> **jambo,** thing, matter; pl. **mambo (ma-ambo)**

Adjectives, including numbers, used with nouns of this class, take no prefix in the singular (unless they begin with a vowel). In the plural they prefix **ma**.

> a big matter, **jambo kubwa;** pl. **mambo makubwa**
> a bad word, **neno baya;** pl. **maneno mabaya**
> a pretty flower, **ua zuri;** pl. **maua mazuri**
> a small field, **shamba dogo;** pl. **mashamba madogo**

Some plural words in this class correspond with nouns used in English in the singular; in Swahili they must have the plural concords, e.g. **maji mabaya,** bad water. Among such words are: **maji,** water; **maziwa,** milk; **mafuta,** oil; **mate,** saliva; **matata,** trouble; **matusi,** abuse; **majani,** grass.

The subject prefix of the verb is li in the singular and **ya** in the plural.

The field has fine maize.	**Shamba lina mihindi mizuri.**
The plans are dangerous.	**Mashauri yana hatari.**
There was enough milk.	**Maziwa yalitosha.**
One egg will be enough.	**Yai moja litatosha.**

NOTES:

1. **Shauri:** anything that can be talked about, from a servant's request for an hour off, to consultations on matters of state.

2. **Jambo.** This word, and sometimes **neno** (see Vocabulary) are used for *thing* in its abstract sense, as distinguished from **kitu** used of a concrete thing.

3. It will be seen that in the singular there is nothing to distinguish nouns of this class from those of the **N** class which have no prefix. But it does not take long to learn which words add **ma** for the plural and which remain unchanged. There is so much variation nowadays in African usage that it will not matter much if a learner puts a word into the wrong class.

Of

The word **of** is formed by prefixing the subject prefix of the verb to the particle * **-a.** The prefixes become slightly altered before the vowel, and are shown in full in the examples below. Note that **of** has two uses: to show the possessor, and to describe the thing spoken of. Be careful to make the *of* agree with the person or thing spoken of, and not with the possessor; e.g. *the child's book = the book of the child*, and *of* must agree with the *book*—**kitabu cha mtoto.**

Examples:

kisu cha mpishi	the cook's knife
vyeti vya mwalimu	the teacher's certificates
mfuko wa chakula	a bag of food
milango ya nyumba	the doors of the house
mwana wa mfalme	the king's son
wenyeji wa nchi	the inhabitants of the country

* The word particle is here used for the little words denoting relationship, association, etc., which do not fit into any of the categories of English grammar.

taa ya mkono	a hand-lamp
habari za furaha	joyful news
soko la mji	the market of the town
maganda ya ndizi	banana skins

It is a good plan to make up phrases like these with all the new words you learn.

Vocabulary

tumbo, stomach		**shoka,** axe	
sikio, ear		**jembe,** hoe	
goti, knee		**soko,** market	
tunda, fruit		**duka,** shop	
chungwa, orange		**kanisa,** church	
embe, mango		**swali,** question	
nanasi, pineapple		**neno,** word	
dafu, coconut with milk in		**wazo,** thought	
ganda, skin, shell		**tendo,** deed	
gunia, sack		**kosa,** fault	
shimo, pit		**bwana,** master	
tundu, hole		**bibi,** lady, grandmother	
sanduku, box		**fundi,** craftsman	
jua, sun		**seremala,** carpenter	
giza, darkness		**karani,** clerk	

Exercise 5

Write in Swahili: oranges and mangoes; questions and answers; three pineapples; nice fruits; two knees; a small church; bad faults; an important thing; long grass; big stones; four large boxes; a deep pit; an axe and two hoes; two ears and two eyes; the guest's food; the cook's baskets; the master's umbrella; the lady's servant; the roots of the trees; the carpenter's sons; a sad day; hours of work; the orange market; the shops of the Indians; the children's teeth; the answers to (of) the questions; thoughts, words and deeds; the clerk's pen.

LESSON 7

THE U CLASS

THERE is little difficulty about this class, as all the nouns begin with **u** in the singular (**w** before a vowel), and most of them have no plural. The others take the plural of the **N** class, except two or three which make a **MA** plural.

Most of the **U** class nouns are abstract—that is, they denote qualities and states; they are formed from adjectives by prefixing **u,** and from nouns by changing the class prefix to **u** or, before a vowel, **w.**

ukubwa	size	**umoja**	unity
ubaya	badness	**uzee**	old age
udogo	smallness	**ufalme**	kingdom
uzuri	beauty	**ujinga**	folly
urefu	length	**wizi**	theft

You can make many others for yourself.

A few of these nouns have a corresponding plural in the **MA** class:

ugonjwa	sickness	**magonjwa**	diseases
ugomvi	quarrelling	**magomvi**	quarrels

Other **U** class nouns denote a substance which can be regarded as a collection of small things:

unga	flour	**uvumba**	incense
uji	gruel	**ufuta**	oil-seed
ugali	porridge	**ushanga**	beads
wali	cooked rice	**utitiri**	chicken fleas
udongo	soil	**wimbi**	bulrush millet

Other **U** class nouns denoting concrete things belonged originally to a different class with the prefix **LU.** The **l** sound is very easily lost in Swahili, and so these words have become assimilated to the **U** class. Most of these nouns can take a plural, which is that of the **N** class. Remember that **n** can stand only before **d, g, j** and **z,** and, as **ny,** before a vowel:

udevu, a hair of the beard; pl. **ndevu**
wimbo, song, hymn; pl. **nyimbo**
wembe, razor; pl. **nyembe**
wavu, net; pl. **nyavu**
wakati, time; pl. **nyakati**

With **b** or **w** n makes **mb,** and with **l** or **r, nd** :

ubao, plank; pl. **mbao**
ubavu, rib; pl. **mbavu**
ubawa, wing; pl. **mbawa**
uwingu, sky; pl. **mbingu**
ulimi, tongue; pl. **ndimi**

With other letters the **N** just disappears:

ufagio, broom; pl. **fagio**
ukuta, wall; pl. **kuta**
upepo, wind; pl. **pepo**

When a noun has only one syllable after the **u** prefix, the **ny** is prefixed to the whole word to make the plural:

uso, face; pl. **nyuso**   **ua,** courtyard; pl. **nyua**
ufa, crack; pl. **nyufa**   **uzi,** cord, thread; pl. **nyuzi**

Some words are used only in the singular:

usiku	night	**umeme**	lightning
usingizi	sleep	**umri**	age
ulimwengu	world	**wino**	ink

The **adjective prefix** is **m** in the singular, and **n** (or **ma**) in the plural:

a long plank	**ubao mrefu**	long planks	**mbao ndefu**
one broom	**ufagio mmoja**	three brooms	**fagio tatu**
a bad disease	**ugonjwa mbaya**	bad diseases	**magonjwa mabaya**

Notice, however, that the old prefix **u** is generally used in the phrases **utu ume,** manhood; **utu uke,** womanhood; **utu uzima,** maturity; **utu wema,** kindness.

The **subject prefix of the verb** is **u** in the singular and **zi** (or **ya**) in the plural:

There was enough string.	Uzi ulitosha.
Two hymns will be enough.	Nyimbo mbili zitatosha.
The night is dark.	Usiku una giza.
The walls have cracks.	Kuta zina nyufa.

Of, with nouns of the **U** class, is **wa** in the singular, and **za** (or **ya**) in the plural:

a dark night   **usiku wa giza**   the children's   **nyuso za**
                                    faces   **watoto**

The prefix **U** is much used to form names of countries, e.g. **Uganda, Unguja** (Zanzibar), **Ureno** (Portugal), but the verb prefixes are generally those agreeing with **nchi,** country; e.g. **Uganda ina watu.** Note that the language of the country takes the **KI** prefix, and so we get:

> **Uingereza,** England; **Waingereza,** the English; **Kiingereza,** the English language.

Ulaya (Europe) is an Arabic word and the **U** is not a class prefix.

All nouns beginning with **U** are in this class, except **ua,** a flower, which belongs to the **MA** class. Distinguish between:

> **ua la mti,** the flower of a tree; pl. **maua**
> **ua wa nyumba,** the yard of a house; pl. **nyua**

Exercise 6

Write in Swahili: good cooking; a long cord; a large plank; a small razor; a bad sickness; a big wind; long nets; large courtyards; bad soil; small cracks; good songs; four walls; three ribs; the child's face; the walls of the cook's house; the cords of the nets. The gruel is hot (has heat). The women's faces are sad (have sorrow). Drunkenness is dangerous (has danger). Was there enough flour?

LESSON 8

PA AND KU

(1)

The **PA class** contains only one word, **mahali,** place or places. This is an Arabic word which has supplanted the old Bantu words formed with the root **-tu** referred to in Lesson 1. The old words were **patu,** a definite place; **kutu,** an indefinite place, and **mutu,** an inside place. Although these words have quite disappeared in Swahili, their prefixes remain, as we shall see under section (3).

Adjectives and verbs agreeing with **mahali** take the prefix **pa:**

a nice place	**mahali pazuri**	one place	**mahali pamoja**
bad places	**mahali pabaya**	three places	**mahali patatu**
A small place will do.		**Mahali padogo patatosha.**	

Of is **pa:**

a place of danger **mahali pa hatari**

Note that **pamoja,** one place, is used for " together ".

(2)

The **KU class** contains all infinitives of verbs, i.e. verbs preceded by " to " in English; e.g.

kusoma	to read	kuingia	to enter
kuandika	to write	kutoka	to go out
kuweka	to put	kuanza	to begin
kutaka	to want	kukaa	to sit, stay
kuenda *	to go	kusimama	to stand

All verbs in the infinitive can be used as nouns in Swahili, requiring the prefix **ku** with adjectives and verbs. They should usually be translated by the English verb in **-ing:**

Kusoma kwa mtoto ni kubaya. The child's reading is bad.

* Usually written **kwenda.**

It is usual to put the statement less baldly, and say:

Kusoma kwa mtoto si kuzuri. The child's reading is not
good.

From these sentences you will see that *of* in the **KU** class
is **kwa;** and that **ni = is,** and **si = is not.**

(3)

We must now consider a useful device in Swahili, namely
the addition of the syllable **-NI** at the end of a noun to
denote place. This really turns the noun into an adverb,
i.e. a word showing " where ", and we can call such nouns
adverbial nouns. The stress is then transferred to the
syllable before the **ni,** and the noun ceases to belong to its
original class and must take the concords of place:

    ḿji, mjíni; nyúmba, nyumbáni; mlángo, mlangóni;
    etc.

The **ni** does not show whether the place is **at, to, in, from,**
or **on;** this is shown by the concords used, or by the
meaning of the sentence:

Wageni waliingia nyu- The visitors entered (into)
mbani.   the house.
Mzee alikaa mlangoni. The old man sat at the door.
Ataweka mayai mezani. He will put the eggs on the
      table.

The " concords " just referred to are those mentioned at
the beginning of the Lesson, **pa, ku** and **mu.**

    PA denotes position at a place, or definite position;
    KU denotes movement to or from a place, or indefinite
      position;
    MU denotes position inside a place.

Combined with **-a,** of, they make **pa, kwa** and **mwa.**

    The children are reading *in* the house of the teacher.
      Watoto wanasoma nyumbani *mwa* mwalimu.
    He went *to* the town of the king. **Alikwenda * mjini**
    kwa **mfalme.**

   * This verb retains the **kw** of the infinitive in most of its tenses.
   B

They will leave the hoes *at* the old man's door.   **Wata-acha majembe mlangoni *pa* mzee.**

They are also used as the verb subject prefixes:

Mjini kuna watu.   Over-there-at-the-town has people.
Mlangoni pana mtu.   At-the-door has a man.
Nyumbani mna watu.   In-the-house has people.

In English we should, of course, say: There are people in the town; There is a man at the door; There are people in the house.   We can put the words in that order in Swahili also:

Kuna wageni shambani.   There are strangers in the field.

Pana mtoto mlangoni.   There is a child at the door.
Mna mayai kikapuni.   There are eggs in the basket.

Note that we do not use the **MU** concords every time we say " in " in English.   **Mu** denotes definite insideness, as in a box, a pit, a house, etc., not vague insideness, as in a field, a town, etc.

Adverbial nouns do not take adjectives.   If we want to use an adjective we must use the ordinary noun with a separate word (preposition) to denote *to, in*, etc.   It will be useful here to learn one of these words, **katika,** *in*.   It has a wider meaning than the English " in ", for we can say **katika meza,** on the table; or **katika sahani,** on the the plate.

The visitors entered the big house.   **Wageni waliingia katika nyumba kubwa.**

There are eggs in the little basket.   **Mna mayai katika kikapu kidogo.**

Exercise 7

Translate into English; then back from the Key into Swahili: Wanaume walikaa mahali pamoja, na wanawake mahali pamoja.   Mpishi aliweka maziwa mahali pabaya. Watu wanaingia kanisani.   Watoto walitaka kwenda nyumbani kwa Mzungu.   Kuna wanyama shambani.   Mna maji kisimani?   Pana watoto wawili mlangoni.   Wanawake wanatoka sokoni.   Mfukoni mna kipande cha nyama na mikate miwili, chakula cha mgeni. Kuna nyoka mkubwa njiani. Kusoma na kuandika ni kazi za watoto shuleni.*

LESSON 9

PERSONS AND ANIMALS

WE have now considered all the eight classes of Swahili nouns. We have seen that most names of people are in the **WATU** class, but nearly all names of animals, and many family names of people, are in the **N** class, and a few other nouns denoting persons or animals are scattered about in other classes. The important thing to remember about them all is that, whatever class they may be in, they take the prefixes proper to the **WATU** class:

a big hippo	**kiboko mkubwa**
long snakes	**nyoka warefu**
two brothers	**ndugu wawili**
bad craftsmen	**mafundi wabaya**

There is, however, one exception to this rule. It concerns the words *my, our, his,* etc. which we call in English " possessive adjectives ". Before learning this exception, it is necessary to know what these possessive adjectives are.

Possessive Adjectives

-angu	my	**-etu**	our
-ako	your (one possessor)	**-enu**	your (many)
-ake	his, her, its	**-ao**	their

These take the same prefixes as the particle **-a,** of; i.e.

kitabu changu, my book; pl. **vitabu vyangu**
mkono wako, your hand; pl. **mikono yako**
mpishi wake, her cook; pl. **wapishi wake**
nyumba yetu, our house; pl. **nyumba zetu**
shoka lenu, your axe; pl. **mashoka yenu**
ubao wao, their plank; pl. **mbao zao**
mahali pake, his place
kusoma kwao, their reading

* **shule** or **skuli,** school.

In English there are different forms for a possessive adjective used with a noun, e.g. *my* book, and a possessive pronoun used without a noun, e.g. This is *mine*. But in Swahili there is no difference.

These possessives, like all adjectives, agree with the noun they refer to, i.e. the thing spoken of. But the distinction between **-ako** and **-enu** depends on the possessors, whether they are one or more than one. It is the old English distinction between " thy " and " your ".

Note that **-ao,** their, is only used in speaking of persons or animals. When speaking of plants or things, **-ake** is used for both " its " and " their " :

watu na watoto *wao*	people and their children
miti na matunda *yake*	trees and their fruit

Animals and Persons of the N Class

We can now state the exception referred to at the beginning of the Lesson :

The possessive adjectives, when used with the names of people or animals in the N class, take the N class prefixes:

    (a) **with animals, in the plural only;**
    (b) **with persons, in both singular and plural.**

For example :

mbuzi wetu	our goat	mbuzi zetu	our goats
ndugu yangu	my brother	ndugu zangu	my brothers

> Ng'ombe zao wakubwa wanaingia mjini. Their big cows are coming into the village.
>
> Mbuzi wangu mmoja na mbuzi zake wawili. My one goat and his two.
>
> Ali na Juma ni ndugu zangu wakubwa, na Bakari ni ndugu yangu mdogo. Ali and Juma are my elder brothers, and Bakari is my younger brother.

With **-a,** of, the usage varies. One can say either **ng'ombe za mfalme,** the king's cows, or **ng'ombe wa mfalme; adui ya mfalme,** the king's enemy, or **adui wa mfalme.**

With all other qualifying words the **WATU** prefixes are used.

This is the ruling of Standard Swahili, but many people do not observe it, and you can, if you find it too puzzling, ignore it for the present.

Some **N** class words, such as **rafiki**, friend; **adui**, enemy; **baba**, father, sometimes take a **MA** class plural, perhaps to express collectivity. When this happens, they usually keep the **N** class concords with the possessive adjectives; e.g. **marafiki zetu**, our friends; **maadui zao**, their enemies; **mababa zetu**, our ancestors; etc.

Vocabulary

NOTE. Where no plural is shown, the word is in the **N** class and does not change.

adui, enemy	**twiga,** giraffe
rafiki, friend	**nyati,** buffalo
askari, soldier	**kifaru(vi),** rhino
raia, subject	**kiboko(vi),** hippo
pepo, a spirit	**tembo,** elephant
malaika, angel	**fisi,** hyena
baba, father	**nyani,** baboon
mama, mother	**tumbili,** monkey
ndugu, kinsman	**sungura,** hare
ng'ombe, cow	**panya,** rat
mbuzi, goat	**chura(vy),** frog
kondoo, sheep	**kobe,** tortoise
nguruwe, pig	**samaki,** fish
farasi, horse	**mamba,** crocodile
punda, donkey	**nyoka,** snake
ngamia, camel	**inzi,*** fly
mbwa, dog	**mbu,** mosquito
paka, cat	**nyuki,** bee
kuku, fowl	**nge,** scorpion
jogoo(ma), cock	**tandu,** centipede
bata, duck	**buibui,** spider
njiwa, pigeon	**mchwa,** termites
simba, lion	**siafu,** biting ants
chui, leopard	**sisimisi,** small ants

* This is the standardised form at present, but the spelling **nzi** is under consideration.

Exercise 8

Write in Swahili: my dog; our dogs; your fowls; his
children; her husband; our fault; our goats; your faces;
your knives; their shoes; the mother and her children;
the Europeans and their servants; the banana plant and
its bananas; the overseers and their dogs; their good
horses; our bad camels; three big cats; five little fish; one
large elephant; my two friends; the king's good subjects;
bad spirits and good angels. A hare has four legs. There
is a hyena in the field. In the river there are crocodiles.
Locusts are bad insects. A giraffe is a tall animal. My
goats are small. My brother's goats are big.

LESSON 10

LARGENESS AND SMALLNESS

BANTU languages had special classes for showing largeness
and smallness, i.e. for augmentatives and diminutives, but
in Swahili these have disappeared. Smallness is shown by
bringing the noun into the **KITU** class, and largeness by
bringing it into the **MA** class:

> **ndege,** a bird; **kidege,** a little bird; **dege(ma),** large
> bird
> **mfuko,** a bag; **kifuko,** a little bag; **fuko(ma),** large
> bag

Diminutives

Nouns are brought into the **KI** class by changing the
prefix to **ki,** or by prefixing **ki** if the noun has no prefix:

mlima	mountain	**kilima**	hill
sanduku	box	**kisanduku**	small box

If the noun is already in the **KITU** class, or if, without its
prefix, it has only one syllable or begins with a vowel, **ji** or
j is inserted after the **ki**:

kitabu	book	kijitabu	little book
mji	town	kijiji	village
mto	river	kijito	stream
mwiko	wooden spoon	kijiko	small spoon

This **ji** must be distinguished from that used to form augmentatives. When used to form diminutives it always follows **ki**.

The **ki** prefix sometimes carries the idea of diminution owing to some physical disability:

kipofu	a blind person	kiziwi	a deaf person
kiwete	a lame person	kilema	a deformed person

Diminutives take the concords of the **KITU** class unless they denote persons or animals. If any special emphasis, either affectionate or contemptuous, is put on the diminutive, even words denoting living things may take the **KITU** concords:

Kisanduku kizuri cha fedha. A pretty little silver box.
Vipofu wawili wameingia mjini. Two blind men have entered the village.
Kitoto changu. My little child.

Augmentatives

A noun is brought into the **MA** class by omitting its prefix in the singular and changing it to **ma** in the plural:

mdudu	insect	dudu(ma)	large insect
kikapu	basket	kapu(ma)	large basket

But where, without a prefix, the noun would have only one syllable, or would begin with a vowel, **ji** or **j** is prefixed:

mtu, man; **jitu,** giant; pl. **majitu**
nyoka, snake; **joka,** big snake; pl. **majoka**
nyumba, house; **jumba,** large house; pl. **majumba**
mwizi, thief; **jizi,** clever thief; pl. **majizi**

The Mombasa * dialect makes these plurals with **mi, mijitu,** etc.

Augmentatives take the concords of the **MA** class.

* No differentiation is made in this book between **Kimvita** and **Kiamu**.

Those denoting living things can be used with either the **MA** concords or those of the **WATU** class, but when emphasis is laid on the hugeness or uncouthness the **MA** concords are more usual:

makapu mawili ya mchele	two large baskets of rice
majitu matatu	the three giants
joka baya	the bad serpent

NOTE: The reader should not equate any Swahili word too closely with its English equivalent. To an African even three houses are a town (**mji**); he might differentiate between **mji mkubwa** and **mji mdogo,** but he does not usually speak of a village as **kijiji.** Any stream is normally called **mto,** and any elevation **mlima.** (Conversely, we may note that the highest mountain in Africa is called Kilima Njaro!) If we want a teaspoon and ask for a **kijiko,** it is disconcerting to be brought a tablespoon, but to an African, accustomed to the large wooden spoons used in his village, even a tablespoon is a little spoon.

Exercise 9

Write in Swahili: the king's palace; two large snakes; a large basket of mangoes; two blind men; little streams of water; huge rivers; two giants. A blind man is going into the house. The three lame men want work. In the basket there is a wooden spoon and two tablespoons.

LESSON II

PREFIXES BEFORE A VOWEL

(I) Adjective Prefixes

The most common adjectives beginning with a vowel are:

-ema	good	**-ekundu**	red
-embamba	narrow	**-epesi**	light (weight)
-erevu	cunning	**-ingi**	much, many
-eupe	white	**-ingine**	other
-eusi	black		

There are only one or two adjectives beginning with vowels other than **e** and **i** and they are little used.

Changes to be noted in the adjective prefixes before **e** and **i** are these:

1. **WATU class.** The singular prefix is **mw.** The plural prefix **wa** with a following **e** or **i** makes **we.**

> **mwalimu mwema,** a good teacher; pl. **waalimu wema**
> **mtu mwingine,** another man; pl. **watu wengine**

2. **MITI class.** The singular prefix is **mw.** The plural prefix **mi** with a following **e** makes **mye,** and with a following **i** makes **mi,** the two **i**'s combining.

> **mzigo mwepesi,** a light load; pl. **mizigo myepesi**
> **mtama mwingi,** much millet; **miiba mingi,** many thorns

3. **N class.** The adjective prefix is **ny** in the singular and plural. EXCEPTION: **-ema** becomes **njema.**

> **mvua nyingi,** much rain   **njia nyembamba,** narrow paths
> **mbegu njema,** good seed   **habari njema,** good news

4. **KITU class.** The prefixes **ki, vi** become **ch, vy** before **e.** With a following **i** the two **i**'s make **one.**

> **kiatu cheusi,** a black shoe; pl. **viatu vyeusi**
> **chakula kingi,** much food; pl. **vyakula vingi**

5. **MA class.** In the singular **j** is prefixed. In the plural the **ma** prefix with a following **e** or **i** makes **me.**

> **ua jekundu,** a red flower; pl. **maua mekundu**
> **shauri jingine,*** another plan; pl. **mashauri mengine**

6. **U class.** The adjective prefixes are **mw** in the singular, and **ny** in the plural. But **-ema** makes **njema** in the plural.

> **uso mwema,** a good face; pl. **nyuso njema**
> **wizi mwingi,** much stealing; **nyimbo nyingi,** many songs

7. **PA class.** The adjective prefix **pa** with a following **e** or **i** makes **pe.**

> **mahali pema,** a good place; **mahali pengi,** many places

---

* **lingine** is sometimes used in place of **jingine.**

8. **KU class.** Before **e** and **i**, the **ku** becomes **kw.**

> **kusoma kwema,** good reading; **kusoma kwingi,** much reading

(2) Subject Prefixes

We have already seen that the particle **-a, of,** and the possessive adjectives and pronouns **my, your,** etc. are made with the subject prefix of the verb. Other words of this kind are

-ote	all	**-enye**	having
-o -ote	any whatever	**-enyewe**	self

and the same changes take place in the prefixes before the vowels. For instance, with the word **miti,** the subject prefix **i** makes:

> **miti ya mzee,** the old man's trees; **miti yangu,** my trees. **miti yote,** all the trees; **miti yo yote,** any of the trees; **miti yenye miiba,** trees having thorns; **miti yenyewe,** the trees themselves.

In the singular of the **WATU** class, however, irregularities occur and the forms taken are these:

> **mtoto wa mzee,** the old man's child; **mtoto wangu,** my child; **mtoto ye yote,** any child; **mtoto mwenye kitabu,** the child with the book; **mtoto mwenyewe,** the child herself.

Look now at the table on pages 154–5. Under the noun classes given there, you will see the adjective prefixes with examples of their use both before consonants and before vowels. Below them, you will see the verb prefixes and the words formed with them. Use this table for reference whenever you are in doubt. Note the order of the noun classes. In the Lessons we began with the **KITU** class as it is the easiest, but the order given in this Lesson 11 and in the Reference Table is the accepted one, and we shall follow it henceforward.

Exercise 10

Write in Swahili: white potatoes; black iron; many islands; any food whatever; other loads; much fire; big roots; white bread; good children; black men; a white cow; many lions; much hunger; a long road; many days; white salt; a narrow box; much wind; a good word; many leaves; much grass; good sleep; red beards; many places; everywhere (all places); anywhere (any place); cunning thieves; the whole arm; a cup of tea; my white shoes; the roots of all the trees; your black umbrella; children having books; the inhabitants of Zanzibar; the length of the plank itself; the teacher's questions and the children's answers.

LESSON 12

THE VERB

WE have learnt how to make the verb agree with the noun which is its subject, by giving it the subject prefix of the right class. We have now to learn the prefixes denoting *I*, *we* and *you*, words which in English we call personal pronouns.

The personal pronouns standing by themselves are these:

mimi	I	**sisi**	we
wewe	you (one person)	**ninyi**	you (more than one)
yeye	he, she	**wao**	they

There is no distinction of gender in Swahili; **yeye** can refer to a man or a woman. It cannot be used for " it ", nor can **wao** refer to things.

It is not necessary to use these pronouns with a verb except for emphasis; the subject prefix of the verb is usually sufficient.

> **Mimi ni nyama, wewe kisu.** I am the meat, you are the knife (i.e. I am in your power).
> **Yeye ni mwema; wao ni wabaya.** She is good, but they are bad.

Here are the subject prefixes for all persons:

		Sing.			*Plur.*
1st person	**ni-**	I		**tu-**	we
2nd person	**u-**	you		**m-**	you
3rd person	**a-**	he, she		**wa-**	they

With the three tenses we have already used they make:

Past Tense (-LI-)

nilisoma	I read	**tulisoma**	we read
ulisoma	you read	**mlisoma**	you read
alisoma	he read	**walisoma**	they read

NOTE: In the 1st person singular, **nali-** is often used instead of **nili-**; **nalisoma**, I read.

Future Tense (-TA-)

nitasoma	I shall read	**tutasoma**	we shall read
utasoma	you will read	**mtasoma**	you will read
atasoma	he will read	**watasoma**	they will read

Present Tense (-NA-)

ninasoma	I am reading	**tunasoma**	we are reading
unasoma	you are reading	**mnasoma**	you are reading
anasoma	he is reading	**wanasoma**	they are reading

Remember that, in all these tenses, the prefix **u** refers to one person only, and **m** to more than one; and **a** refers to she as well as he.

There is another present tense, a simple or indefinite present with no special note of time. Its tense prefix is **-a-**; note the changes that take place in the subject prefixes before this vowel:

Simple Present Tense (-A-)

nasoma	I read	**twasoma**	we read
wasoma	you read	**mwasoma**	you read
asoma	he reads	**wasoma**	they read

With the other noun classes the changes which take place before the vowel are the same as before the **-a** of **of**.

Grammatically, the **NA** tense is a continuous present, and should only be used when the action is going on at the time of speaking. Note the difference between the sentences

	Ndege wanaruka.	The birds are flying
and	**Ndege waruka.**	Birds fly.

In practice, the **NA** tense is becoming increasingly used, and the simple present is tending to go out of fashion.

Another tense shows an action completed at the time of speaking, the result of which is still present:

> **Mgeni amefika.** The visitor has arrived (and is here now).
> **Kikombe kimejaa.** The cup has become full (and is full now).

When considering especially the resulting state, it is often better to translate by the verb *is*; e.g. The visitor *is* here; The cup *is* full. The tense is called the *perfect*, or *present perfect*, and is made with the tense prefix **me.**

PERFECT TENSE (-**ME**-)

nimesoma	I have read	**tumesoma**	we have read
umesoma	you have read	**mmesoma**	you have read
amesoma	he has read	**wamesoma**	they have read

In the case of reading, the use of this tense would imply that the lesson or school session was still going on, not that the actual child was still reading.

There is no difference in form between a verb making a statement and one asking a question:

> **Amesoma.** He has read. **Amesoma?** Has he read?

Monosyllabic Verbs

There are a few verbs which, without the **ku** of the infinitive, have only one syllable, e.g. **ja,** come; **fa,** die; **la,** eat. For ease of pronunciation these verbs keep the **ku** in many of their tenses. So do two other verbs, **isha,*** finish, and **enda,*** go. In the five tenses of this lesson, **ku** is kept in all except the simple present; e.g. **alikuja, nitakula, wanakwenda, amekufa,** etc.; but **aja,** he comes; **wala,** they eat, etc.

Nakuja, I come; **nakwenda,** I go, etc. are heard, but these may be abbreviated forms of the **NA** tense; **n'nakuja,** I am coming; **n'nakwenda,** I am going.

* With these two verbs the **ku** generally takes the form of **kw.**

Vocabulary

sema, say	**fika,** arrive, reach
sikia, hear	**rudi,** return, go back
ona, see	**pata,** get
jua, know	**nunua,** buy
weza, be able to	**uza,** sell
fanya, do, make	**faa,** be useful

Revise the verbs given in Lesson 8.

Exercise 11

Write in English; then put back into Swahili: Anaandika;
wamefika; nitakuja; waliona; utasoma? amekwisha;
mnarudi? twajua; tumesema; ataweza; nataka; uta-
pata; wanaingia; tumekwenda; ametoka; tumekwisha.
Atapata kazi. Wataka kuona? Ninaandika barua (*letter*).
Walisoma kitabu. Walikuja nyumbani. Utafika Unguja?
Tutakwenda kwetu. Nimeanza kazi. Mmesikia habari?
Unajua njia? Twaweza kwenda na kurudi. Amenunua
mayai yote. Nauza kuku wawili. Wanafanya kazi.
Ameweka fedha mezani. Kazi yake itafaa.

LESSON 13

THE OBJECT PREFIX

JUST as subject prefixes are put before the verb stem to
show the person or thing about which something is said,
so object prefixes are used when it is necessary to show the
object of the verb—I read *what*? They will suffice *whom*?
These prefixes always come immediately before the verb
stem.

> **Nili*ki*soma.** I read *it* (the book).
> **Zita*tu*tosha.** They (bananas) will suffice *us*.

Object prefixes are used, even if the noun is expressed, if it
is desired to emphasise a particular thing:

> **Umeleta kitabu?** Have you brought a book?
> **Umekileta kitabu?** Have you brought the book (the
> particular one I wanted)?

The object prefixes used with the various noun classes are the same as the subject prefixes. No change occurs when they come before a vowel:

Nakiona kitabu. I see the book.
Naiona miti. I see the trees.

But in referring to persons the object prefixes differ somewhat from the subject prefixes given on page 35. The object prefixes are these:

-ni-	me	**-tu-**	us
-ku-	you (one)	**-wa-**	you (more than one)
-m-	him, her	**-wa-**	them

The only change before a vowel is that **m** becomes **mw**:

Aniona, he sees me; **Amwona,** he sees him.

It will be noticed that the object prefixes for *you* (plur.) and *they* are the same. This is because the old prefix **mi** (you) has been lost in Swahili, though it is still found in poetry, and **wa** has taken its place. Other forms for showing *you* in the plural are made by adding **ni** (from **ninyi,** you) to the end of the verb, and changing the final **a** of the verb stem to **e.** So that " I beg you", speaking to more than one person, can take three forms:

nawaomba, nawaombeni, and **nakuombeni.** And, " I tell you ", **nawaambia, nawaambieni,** and **nakuambieni. Nawaombeni** means " I ask you all collectively "; and **nakuombeni,** " I ask each one of you ". These forms in **-ni** are not known everywhere, and the learner had better use the first form.

The reflexive prefix **ji** is used to denote *myself, himself,* etc. when the subject and object of the verb are the same:

Najiuliza, I ask myself.
Watoto walijitazama katika kioo. The children looked at themselves in the glass.

This reflexive prefix sometimes changes the meaning of the verb; **kujiona,** for instance, usually means to be conceited; **kujifanya,** to pretend; etc.

Grammatically, we should use an object prefix wherever the object is definite, but in practice it is often omitted, especially where the object is a thing. If the object is mentioned first, as is sometimes done for emphasis, the object prefix must be used:

> **Kitabu changu umekileta?** My book, have you brought it?

In writing, if *the* things are specified, you should put in the prefix.

Vocabulary

omba, beg, ask for	**penda,** love, like
uliza, ask (question)	**vunja,** break
jibu, answer	**haribu,** destroy
ambia, say to, tell	**jaribu,** try
tazama, look at	**tia,** put in
tafuta, look for	**toa,** take out, put forth

Exercise 12

Write in English; then put back into Swahili: Nitamwambia. Tutawauliza. Alituomba. Umemwona? Mnaniuliza? Wanakuuliza. Najiuliza. Nawaambieni. Ulimpata? Twakusikia. Nakujibu. Alimwambia. Nimemtazama. Nakupenda. Mvua imeiharibu nyumba yake. Wevi waliuvunja mlango wa nyumba. Watoto wote wapenda matunda. Nitavitia vyombo nyumbani. Je, watoto wamepata mikate; umeitoa? Ninatafuta kisu changu; umekiona? Ninajaribu kufanya hesabu, nimekwisha kufanya tatu.

LESSON 14

THIS AND THAT (Demonstratives)

That, and its plural, **those,** are formed from the syllable **-LE,** preceded by the subject prefixes of the verb; except in the singular of the **WATU** class, where the old subject prefix **yu** has taken the place of **a.** Like the English words, they can be used either as adjectives, with a noun, or as pronouns, without a noun. When used as adjectives in their proper sense of *that, those,* they follow the noun; but they can also be used before a noun in the sense of *the* when referring to something which is the subject of conversation. This use tends to be overdone by present-day writers; it should be used sparingly.

The forms taken with the various noun classes are these:

1. mtu *yule*   watu *wale*   5. yai *lile*   mayai *yale*
2. mti *ule*   miti *ile*   6. ubao *ule*   mbao *zile*
3. nyumba *ile* nyumba *zile* 7. mahali *pale*
4. kitu *kile*   vitu *vile*   8. kusoma *kule*

When *that*, referring to place, is used with the noun **mahali**, it can take only the form **pale**, as a definite place is denoted. But without a noun, in the sense of " where ", it can take any of the three place concords:

Simama pale. Stand there.
Ametoka kule. He has come from over there.
Aliingia mle. He went in there.

Increasing distance is shown by lengthening the last syllable and raising the voice—**Kuleee! Yuleee!**

For nearby things, where we should say *this* or *these*, the same subject syllables are used, preceded by a syllable formed by **h** with the same vowel as in the following syllable. The forms taken with the different classes are these:

1. mtu *huyu*   watu *hawa*   5. yai *hili*   mayai *haya*
2. mti *huu*   miti *hii*   6. ubao *huu*   mbao *hizi*
3. nyumba *hii* nyumba *hizi* 7. mahali *hapa*
4. kitu *hiki*   vitu *hivi*   8. kusoma *huku*

The forms denoting place are **hapa, huku** and **humu**:

Alisimama hapa. He stood here.
Watakuja huku. They will come here.
Aliingia humu. He went in here.

A third form of demonstrative is used when referring to something already mentioned. It is similar to the *this* form, but the last letter is **o**; this **o** has caused slight changes as will be noted. The forms taken are these:

1. mtu *huyo*   watu *hao*   5. yai *hilo*   mayai *hayo*
2. mti *huo*   miti *hiyo*   6. ubao *huo*   mbao *hizo*
3. nyumba *hiyo* nyumba *hizo* 7. mahali *hapo*
4. kitu *hicho* vitu *hivyo* 8. kusoma *huko*

The place forms are **hapo, huko** and **humo.**

This **o** form is only used when referring to something already spoken of, and it is not really necessary to use it even then if the thing has only just been mentioned. It must never be used with reference to something about to be mentioned. If, for instance, you say " maneno hayo " you are referring to words already said. If you are about to write the words, you must say " maneno haya ".

Huko seems to be an exception to this rule; it is the common word for *there* where no definite place is pointed out.

When demonstratives of place are used with an adverbial noun, they generally precede it :

> **hapa mjini,** here in the village; **mle nyumbani,** there in the house ; **huko shambani,** over there in the field.

NOTE : In Swahili the two forms *this* and *that*, or the place forms *here* and *there*, should not be used in contrast as is customary in English, although many Africans, in imitation of the English construction, are beginning to do so. Swahili idiom says :

Wataka hiki au hiki ?	Do you want this or that ?
Huyu ni mwema na huyu ni mbaya.	This man is good and that one bad.
Walikwenda huko na huko.	They went here and there.

Exercise 13

Write in Swahili: this well; these months; that day; those stones; this world; that place; those sores; those foolish people; these lamps; this soil; those songs; this year; this eye; that disease; this place; here in this house; there in that house; over there in the field.

Write the following as you would do if the thing had been already referred to: this food; these loads; these Englishmen; this sorrow; these faults; this place; these cloths; these hills; this European; these joys; this market.

LESSON 15

NEGATIVE TENSES

WE will now consider the negative forms of the tenses given in Lesson 12. They are formed with the negative particle **ha**. In the **WATU** class some contraction has taken place, and the subject prefixes have become

si- (*not* hani-)	I	**hatu-**	we
hu- (*not* hau-)	you	**ham-**	you
ha- (*not* haa-)	he	**hawa-**	they

With the other noun classes there is no irregularity, the prefixes being **haki-, havi-, hau-, hai-,** etc.

PRESENT TENSE (**HA-I**)

sisomi	I do not read	**hatusomi**	we do not read
husomi	you do not read	**hamsomi**	you do not read
hasomi	he does not read	**hawasomi**	they do not read

It will be seen that there is no tense prefix, but the final vowel of the verb stem is changed to **i**. This change does not take place in verbs derived from the Arabic which end in some other vowel; e.g. **hajibu,** he does not answer.

This tense serves as the negative of both the **A** and **NA** present tenses. Examples of its use with other noun classes are:

Chakula hiki hakitoshi.	This food is insufficient.
Vitabu hivi havitoshi.	These books are too few.
Mwezi mmoja hautoshi.	One month is not long enough.
Miti hii haitoshi.	There are not enough poles.

PAST TENSE (**HA-KU**)

sikusoma	I did not read	**hatukusoma**	we did not read
hukusoma	you did not read	**hamkusoma**	you did not read
hakusoma	he did not read	**hawakusoma**	they did not read

Mvua haikutosha.	There was too little rain.
Siku mbili hazikutosha.	Two days were not enough.

This past tense is made with the tense prefix **KU.** If the verb is a monosyllable no second **ku** is needed.

FUTURE TENSE (**HA-TA**)

sitasoma	I shall not read	**hatutasoma**	we shall not read
hutasoma	you will not read	**hamtasoma**	you will not read
hatasoma	he will not read	**hawatasoma**	they will not read

Gunia halitatosha.   The sack will not be big enough.
Mafuta hayatatosha.   The oil will not be enough.

This tense is of the same form as the past negative, with the future prefix **TA** instead of **KU.**

The present negative is often preferred to the future in general statements, e.g. **Siendi leo,** I shall not go today; **Haji tena,** He won't come again.   But with the verb **weza,** be able, the reverse is the case, for here the present tense has taken the special meaning of " I am ill " and therefore the future tense, **Sitaweza,** is generally used for " I cannot ".

THE NOT-YET TENSE (**HA-JA**)

sijasoma	I have not yet read	**hatujasoma**	we have not yet read
hujasoma	you have not yet read	**hamjasoma**	you have not yet read
hajasoma	he has not yet read	**hawajasoma**	they have not yet read

Unga haujatosha.   The flour is still not enough.
Ndizi hazijatosha.   There are not enough bananas yet.

This tense is a kind of negative of the perfect **ME** tense, as it implies that something has not happened up to the present time.   It is often followed by **bado,** not yet.   It is only used where there is still hope of the event occurring; if there is no hope, the past tense is used:

> **Amefika?** Has he come?   If he is still expected, the answer will be: **Hajafika;** or, **Hajafika bado,** or just **Bado.**   But if the time of his coming is now past, the answer may be, **Hakufika.**

The word **kabla** (before) used with this tense makes the equivalent of " Before I read ", etc. **Kabla hajafika,** Before he arrives.

In all these tenses, the object prefix, if used, comes in its usual place, immediately before the verb stem:

Hawatuoni.	They do not see us.
Hujamsikia.	You have not heard him.
Mahali hapatatutosha.	The place will not be big enough for us.

Monosyllabic Verbs

These verbs (including **isha** and **enda**) retain their **ku** in the **TA** tense only: **Haji,** he does not come; **Hakuja,** he did not come; **Hajaja,** he has not come; but **Hatakuja,** he will not come. Similarly, **Haendi, hakuenda, hajaenda, hatakwenda.**

Vocabulary

iva, get ripe, be cooked	**ogopa,** be afraid
oza, go bad, rot	**ongea,** converse
kosa, fail, make mistake	**zoea,** get used to
pona, get well	**zuia,** hinder
vizuri, nicely, well	**sana,** very

Exercise 14

Write in English; then put back into Swahili: Sijui. Hukusema. Hatafika. Hatuogopi. Hamtakuja? Hawauzi. Huingii? Hamjazoea. Sitakwenda. Hajaja bado. Hatujaandika. Sijamwuliza. Hawajamwona. Hutalipata jembe. Hamniogopi? Hatukumpenda. Hakuniambia. Sikumzuia. Sijamwona mbwa wako. Hampendi mgeni wetu. Hatutapata ruhusa. Hujayasikia mashauri? Nyama haijaiva bado. Hawakutoa fedha. Ugomvi haufai. Ugonjwa wake hauponi. Sitakosa kukuambia. Mihindi haijaiva. Sikuzoea kuona walevi. Mwizi yule ni mbaya, hamwogopi Mungu. Wazungu hawa hawajui Kiswahili. Kidonda changu hakijapona. Ndizi hazikuoza, zimeiva vizuri. Watoto hawakuongea, walimwogopa mwalimu. Shauri lake halitafaa. Mke wangu hajaizoea nchi hii. Chakula hakikufaa sana, hakikuiva.

LESSON 16

THE INFINITIVE, IMPERATIVE AND SUBJUNCTIVE

THE **INFINITIVE** is the form of the verb beginning with **ku** in Swahili and **to** in English. We have already spoken of it in connection with the noun classes, for any verb in the infinitive can be used as a noun, e.g. **kusoma,** to read, reading; **kuandika,** to write, writing.

The negative infinitive is formed with a verb **kuto(w)a,** to lack. Occasionally the full form **kutoa kusoma** is found, but usually it is shortened to **kutokusoma,** or even **kutosoma,** The monosyllabic verbs never take this last form, but always retain their **ku;** e.g. **kutokuja,** not to come; **kutokwenda,** not to go.

Examples of the use of the infinitive:

> **Kusema ni kuzuri, na kutokusema ni kuzuri.** To speak is good, and to be silent is good.
> **Najua kusoma na kuandika.** I know how to read and write.
> **Kusoma kwafaa sana.** Reading is very useful.

The infinitive has two special uses:

1. It can be used instead of repeating the verb tense:

> **Watoto wanaandika na kusoma.** The children are reading and writing.
> **Watoto hawakusoma wala kuandika.** The children did not read or write.

NOTE: **Wala** is used instead of **na** in negative sentences.

2. It can be used before the verb of the sentence to call attention to a fact:

> **Kufa tutakufa wote.** As for dying, we shall all die.

The **IMPERATIVE** is the form used in giving orders or directions. In Swahili, as in English, it is the simplest form of the verb:

> **Soma.** Read. **Andika.** Write. **Imba.** Sing.

When giving an order to more than one person the plural form must be used. This is made by adding **-ni** (from **ninyi,** you). Under the influence of this **ni,** the final vowel of the verb stem, if **a,** is changed to **e***. We have seen this happen before; see page 39:

Someni. Read (ye). **Andikeni.** Write (ye).
Imbeni. Sing (ye)

This change of the final **a** to **e*** takes place in the singular also, when an object prefix comes before the verb:

Visome. Read them (books). **Ziandike.** Write them (letters).

NOTE : Monosyllabic verbs retain the **ku** in the singular, unless there is an object prefix. The **ku** is not necessary in the plural, but is frequently used: **Kula!** Eat! **Leni!** Eat (ye)! The monosyllabic verb **pa,** give, is never used without an object, and therefore the **ku** is not needed: **Nipe!** Give me! **Mpeni!** Give (ye) him!

Ja, come, has an irregular imperative, **Njoo! Njoni!**
Enda, go, makes the imperative, **Nenda! Nendeni!** or **Enenda! Enendeni!**
Leta, bring, makes **Lete! Leteni!**, the **e** being used in the singular even without an object prefix.

There is a negative imperative in existence:

Sisome! Do not read. Pl. **Sisomeni!**

but the subjunctive (see below) nearly always takes its place. The subjunctive is used instead of the imperative in the affirmative also, when a more courteous form of request is needed; and, when two imperatives follow one another, the second is put into the subjunctive: **Njoo usome!** Come and read!

The **SUBJUNCTIVE** is formed with the subject prefix followed by the verb stem with its final **a** changed to **e**; no change takes place if the verb does not end in **a**. To form the negative subjunctive **si** is inserted between the subject prefix and the verb stem. If there is an object prefix, it comes just before the verb stem, after the **si.**

* In the Mombasa dialect this change is not always made.

Affirmative		*Negative*	
(that I may read, etc.)		(that I may not read, etc.)	
nisome	tusome	nisisome	tusisome
usome	msome	usisome	msisome
asome	wasome	asisome	wasisome

With the other noun classes the appropriate prefixes are used:

Chakula kipate moto.	Let the food get hot.
Mbegu zisipate maji.	Don't let the seeds get wet.

The subjunctive primarily denotes purpose or intention, but it can be translated in many different ways:

Nipe kitabu nisome.	Give me a book that I may read.
Nisome kitabu hiki?	Shall I read this book?
Nisome hiki.	Let me read this.
Watoto wasome?	Are the children to read?
Wasisome.	Don't let them read.

Besides the ordinary meaning of an intention or purpose not to do, the negative subjunctive can bear the meaning of an intention or purpose which fails:

Alinitafuta asinione. He looked for me without finding me.

Tulijaribu kila dawa isifae. We tried every medicine but they were all useless.

Walimwuliza maswali mengi asiseme (neno) lo lote. They asked him many questions without his answering a word.

Walisikia sauti wasimwone mtu. They heard a voice without seeing anyone.

NOTES:

1. The subjunctive should be used in Swahili whenever purpose or intention is denoted, except with verbs of *going* and *coming*, which are usually followed by the infinitive:

I gave the cook money to buy rice. **Nilimpa mpishi fedha anunue mchele.**

I am looking for the cook to give him the money. **Ninamtafuta mpishi nimpe fedha.**

They have gone to the field to hoe. **Wamekwenda shambani kulima.**

I have come to see the baby. **Nimekuja kumtazama mtoto.**

But, by modern usage, the infinitive can be used, preceded by **ili,** in order that, if there is no change of person:

I am working in order to get money. **Ninafanya kazi ili kupata fedha.**

If there is a change of person, the subjunctive must be used:

I am working in order that my child may get clothes. **Ninafanya kazi (ili) mtoto wangu apate nguo.**

It is not necessary to use **ili** when the subjunctive is used, as the meaning is contained in the verb itself, but it is often added. The verb **pata,** get, can be used when there is some idea of managing or contriving:

Imbeni nyimbo zenu (ili) nizisikie. Sing your songs that I may hear them.

Imbeni nyimbo zenu nipate kuzisikia. Sing your songs so that I may have a chance of hearing them.

2. The subjunctive must be used after verbs of *telling, commanding* or *requesting,* and after words like **lazima, sharti,** which denote compulsion or obligation:

Tell the child to read. **Mwambie mtoto asome.**
Ask him to give us an answer. **Mwombe atupe jibu.**
He must go. **Lazima aende.**

3. After verbs implying *not* to do something, such as verbs of forbidding, refusing and preventing, the *negative* subjunctive must be used. Among such verbs are **kataa,** refuse; **kataza,** forbid; and **zuia,** prevent:

The parents have forbidden their children to do this. **Wazee wamewakataza watoto wao wasifanye hivi.**

Mother has refused to let me go. **Mama amekataa nisiende.**

Prevent the child from going there. **Mzuie mtoto asiende kule.**

Vocabulary

angalia, observe, take care
ngoja, wait
ondoa, take away
ondoka, go away

iba, steal
imba, sing
acha, leave, let alone
pika, cook

Exercise 15

Write in Swahili: Look out! Go away (all of you)!
Wait! Don't let him wait. May I go away? Stop speaking. Shall I bring the food? Give me a pen. Take away
the cups. Do not steal. Don't let them sing here. Don't
wait. Let us take care. Don't go away. Come here.

Write in English; then put back into Swahili: Ondoka
hapa uende mjini. Ngojeni, msiondoke bado. Mlete
mbwa wako tumwone. Tuimbe nyimbo zetu ili wageni
wapate kuzisikia. Mpishi anauliza, je, apike chakula?
Mwambie aanze kupika nyama, asipike viazi bado. Mwangalie mgonjwa asiondoke kitandani. Je, wataka nikae
nyumbani au niende kazini? Mwalimu aliwakataza watoto
wasiimbe wala kuongea. Waambie watoto waondoe vitabu
vyao na kuondoka, ili wageni waingie wale chakula.

LESSON 17

THE KI AND KA TENSES

THE **KI** tense shows simultaneous action; the **KA** tense
consecutive action. The two tenses are quite distinct in
Swahili, though many Bantu languages have only one
form for both. The tenses are formed by putting **KI** or
KA between the subject prefix and the verb stem.

Ki Tense

(if I read, when I read, I reading)

nikisoma
ukisoma
akisoma

tukisoma
mkisoma
wakisoma

After another verb this tense is equivalent to an English
verb in *-ing:*

Nilimwona akilia.	I saw him crying.
Alipita akiimba.	He went by singing.
Nalimsikia akisema.	I heard him saying.

In other cases it is best translated by using *if* or *when* :

Akiniomba, nitampa.	If he asks me, I will give (it) to him.
Wakija, wape vitabu.	When they come, give them the books.
Ukitazama utaviona.	If you look you will see them.

When the sense of *if* predominates, the conjunction **kama,** if, is often used as well:

Kama mpishi akipata samaki asinunue nyama. If the cook gets fish he is not to buy meat.

Ka Tense

(and I read)

nikasoma	tukasoma
ukasoma	mkasoma
akasoma	wakasoma

This tense always expresses an action or state which follows another. It is most commonly found after the past **LI** tense, and is much used in stories and narrations:

Tulikwenda mjini tukamwona Ali, tukasema naye, tukaondoka, tukarudi kwetu. We went to the village and saw Ali and spoke with him, and came away and returned to our home.

It is, however, found after any tense, and its use seems to be becoming more frequent. More about this will be said in a later chapter. For the present the reader is advised to use it only after the **LI** tense. Remember that, unless the action of the second verb is subsequent to that of the first, the infinitive should be used:

Nilikwenda sokoni nikarudi.	I went to the market and came back.
Watu wanakwenda na kurudi.	People are going and coming.

The **KI** tense has a negative counterpart, denoting *if not, unless*, etc. **SIPO** is used in place of **KI**.

The Sipo Tense

(if I do not read)

nisiposoma	tusiposoma
usiposoma	msiposoma
asiposoma	wasiposoma

Asipokuja, sitaweza kumwambia. If he does not come I shall not be able to tell him.

Tusipopata mvua, mihindi haitafaa. Unless we get rain the maize will be no good.

Monosyllabic verbs, as also **isha** and **enda,** retain the **ku** in the **SIPO** tense, but not in the **KI** and **KA** tenses: **akija,** if he comes; **akaja,** and he came; **asipokuja,** unless he comes.

There is no difficulty about forming these tenses with nouns of the other classes:

Viazi vyako vikifaa nitavinunua. If your potatoes are good I will buy them.

Tulipata mvua kubwa ikaharibu maua. We got a heavy rain and it destroyed the flowers.

Chakula kisipoiva hakitafaa. If the food does not get cooked through it will be no good.

Vocabulary

lima, dig, hoe	**jenga,** build
panda, sow, plant	**ng'oa,** uproot
ota, grow	**chuma,** pick
palia, hoe up weeds	**chukua,** carry
linda, guard	**chagua,** choose
zaa, bear fruit	**pita,** pass
vuna, reap	**pima,** measure
mavuno, harvest	**asante,** thank you
asubuhi, morning	**pole !** I am sorry

Exercise 16

Read and translate; then translate back from the Key:
Nilimwona mzee wa mji akijenga nyumba yake. Nika-mwuliza, " Je, baba, mwaka huu mmepata mavuno

mazuri? " Akasema, " Bwana, hatukupata kitu." Nika-
mwuliza, " Hamkulima? " Akasema, " Kulima, tulilima ;
tukapanda mbegu zikaota. Tukapalia majani, tukalinda
kila siku ili nyani na nguruwe wasiharibu mihindi yetu.
Mihindi ikazaa, ikaiva. Tukataka kuvuna. Lo-o-o!
Tembo wakaja usiku wakauvunja ukuta wa shamba, waka-
ingia, wakaliharibu shamba lote. Tumepata hasara
kubwa." Nikamwambia, " Pole! baba. Huna shamba
lingine? " Akasema, " Nina shamba kubwa la muhogo,
sitakosa chakula. Asubuhi nalikwenda kung'oa muhogo
na kuchuma machungwa. Ngoja nikupe machungwa."
Akamwambia mke wake, " Lete machungwa hapa."
Akaleta, akaniambia, " Chukua, bwana. Chagua machungwa makubwa, yameiva vizuri." Nikachukua machungwa matano, makubwa sana, nikayatia katika mfuko
wangu. Nikamwambia, " Baba, asante sana, yatanifaa
sana njiani."

LESSON 18

THE NGE AND NGALI TENSES

THESE are the tenses which, in English, are often called
conditional, that is, they express a supposition depending
on a certain condition. When referring to present time the
NGE tense is used; when referring to past time and the
condition is now impossible of realisation, the **NGALI** tense
should be used:

> **Kama ningejua kusoma ningenunua kitabu.** If I knew
> how to read I should buy a book.
> **Kama ningalijua kusoma ningalinunua kitabu.** If I
> had known how to read I should have bought a
> book.

In actual practice, few natives make this distinction con-
sistently; they are as uncertain about the use of **nge** and
ngali as many English people are about the use of *should*
and *would*. But it is the accepted ruling, and should be
observed.

Both tenses are made by inserting the tense prefix **NGE** or **NGALI** between the subject prefix and the verb stem. No stress can fall on these two tense prefixes; the words given above are pronounced **níngejúa, níngenunúa, níngalijúa, níngalinunúa.** Hence verbs of one syllable have to retain their **ku** unless they have an object prefix to take the stress:

> **Angalikuja ningalimpa.** If he had come I should have given (it) to him.

As will be seen from the above example, **kama** is not always used; but its use makes clear which part of the sentence shows the condition and which the consequence.

It should be remembered that the English *should* does not always express a condition; sometimes it denotes duty or advisability, e.g. You should go. In this case it must be translated in some other way, e.g. **Yafaa uende.** It is good that you go.

The negative form of these tenses is the same as the affirmative, with **SI** inserted after the subject prefix.

Nge Tense

I should (not) read

Affirmative		*Negative*	
ningesoma	tungesoma	nisingesoma	tusingesoma
ungesoma	mngesoma	usingesoma	msingesoma
angesoma	wangesoma	asingesoma	wasingesoma

Ngali Tense

I should (not) have read

ningalisoma	tungalisoma	nisingalisoma	tusingalisoma
ungalisoma	mngalisoma	usingalisoma	msingalisoma
angalisoma	wangalisoma	asingalisoma	wasingalisoma

With the other noun classes the formation is regular:

> **Miti isingetoa maua kama tusingepata mvua.** The trees would not flower if we did not get rain.
>
> **Kama jua lingetoka mihindi ingepona.** If the sun would come out the maize would be saved.

Kama vitabu visingalifika watoto wasingaliweza ku-soma. If the books had not come, the children would not have been able to read.

There is a second form of the negative tenses which you should be able to recognise when you meet it. Instead of using the ordinary subject prefixes followed by **si**, it uses the negative subject prefixes (see page 43) without **si**:

Nge Tense		Ngali Tense	
singesoma	hatungesoma	singalisoma	hatungalisoma
hungesoma	hamngesoma	hungalisoma	hamngalisoma
hangesoma	hawangesoma	hangalisoma	hawangalisoma

So also, **Chakula hakingetosha, vitabu havingalitosha,** etc. You will probably find it easier to keep to the first form for your own use.

In the present and the future, unless the condition is very much emphasised, the **KI** tense is all that is needed:

Kama jua likitoka, mihindi itapona. If (when) the sun comes out the maize will recover.

Study carefully the Swahili of the Exercise and translate it into English. Then turn the English back into Swahili. No new verbs are introduced.

Exercise 17

Kama ungetoa fedha ungepata chakula. Kama wasi-ngetoa fedha wasingepata chakula. Kama tungalitoa fedha tungalipata chakula. Kama tusingalitoa fedha tusingalipata chakula. Kama angepanda mihogo asingeo-gopa njaa. Kama asingalipanda mihogo angaliona njaa. Kama ungechuma machungwa yako ungeweza kuyauza sokoni. Kama tungalilima mwaka huu tungalipata mavuno. Kama askari wasingalipata maji wangalirudi. Kama nchi hii ingepata mvua watu wengi wangejenga hapa. Kama watoto wangaliangalia kazi yao wasingalifanya makosa mengi. Kama tukipata nyama hatutanunua samaki.

LESSON 19

IMPERSONAL FORMS

The HU Tense

This is a very useful, easy, and much used tense, showing customary, frequent or habitual action. It makes no distinction between persons and times, the one form (**HU** with the verb stem) being used for all persons and any time. No **ku** is needed in the monosyllabic verbs.

> **Ulevi huondoa akili.** Drunkenness takes away sense.
> **Magari * hupita kila siku.** Trains go by every day.
> **Kila mwaka baba yangu hulima shamba la mpunga.** Every year my father cultivates a field of rice.

Note : **kila,** every, unlike other adjectives, precedes the noun.

There Is

The equivalent of the English construction " There is " is made in Swahili with the verb *has*, as was shown in Lesson 8 :

There is a man at the door.   **Pana mtu mlangoni.**
There is water on the way.   **Kuna maji njiani.**
In the bag there is a loaf.   **Katika mfuko mna mkate.**

The negative forms are made by prefixing **ha: hapana, hakuna, hamna:**

Hapana mtu.   There is no one here.
Hakuna watu.   There are no people about.
Hamna mtu.   There is no one in.

Note: **Hapana** is frequently used in the sense of **No!**:

> " **Bwana, nataka ruhusa.**" " **Hapana!** " " Sir, I want leave." " No!"
> " **Niende sasa?** " " **Hapana, ngoja kidogo.**" " Shall I go now? " " No, wait a little."

---

* Any wheeled vehicle, from a train to a wheelbarrow.

It is also used, quite inexcusably, as a general negative by those who do not take the trouble to learn Swahili—**Hapana kwenda!** Don't go. Never use it like this.

The past tenses will be dealt with later.

It

The impersonal *it* is denoted in Swahili by the singular prefix of the **N** class, **i.** The following verbs are very commonly used this way:

(a) **pasa,** it is right, it is proper, it behoves:

Yatupasa kusali kila siku. It is right to pray every day.
Inanipasa kurudi sasa. I must go back now.
Imekupasa kulipa. It behoves you to pay.

(b) **bidi,** used very much like **pasa,** but usually implying more moral compulsion:

Ilinibidi kwenda. I was obliged to go.
Yanibidi kusema hivi. I feel I must say this.
Imekubidi kumtii mwalimu. You must obey your teacher.

(c) **faa,** be of use, be good.

Yafaa tuondoke sasa. We had better go now.
Itafaa kuandika habari hii. It will be a good thing to write this matter down.
Haifai kuongea saa za shule. It is not fitting to talk in school hours.

(d) **haidhuru,** never mind, it does not matter, from **dhuru,** cause harm:

" Bwana, hakuna nyama sokoni." " Haidhuru." " Sir, there is no meat in the market." " Never mind, it does not matter."

(e) **wezekana,** be possible, from **weza,** be able. The commonest phrase is **Haiwezekani!** It can't be done!

The verb TO BE gives many impersonal forms which will be discussed later.

c

Vocabulary

fuata, follow	**sana,** very
ficha, hide	**sasa,** now
tumia, use	**leo,** today
lia, cry, as person or animal	**upesi,** quickly
piga, beat	**tu,** only

EXERCISE 18

Write in English. Then put back into Swahili: Ugomvi huleta matata. Simba hulia sana siku hizi. Furaha hufuata huzuni. Haifai kupiga watoto sana. Yafaa uondoke sasa uende nyumbani. Haiwezekani kufanya kazi leo. Yakupasa uende shule kila siku. Haifai kufuata njia hii; njiani kuna maji. Haidhuru, nitaweza kupita. Yafaa turudi upesi. Taa hizi hutumia mafuta mengi. Nairobi hakuna mbu. Hapana simba hapa. Pana watu hapa, wanatafuta mayai. Kisimani mna maji? Hamna. Kama watu ni watatu tu, kazi haitawezekana leo.

LESSON 20

WHO AND WHICH (Relatives)

In Lesson 14, when studying the demonstratives *this* and *that*, we found a form in **o** used when referring to something already mentioned. This **o**, which has aptly been called the **o** of reference,* is used as a relative particle with verbs, referring back to the person or thing mentioned and denoting *who*, *which*, or *that*

Chakula kilitosha.	The food was enough.
Chakula kili*cho***tosha.**	The food *which* was enough.

This relative particle follows the tense prefix, and takes the same form as the **o** used in the demonstratives (see page 41), except in the singular of the **WATU** class, where **ye** is used instead of **yo** for all three persons:

---

* *Swahili Grammar* by E. O. Ashton.

(mimi) niliyesoma	I who read	**(sisi) tuliosoma**	we who read
(wewe) uliyesoma	you who read	**(ninyi) mliosoma**	you who read
(yeye) aliyesoma	he who read	**(wao) waliosoma**	they who read

It is not necessary to use the personal pronouns except for emphasis:

> **Waliosoma jana wasimame.** Those who read yesterday, stand up.
>
> **Mimi niliyeona nasema hivi.** I who saw (the matter) say thus.

The following sentences show the use of the relative particle with the other noun classes. The particles are shown for all the classes in the Table of Concords at the end of the book.

> **Ndizi zilizoiva ni hizi.** The bananas which ripened are these.
>
> **Nimeijibu barua iliyokuja jana.** I have answered the letter which came yesterday.
>
> **Unga uliotoka sokoni ni mzuri?** Is the flour which came from the market good?

If there is an object prefix, it comes, as always, immediately before the verb stem:

> **Chakula kilicho*tu*tosha.** The food which sufficed *us*.

The relative particle is used in the same way with the NA present tense, e.g. **mimi ninayesoma,** I who am reading. But with the future tense **TAKA** is used as the tense prefix, instead of **TA,** when a relative particle is added, as neither the **ta** nor the relative particle can take a stress:

> **Watoto watakáosoma kitabu hiki.** The children who will read this book.

NOTE : The tense prefix **TA** is derived from **taka,** want; therefore the **ka** is not really an addition; it is the whole verb stem being used for ease of pronunciation instead of its shortened form.

The **LI, NA** and **TA** tenses are the only affirmative tenses in which a relative particle can be inserted. The relative form of the **LI** tense is used for the **ME** tense also, for it is obvious that someone who *has read* is he who *read*.

But there is also a *general relative* with no special note of time. It is formed by the subject prefix, the verb stem, and the relative particle at the end:

mtoto asomaye	a child who reads
shamba litoshalo	a field which is big enough
simba aliaye kila siku	the lion who roars every day

As there is no tense prefix, the object prefix follows the subject prefix immediately:

ani̱sikiaye	he who hears *me*
tumwonao	we who see *him*
shamba litufaalo	a field that suits *us*

There is only *one negative relative tense*, which, having no special note of time, can be used for past, present or future. It is formed by prefixing the subject prefix, the negative particle **si**, and the relative particle to the verb stem:

mimi nisiyesoma	I who do not read
chakula kisichotosha	food which is insufficient
miti isiyofaa	poles which are no use

It is often possible to translate such verbs by adjectives: e.g. *insufficient food; useless poles;* etc.

The object prefix takes its usual place:

asiyenijua	he who does not know *me*
shoka lisilotufaa	the axe which does not suit *us*

It is owing to this adjectival sense that the one form can be used for any time, as shown in the following sentences:

Watu wasiokuja kazini jana waende kwa Bwana. The men who did not come to work yesterday, let them go to the master.

Watu wasiokuja kazini leo wasipate fedha yao kesho. The men who are not at work today, let them not get their money tomorrow.

Watu wasiokuja kazini kesho watapata matata. Men who do not come to work tomorrow will get (into) trouble.

We can speak of the child who reads a book, and we can speak also of the book the child reads. In both cases the *child* is the subject of the verb *reads*, but in the first case the relative refers to the child, and in the second case to the book, which is the thing read, i.e. the object. In the second case the relative particle must refer to the book, not to the child, and, as one particular book is now specified, there must be an object prefix in the verb. In order that the relative may be near the word to which it relates, it is usual to put the subject after the verb instead of in its usual place before it. Notice carefully the difference between the following sentences:

The child who read a book.	**Mtoto aliyesoma kitabu.**
The book which the child read.	**Kitabu alichokisoma mtoto.**
The old man who cultivated a field.	**Mzee aliyelima shamba.**
The field which the old man cultivated.	**Shamba alilolilima mzee.**
I who read books.	**Mimi nisomaye vitabu.**
The books which I read.	**Vitabu nivisomavyo.**
I who do not read books.	**Mimi nisiyesoma vitabu.**
The books which I do not read.	**Vitabu nisivyovisoma.**

Make quite sure to what thing the relative *which* or *who* refers, and then make the particle agree with the right noun class.

As the relative particle cannot bear a stress, **ku** must be retained in monosyllabic verbs and the two verbs **isha** and **enda,** unless they have an object prefix:

watu walio*ku*la mikate.	The people who ate bread.
Watu walio*i*la mikate.	The people who ate *the* bread.

Vocabulary

anguka, fall down	**jana,** yesterday
amkia, greet	**kesho,** tomorrow
aga, take leave of	**vizuri,** well
potea, get lost	**v(y)ema,** well
pungua, get less	**vibaya,** badly

Exercise 19

Write in Swahili: The sore which does not heal; the certificates which got lost; the bread which was no good; the date trees which are bearing; the trouble (**shida**) which will come upon (get) us; the bananas which do not ripen; a plan which I heard; the words which they will speak; rice which we are eating; the songs which they sang; a place which is not suitable; the dog which they are beating; the mother who bore me; the things which we have got used to; a suitable time (which is suitable); coming days (which come); lions which roar at night; the lightning which struck my house; the rain which is destroying the maize; the wind which broke that coconut palm; words which caused (put into) us grief; the visitors who looked at our work; our work which they looked at; the food which the cook will cook; laziness (**uvivu**) which brings hunger; quarrelling which follows drunkenness; the songs which they sang well; the rain which does not get less; the old men we took leave of.

LESSON 21

MORE ABOUT THE RELATIVE

Place and Time

The relative particles of place are **po**, **ko** and **mo**, referring to a *definite*, an *indefinite*, and an *inside* position:

Hatujui alikokwenda.   We do not know where he has gone.

Hatujui alipoviweka.   We do not know where he put them.

Hatujui alimoingia.   We do not know where he went in.

With an adverbial noun ending in **-ni**, these relative particles must be used, for such a noun no longer belongs to its original class:

Je, wamepata maji nyumbani wana*mo*kula?   Have they got water in the house where they are eating?

Twataka kujenga kanisa hapa mjini tuna*po*kaa. We want to build a church here in the village where we live.

Ku*le* mjini ana*ko*kwenda kuna mashauri. There in the town where he is going there are discussions (going on).

The relative **po** is used also of *time*:

Aliponiona aliniamkia. When he saw me he greeted me.

Simba anapolia, tunaogopa sana. When the lion roars we are much afraid.

Nitampa kisu chake nitakapomwona. I will give him his knife when I (shall) see him.

Manner

The **VI** concords, as well as being used with nouns of the plural of the **KITU** class, are also used to express *manner*:

vibaya	badly	hivi	in this way
vizuri	well	vile	in that way
vema	well	hivyo	in the way referred to
Alisoma vibaya.			He read badly.
Alisema hivi.			He said thus.
Fanya hivyo.			Do like this.

Hence the relative particle **vyo,** as well as referring to things of the **KITU** class, has also the meaning of *thus, in this way,* etc. **Kama,** here meaning *like* or *as,* or **jinsi,** *how,* is often used as well:

Nionavyo mimi hatakuja. As I think (see), he will not come.

Fanya kama utakavyo. Do as you like.

Walifanya walivyoweza. They did what they could (as they were able).

Ngoja, tumtazame mbwa atakavyofanya. Wait, let us see what (how) the dog will do.

Kama wazee wanavyosema. As the old men say.

Nionyeshe jinsi ulivyopotea. Show me how you got lost.

Po pote, ko kote, vyo vyote, are frequently used with relatives of place and manner:

Ko kote tuendako.	Wherever we go.
Po pote ninaposimama.	Wherever I stand.
Vyo vyote upendavyo.	Anyhow you like.

After **nani?** *who?* and **wapi?** *where?*, and other words denoting *which?, what kind of?*, etc.; the relative is usually used:

Nani aliyesema hivi?	Who said this?
Ni nani wanaoongea?	Who are talking?
Asiyesoma ni nani?	Who has not read?
Ni wapi ulipomwona?	Where did you see him?

Amba

There is another way of constructing the relative which is becoming increasingly used now. This is by attaching the relative particle to **amba-** and making no change in the verb. The construction is therefore similar to the English, using **ambaye, ambacho,** etc. instead of *who, which,* or *that*:

Mtu *ambaye* aliijenga nyumba yangu ni huyu. The man *who* built my house is this one.

Nyumba *ambayo* ilianguka ni hii. The house *which* fell down is this.

Usiseme maneno *ambayo* hujayapima vema. Do not say words *which* you have not weighed carefully.

Good Swahili got on for years without these forms, but they are likely to become more common as time goes on, and more will be said about them later.

Vocabulary

tupa, throw	**cheka,** laugh
kata, cut	**cheza,** play
lala, lie down, sleep	**sahau,** forget
amka, wake	**saidia,** help

Exercise 20

Write in Swahili: Who gave you these eggs? If this tree does not bear fruit I shall cut it (down). I do not know where he lives. He does not know where he comes from or where he is going to. He came yesterday as he said. When the visitors (will) come they will want food. When the bananas went bad, the cook threw them (away). Do as your teacher told you. We shall do the best we can. I don't know how the discussions went. The news of this place is as you have heard. Who built this house? When we saw them playing we laughed very much. I shall follow you wherever you go. Help me now, as I helped you yesterday. Do not forget to give them the news where you are going. When he wakes I shall go to greet him.

LESSON 22

THE PASSIVE

So far, most of the changes we have noted in Swahili verbs have been made by the addition of prefixes at the beginning, but there are several possible modifications of the end of the verb stem. Most of these will be explained in a later lesson, but it is a good thing to learn how to make the passive form of a verb (to *be* read, to *be* loved, etc.) before learning the verb TO BE. If you do not know the verb TO BE, you will not be able to make the mistake of using it in the Swahili passive.

In English we make the passive form with the verb TO BE—I *am* loved; the book *was* read, etc., but in Swahili all we do is to change the final **a** into **wa**:

jenga, build; **jengwa,** be built; **piga,** beat; **pigwa,** be beaten; **andika,** write; **andikwa,** be written; etc.

All the tenses are the same as in the verbs we have studied; the only difference is the **w** in the ending of the verb stem.

Most verbs ending in **ia** or **ea** make their passive in the same way:

sikia, hear; **sikiwa**   **amkia,** greet; **amkiwa**
tia, put in; **tiwa**   **lemea,** press upon; **lemewa**

But those ending in **aa**, **oa** and **ua**, where the inserted **w** would not be easily recognised in pronunciation, insert **li** or **le** as well:

zaa, bear fruit; **zaliwa**	**toa,** take out; **tolewa**
jua, know; **juliwa**	**ondoa,** take away; **ondolewa**
nunua, buy; **nunuliwa**	**ng'oa,** uproot; **ng'olewa**
fungua, open; **funguliwa**	**chukua,** carry; **chukuliwa**

NOTE: These verbs were originally **zala, tola,** etc., and the l has dropped out. Moreover, there are two passive formations common in Bantu languages, one in **wa** and the other in **iwa**. So that these are not really cases of an inserted **li,** but of reversion to the old form. Notice that when the vowel in the preceding syllable is **e** or **o**, **iwa** becomes **ewa**.

This distinction between **i** and **e** in modifications of the endings of the verb stem will frequently be needed later, so it is well to get it quite clear now. If we write the vowels in their proper order, **a e i o u,** the first, middle and last are followed by **i,** and the intermediate ones by **e**.

The verb **lea,** bring up a child, makes its passive **lelewa,** to distinguish it from **lewa,** get drunk.

Verbs of Arabic origin, ending in **i, u** or **e,** make their passive in **iwa** or **ewa**:

jibu, answer; **jibiwa**	**kubali,** agree to; **kubaliwa**
haribu, destroy; **haribiwa**	**samehe,** forgive; **samehewa**

Those ending in **au** add **liwa** to the stem:

sahau, forget; **sahauliwa**	**dharau,** despise; **dharauliwa**

BY, after a passive verb, denoting the agent, is rendered in Swahili by **na**:

Mtoto alipigwa na baba yake. The child was beaten by its father.

In addition to the passive, there is another form in Swahili to denote state, or possible state, where no particular agent is denoted. This form ends in **IKA** or **EKA** according to the vowel in the verb stem. The difference between the passive and the **IKA** form, generally called the STATIVE, is shown in the following sentences:

Kikombe kimevunjwa na mtoto. The cup has been broken by the child.

Kikombe kimevunjika. The cup has been (is) broken.

Nguo zimeharibiwa na mvua. The clothes have been spoilt by the rain.

Nguo zimeharibika. The clothes are spoilt.

Shauri lilikubaliwa na wazee. The plan was accepted by the elders.

Shauri lilikubalika. The plan was agreed to.

Barua ilisomwa na mwalimu. The letter was read by the teacher.

Barua haisomeki. The letter is unreadable.

Of course, not all words can have a passive, and fewer still a stative form.

The passive and stative of the monosyllabic verbs in common use are:

La, eat; **liwa,** be eaten; **lika,** be eatable.

Nywa, drink; **nywewa,** be drunk; **nyweka,** be drinkable.

Pa, give; **pewa,** be given. (In the Mombasa dialect often **pawa.**)

In these forms the verbs are no longer monosyllabic, and do not retain the **ku** in any tense.

NOTES:

1. **Oa,** marry; **olewa**, be married. **Oa** is used only of the man, and **olewa** of the woman; it is always the man who marries, and the woman who is married. Another form, **oza,** make to marry, is used for the " marrying " done by the father or the priest.

2. **La, liwa, lika.** One would expect **lika,** be eatable, to be used with reference to edible fruits, etc. But this does not seem to be the case. Africans say:

" **Matunda haya yaliwa ?** " " **Hayaliwi.** " " Are these fruits edible ? " " No."

Hayaliki would be used of food spoilt by too much salt, etc.

3. **Pa,** give to. Passive verbs, of course, have no object. But the verb **pa,** which normally takes two objects,

a person and a thing, keeps one in the passive, though it cannot have an object prefix in the verb:

Nimepewa fedha na baba yangu.   I have been given money by my father.

4. **Ua,** kill, has an irregular passive, **uawa.**   The word is not used of slaughtering animals for food; for this **chinja** is used.   **Iba,** steal, generally takes the passive form **ibiwa:** **Fedha imeibiwa.**   The money has been stolen.

Exercise 21

Write in Swahili: A child has been born.   Many people were killed by the lion.   This plan has not yet been accepted by the natives.   My letter has been answered unsatis-factorily (badly).   The drum will be heard at night.   This affair was thoroughly looked into (**angaliwa**).   Coconut oil is usually used by cooks.   The children will not be forgiven. We were given a goat by the elders of the village.   If the milk were put into a bottle it would be able to be carried by the child.   If the maize is not destroyed by baboons, it will bear well.   The cassava plants have been uprooted by pigs.   This road is impassable.   His words are not for-gotten.   This work was not well done.

LESSON 23

TO BE (I)

THE verb TO BE is a monosyllabic verb **WA**, but in most of the forms of the present tense an old verb **LI** is used instead.   In this chapter we shall deal only with the verb **WA,** omitting the **LI** tenses.   All the tenses given in this chapter are regularly formed, but most retain the **ku** of the infinitive, as is usual with monosyllabic verbs.   The verb TO BE cannot take an object, so there are no object prefixes to be considered.

The PAST, FUTURE, and PRESENT CONTINUOUS TENSES are: **nilikuwa** or **nalikuwa,** I was; · **nitakuwa,** I shall be; **ninakuwa,** I am being.   The relative forms are **nilipokuwa,** when I was; **nitakapokuwa,** when I shall be; **ninapokuwa,** when I am, etc.

> **Tumeyala mayai yaliyokuwa mazuri.** We have eaten the eggs which were good.
>
> **Nyumba itakapokuwa tayari, nipe habari.** When the house is ready, let me know.
>
> **Anapokuwa katika kazi yake hasemi na mtu.** When he is (engaged) in his work he does not speak to anyone.

NOTE that this **NA** tense is chiefly used to express duration.

The PERFECT TENSE, **nimekuwa,** is best translated *I have become.* In Swahili it shows a completed action resulting in a state still existing, but in English, *I have been* is usually equivalent to a past tense. Therefore, in Swahili, **Je, umekuwa mwivi?** should be translated, *What! Have you become a thief?*

In translating the English *I have been*, use a past tense if the action is past and over, and a present if the state still endures:

> I have been ill (and am now better). **Nalikuwa mgonjwa.**
>
> I have been ill since January. **Ni mgonjwa tangu Januari.**

The **ME** tense, as noted before, has no relative form. The general relative, given in the next chapter, may be used, or the **amba-** form:

> **Watoto hawa wawili, ambao wamekuwa wevi, wataondoka mjini.** These two children, who have become thieves, will leave the town.

The negative tenses are given in full:

NEGATIVE PRESENT TENSE (**HA-I**)

siwi	I am not	**hatuwi**	we are not
huwi	you are not	**hamwi**	you are not
hawi	he is not	**hawawi**	they are not

Like the **NA** tense, this is not very often used; the tenses formed with **LI** are much more common. It is used when the emphasis is on existence in a certain state:

> **Hatuwi sasa watu wanaoogopa uchawi.** We are not now people who fear witchcraft.

NEGATIVE PAST TENSE (**HA—KU**)

sikuwa	I was not	**hatukuwa**	we were not
hukuwa	you were not	**hamkuwa**	you were not
hakuwa	he was not	**hawakuwa**	they were not

Ndizi hazikuwa nzuri. The bananas were not nice.

NEGATIVE FUTURE TENSE (**HA—TA**)

sitakuwa	I shall not be	**hatutakuwa**	we shall not be
hutakuwa	you will not be	**hamtakuwa**	you will not be
hatakuwa	he will not be	**hawatakuwa**	they will not be

Nguo haitakuwa ndefu. The garment will not be long.
Majibu hayatakuwa mazuri. The answers will not be favourable.

NOT-YET TENSE (**HA—JA**)

sijawa	I am not yet	**hatujawa**	we are not yet
hujawa	you are not yet	**hamjawa**	you are not yet
hajawa	he is not yet	**hawajawa**	they are not yet

NOTE: The note given under the **ME** tense applies here as well. The meaning of the Swahili is, *I have not yet become*, i.e. *I am not*.

> **Hajawa tayari.** He is not ready yet.

As with other verbs, there is a *general negative relative*, formed with the subject prefix, the negative prefix **si**, and the relative particle, followed by the verb stem which, in this case keeps the **ku** of the infinitive:

> **Watu wasiokuwa tayari hawakwenda.** The people who were not ready did not go.
> **Watu wasiokuwa tayari hawatakwenda.** Those who are not ready will not go.
> **Watu wasiokuwa tayari wasiende.** Those who are not ready are not to go.

The general relative exists also in the affirmative, but is little used. It is most often found in the form **awaye yote,** *whoever he be,* and in the impersonal form **iwapo,** *when it be,* i.e. *supposing.*

Other Tenses

As all the other tenses are also regular there is no need to give them in full. Complete them yourself, with reference, if necessary, to Lessons 16–18.

nikiwa	if I am	**nisipokuwa**	if I am not
ningekuwa	I should be	**nisingekuwa**	I should not be
ningalikuwa	I should have been	**nisingalikuwa**	I should not have been
nikawa	and I was		
huwa	I usually am		
niwe	may I be	**nisiwe**	may I not be

The infinitive is **kuwa,** to be, and the negative infinitive, **kutokuwa,** not to be. There is an irregular imperative, **iwe,** be (thou), **iweni,** be (ye), but it is very little used. The usual imperative is **uwe, mwe,** in the affirmative, and **usiwe, msiwe,** in the negative.

Some examples:

Mayai yakiwa mazuri, nitayanunua. If the eggs are good, I will buy them.

Machungwa yaliiva yakawa mazuri sana. The oranges ripened and were very nice.

Kama ungekuwa mtoto ningekupiga. If you were a child I should beat you.

Kama asingalikuwa mvivu angaliweza kupata kazi. If he had not been idle, he would have been able to get work.

Usipokuwa mwema hutapendwa. If you are not good you will not be loved.

Uwe mtoto mwema, usiwe mbaya. Be a good child; don't be naughty.

Siku za baridi zinapoingia, watu wengi huwa wagonjwa. When the cold weather comes in, many people get ill.

Ikiwa huna nafasi, haidhuru. If you have no time, never mind.

Exercise 22

Write in English; then put back into Swahili: Alikuwa
mtu mwema asiyekuwa na matata. Nyumba haikuwa
kubwa, na milango ilikuwa midogo. Mashauri hayatakuwa marefu. Usiwe mtu wa maneno mengi. Ikiwa huna
fedha, yafaa ufanye kazi. Tuliuza ng'ombe wawili walio-
kuwa wakubwa sana. Makosa yatakuwa mengi. Nimekuwa mzee sasa. Mavuno hayakuwa mengi mwaka huu.
Nzige watakapokuwa wakubwa, wataharibu mihindi yetu.
Mvua ikiwa nyingi sitaweza kuondoka. Sikununua matunda yasiyokuwa mazuri. Kama angalikuwa rafiki yangu
asingaliniacha katika hatari.

LESSON 24

TO BE (2)

THE present tenses of the verb TO BE which will be considered in this chapter are those formed from the old verb
LI of which only the root now remains. As we have
already seen, the l sound disappears very easily in Swahili,
and, except where the **LI** was stressed in pronunciation,
even the root has now got lost.

We will take first the forms in which the **LI** still remains:

THE GENERAL RELATIVE

As we saw with the verb **SOMA,** this is a relative tense
formed by the subject prefix, the verb stem, and the relative
particle at the end, **nisomaye,** I who read. We have just
seen one form of this tense made with the verb **WA, niwaye,**
I who am, but it is very little used, and the form made
with **LI** is the common one:

niliye	I who am	**tulio**	we who are
uliye	you who are	**mlio**	you who are
aliye	he who is	**walio**	they who are

The formation with the other noun classes is the same:

Chai iliyo nzuri; Unga ulio mbaya; Vitabu vilivyo vidogo;
etc.

There is a similar form in the negative, with **si** instead of **li**:

nisiye	I who am not	**tusio**	we who are not
usiye	you who are not	**msio**	you who are not
asiye	he who is not	**wasio**	they who are not

It will be noticed that it is similar to the negative relative given in the last lesson, but without the **kuwa**. It is used chiefly as a connective between a noun and its adjective:

Chai isiyo nzuri; Unga usio mbaya; Vitabu visivyo vingi; etc.

Other tenses in which the **LI** is still seen are the durative forms **ningali** and **nikali**. Probably these were two different tenses originally, the former suggesting the meaning of *although*. But now both seem to be used with the same meaning of *still*, the former in Zanzibar Swahili and the latter in Mombasa:

Ningali mgonjwa.	I am still ill.
Wangali watoto tu.	They are still just children.
Akali anavitafuta.	He is still looking for the things.

The Present Tense

The simple form of the present tense has been left until last, as in it the **LI** has entirely disappeared and all that remains is the subject prefix. So that the present tense may now be written:

ni	I am	**tu**	we are
u	you are	**m**	you are
yu	he is	**wa**	they are

NOTE: **yu** is a very old form of the subject prefix *he* or *she*. It is still found in **huyu, yule** (this, that) and a few other places, but has generally been displaced by *a*. In the **ningali** tense given above, **yungali** is as common as **angali** for the third person, and forms such as **yuasoma** (he reads) are found in the Mombasa dialect.

U mgonjwa?	Are you ill?	**Tu wageni.**	We are strangers.
Yu tayari.	He is ready.	**M nani?**	Who are you?

Notice the idiom **Yu macho,** he is eyes, for *He is awake*.

With the other noun classes the subject prefix of the class is used:

Kitabu ki wapi?   Where is the book?

It is more usual, however, for **ni** to take the place of these prefixes for all persons and things in the affirmative, and **si** in the negative:

Miti ni mali.	Trees are wealth.
Watoto ni wagonjwa.	The children are ill.
Unga huu si mzuri.	This flour is not good.

In some cases even **ni** is omitted:

Mimi Yohana.	I am John.
Unga huu mzuri.	This flour is good.
Kisu chako kikubwa.	Your knife is big.

Notice the idiom: **Jina lako nani?** What is your name? **Jina langu Ali.** My name is Ali.

The Emphatic Form

From other Bantu languages we gather that the original form of the present tense was **nili,** I am. In ordinary use the **li** dropped out in Swahili, but where there was emphasis it became **nli** and hence **ndi.** From this we get the emphatic forms:

ndimi	it is I	**ndisi**	it is we
ndiwe	it is you	**ndinyi**	it is you
ndiye	it is he	**ndio**	it is they

It will be seen that the second syllable is a shortened form of the personal pronouns, **mimi, wewe,** etc. Where things are denoted, the second syllable is that used as a relative particle: **Ndicho kitabu,** It is this book; **Ndizo nyumba,** It is these houses, etc.

In the negative, **si** takes the place of **ndi: Sicho hiki,** It is not this; **Sio hawa,** It is not they.

As a thing generally gets emphasised because something is being said about it, these forms are often found with a relative:

Ndicho kitabu nilichokitaka. This is the very book which I wanted.

Huyu siye mtu aliyeijenga nyumba yangu. This is not the man who built my house.

Hapa ndipo tulipomwona. Here is the place where we saw him.

Sivyo nilivyosema. It is not thus that I said—I didn't say any such thing.

Yes and No

Ndivyo or **sivyo** are used in assenting or dissenting when something is being related, in the sense of *It is so* or *It is not so*. But in the more general sense of *Yes* or *No*, the forms **Ndiyo, Siyo,** are used.

It is important to remember that **Ndiyo** means *It is so* and is not always equivalent to the English *Yes*. If one answers **Ndiyo** to a negative question, one is agreeing with the negative statement, and the answer is therefore equivalent to the English *No*:

"**Hukumpa fedha?**" "**Ndiyo, Bwana.**" "Didn't you give him the money?" "I did not, sir."

Conversely, **Siyo** may be equivalent to the English *Yes*:

"**Kuku hawajataga!**" "**Siyo, bwana, wametaga.**" "The hens have not laid yet!" "Not so, sir, they have laid."

This causes many misunderstandings between Europeans and Africans, and as much difficulty to an African learning English as to an Englishman learning Swahili.

Two Arabic words are used as well, **Naam,** yes, and **La,** no. They express agreement and disagreement in the same way as the English words. Another Arabic word **Hasha!** is an emphatic negative, Certainly not! God forbid!

The reader, however, has probably noticed that most answers repeat the whole sentence, or, at least, the verb:

Chakula kilitosha? Kilitosha. Was there enough food? Yes.

Ulimwona? Sikumwona. Did you see him? No.

Wamekuja? Hawajaja bado. Have they come? Not yet.

Bwana yupo? Hayupo. Is the master there? No.

Umesikia? Ndiyo, nimesikia. Do you hear? Yes, I hear.

The more we accustom ourselves to this way of answering, the fewer misunderstandings we shall have.

We close this chapter with two idiomatic ways of using **Ni** and **SI**:

Ndiyo kwanza, followed by the subjunctive, bears the meaning *only just*: **Ndiyo kwanza aingie,** He has only just come in. Sometimes it is equivalent to *the first time*, **Ndiyo kwanza afike kwetu.** It is the first time he has come to us.

Si, *is not*, is used in proverbs to denote that the first thing mentioned is worth more than the second:

Padogo pako si pakubwa pa mwenzio. Your little place is better than the big place of your companion.

Moja shika si kumi nenda uje. One "take hold of it" is better than ten "go and come again"; i.e. A bird in the hand is worth two in the bush.

Kweli iliyo chungu si uongo ulio mtamu. A bitter truth is better than a pleasant falsehood.

Vocabulary

nani ?	who?	**kweli**	truth, true
nini ?	what	**uongo**	falsehood
lini ?	when	**-tamu**	sweet
wapi ?	where?	**-chungu**	bitter
gani ?	what kind of?	**-fupi**	short

Exercise 23

Write in English; then put back into Swahili: U mgeni hapa? Ndiyo, mimi mgeni; kwetu ni Nairobi. Jina lako nani? Jina langu Abdala. Mtu gani * wewe? Mimi Mkikuyu. Sasa unakaa wapi? Nakaa hapa mjini, ndipo ninapofanya kazi. Nini hii? Ni mafuta. Ya nani? Ya mke wangu. Ni mafuta gani? Ni mafuta ya nazi yaliyo mazuri sana; yale yasiyo mazuri sisi hatununui. Sisi tulio watoto hatujui habari hii. Wale walio wagonjwa hawataweza kuja. Kanisa letu ndilo hili. Huyu ndiye baba yangu, na hawa ndio ndugu zangu. Njia iliyo fupi ndiyo hii. Maneno yake ndiyo hayo; ndivyo alivyoniambia. Humu ndimo alimoingia nyoka.

* **Mtu gani** means What tribe?

LESSON 25

TO BE IN A PLACE

In most cases, when we speak of a person or a thing " being " it is in connection with a place. When this is so, we join on to the end of the verb one of the three place syllables **po, ko** or **mo.** Which one we use depends on whether we are speaking of a definite place, an indefinite position, or somewhere inside. The present tense then becomes:

nipo	I am here	**tupo**	we are here
upo	you are here	**mpo**	you are here
yupo	he is here, there	**wapo**	they are here, there

Or, with the other syllables, **nimo,** I am in here; **yuko,** he is over there, etc.

There is also a negative present:

sipo	I am not here	**hatupo**	we are not here
hupo	you are not here	**hampo**	you are not here
hayupo	he is not here	**hawapo**	they are not here

With **mo,** this negative present often carries the meaning of not being in some business, or washing one's hands of it:

Simo. I am not in this! **Humo!** Keep out of this!

With the other noun classes the verb is formed in the same way:

Kitabu kipo hapa.	The book is here.
Visu havimo nyumbani.	The knives are not in the house.
Miti iko wapi? Ipo hapa.	Where are the poles? They are here.
Maziwa yakiwapo, lete.	If the milk is there, bring it.

When we are inquiring about position, the syllables of place must be added:

Bwana yuko? Hayuko, amekwenda mjini. Is the master there? No, he is not here, he has gone to the town.

Sukari yetu iko wapi?   Imo katika kopo.   Where is
our sugar?   It is in the tin.

In Mombasa Swahili the syllable of place is frequently
omitted.

The same place syllables are affixed to the other tenses:

Nitakuwapo hapa kesho.   I shall be here tomorrow.

Nyumba ilipoanguka, watu hawakuwamo.   When the
house fell, the people were not inside.

Akiwapo hapa mtu anayetaka kusema, asimame.   If
there is anyone here who wants to speak, let him
stand up.

**Kama vitu vingalikuwamo nyumbani visingalipata
maji.**   If the things had been in the house, they
would not have got wet.

They are suffixed to the relative tenses as well:

Unga uliokuwako sokoni haukuwa mzuri.   The flour
which was at the market was not good.

Wape habari wale wasiokuwapo hapa.   Inform the
people who were not here.

Waambie watu waliomo nyumbani watoke.   Tell the
people who are in the house to come out.

Nataka kujua mahali utakapokuwapo.   I want to
know the place where you will be.

NOTE: **nilioko, uliopo, aliomo,** etc., are almost everywhere used instead of **niliyeko, uliyepo, aliyemo,** etc.   But
you will find the latter forms in some recently published
books.

The syllable of place is not necessary when the stress is
on the *being* and not on the *position*.   We say in the Lord's
Prayer, **Baba yetu, uliye mbinguni.**   And, as noted above,
it is frequently omitted in Mombasa Swahili even where
place is stressed: **Watu walio Nairobi,** people who are in
Nairobi.

We have seen that **po** can be either a relative particle of
place or time, denoting *where* or *when*, or a syllable of place
denoting *here* or *there*.   In the present tense, where the
relative particle, like the syllable of place, comes at the end,
you may not find it easy to distinguish them; so it is well
to get the following forms clear in your mind:

I am here		*I who am here*		*where I am*	
nipo	tupo	niliopo	tuliopo	nilipo	tulipo
upo	mpo	uliopo	mliopo	ulipo	mlipo
yupo	wapo	aliopo	waliopo	alipo	walipo

Remember that **niliopo, uliopo, aliopo,** are sometimes written **niliyepo, uliyepo, aliyepo.**

Note the following proverbs and idioms:

Alioko juu, mngoje chini. He who is there above, await him below (Pride will have a fall).

Asiopo, na lake halipo. He who is not here, and his (business) is not here (Out of sight, out of mind).

Iliyopo sasa ni kuandika yote tena. There is nothing to be done now but to write it all again.

Vocabulary

lakini	but	sahani	plate
kabisa	entirely	kijana(vi)	youth
tena	again	nafasi	time, opportunity

Exercise 24

Write in Swahili: Where are the planks? They are here at the door. Where is your father? He is in the house. Where is the milk? It is in the bottle. The cups are here, but the plates are not. Will you be here tomorrow? The people who are at the door, what do they want? Those who are not here today will get their money tomorrow. Father is asking, Who are in the house? The young men who were in the town have gone away. When I was in England I saw the King. The baboons have utterly spoilt our field; all that can be done is to sow again. I am not in this; I have no time.

LESSON 26

TO HAVE

THERE is no special verb in Swahili for TO HAVE; to have is TO BE WITH. If we remember this, we shall not be surprised when, on asking a child for his pencil, he says, " **Kalamu ina mwalimu** ". He does not mean that the pencil *has* the teacher, but that it *is with* the teacher.

To make the tenses of the verb TO HAVE, all we have to do is to use **na** (*and* or *with*) after the tenses of the verb TO BE.

It is obvious that one must have, or be with, something, and, unless this something is denoted by a noun following the verb, a particle denoting the object is attached to the **na**. If a noun follows, the particle is not usually used unless we wish to make the object definite. These particles are the same as those used with the verb TO BE in its emphatic form (see page 74). The following examples will show the construction:

Ulikuwa na fedha? Nilikuwa nayo. Had you any money? (Yes), I had (it).

Kama nisingalikuwa nayo ningalirudi. If I had not had it, I should have come back.

Kama ukiwa na ndizi kesho, nitanunua. If you have any bananas tomorrow, I will buy (some).

Kesho sitakuwa nazo. Tomorrow I shall not have any.

Sometimes the relative particle is present in the verb, as well as the object particle attached to the **na**:

Mayai tuli*yo*kuwa na*yo*. The eggs which we had (lit. which we were with-them).

Vitabu wali*vyo*kuwa na*vyo*. The books which they had (which they were with-them).

Kisu ali*cho* na*cho*. The knife which he has (which he is with-it).

Fedha nisi*yo*kuwa na*yo*. (The money which I did not have (which I was not with-it).

The PRESENT TENSE of TO HAVE is made by attaching the **na** to the subject prefixes which, now that the **LI** has been lost, are all that remains of the present tense. We have used this tense in the earlier chapters of the book. With the **WATU** class the forms used are:

Affirmative		Negative	
(*I have*)		(*I have not*)	
nina	tuna	sina	hatuna
una	mna	huna	hamna
ana	wana	hana	hawana

Note that the **yu** used for *he is*, has here become **a**.

The object particle, when needed, is attached to the end:

Una sukari? Ninayo. Have you any sugar? I have (it).

Mnavyo vitabu vile? Hatunavyo. Have you those books? We have (them) not.

Mgonjwa ana dawa? Hana. Has the sick man medicine? He has not.

Sokoni kuna watu? Hakuna. Has there-at-the-market people? It has not.

Note that in the negative of the present tense no object particle need be attached to the **na** unless the object is specially defined; it is enough to say " **Sina** ", " **Hatuna** ", etc. But where the **na** is separate we cannot say " **Sikuwa na** " and leave it at that; we must complete the verb by saying " **Sikuwa nayo** ", etc.

The relative of the present tense is made in the ordinary way with a separate **na**:

Aliye na nguvu. He who has strength.

Wasio na hofu. They who have no fear.

Kikapu kilicho na machungwa. The basket which has oranges.

Furaha tuliyo nayo sisi. The joy which we have.

Unga alio nao mpishi. The flour which the cook has.

Place

We have learnt the forms of the verb TO HAVE used to express *There is, There is not*:

Kuna watu njiani? Hakuna. Are there people on the road? There are not.

Pana mtu hapa? Hapana. Is there anyone here? There is not.

Mna watu ndani? Hamna. Are there people inside? There are not.

The other tenses are used in the same way:

Kulikuwa na watu wengi sokoni. There were many people at the market.

Patakuwa na maji mengi hapa. There will be much water here.

Nyumbani hamkuwa na mtu. In the house there was no one.

Note the common beginning of Swahili stories: **Hapo zamani palikuwa na mtu.** Once upon a time there was a man: and the two phrases, **Unazo habari za . . .?** Have you heard about . . .? and **Sina (neno) la zaidi,** I have no more to say.

Exercise 25

Write in Swahili: We have no money. He has no sense. The well has no water. Have you any eggs? I have none. Have they pencils? They have. Have you lamps? We have not. There is no answer. There is nothing inside. There is no time. The boxes which had clothes. All the things which he has. All the seeds which I had. Every fowl which he had. That (man) who had bananas. The men who will have hoes. The pens I had. The books you have. A rainless country. A waterless place.

Read and translate into English: Hapo zamani palikuwa na mtu mmoja aliyekuwa na ng'ombe walio wazuri sana, wala hapakuwa na mtu mwingine aliyekuwa na ng'ombe wazuri kama yeye. Zile mbegu alizozipanda mwaka ule sasa zimekuwa miti mikubwa itoayo matunda yanayowafaa watu. Kitu cho chote alicho nacho ni chake mwenyewe. Nilicho nacho ndicho nikupacho.

LESSON 27

ADJECTIVES

An adjective is a word used with a noun to describe the thing denoted by the noun. We have seen that the Swahili adjective has to take the prefix of the class to which the noun belongs. In a dictionary you will find the adjectives listed under the first letter of their stem, e.g. **-baya, -refu,** etc.

Besides these Bantu adjectives which agree with the noun they qualify, there are others derived from the Arabic which do not vary. When using the adjective **safi,** clean, for instance, we say **maji safi,** pure water ; **nguo safi,** clean clothes ; **unga safi,** fine flour, without adding any prefixes.

The interrogative adjective, **gani?,** is also invariable. It is much used in such phrases as :

Mahali gani?	Where?	**Jinsi gani?**	In what way?
Wakati gani?	When?	**Habari gani?**	What news?
Namna gani?	What kind?	**Kitu gani?**	What is it?
Sababu gani?	Why?	**Mtu gani?**	What tribe?

There is one monosyllabic adjective **-pya,** new. With the **N** prefix this becomes **mpya,** and with the singular of the **MA** class, **jipya:**

nguo mpya	new clothes	**duka jipya** a new shop

If you are not quite sure of the right prefixes for each noun class, consult the Reference Table on pages 154–5. You will find more useful adjectives in the Vocabulary at the end of this lesson. Almost all of them are found also as abstract nouns beginning with the **U** prefix (**w** before vowels) :

> **weupe,** whiteness ; **wema,** goodness ; **utamu,** sweetness ;
> **wingi,** abundance, etc.

Order of Words

Adjectives follow the noun they qualify, except **kila,** every, which always precedes the noun. As in English, an adjective can get separated from its noun and be found at the end of the sentence :

> *Machungwa* niliyonunua sokoni jana ni *mazuri* sana.
> The oranges which I bought in the market yesterday are very good.

When two or more adjectives follow a noun the order varies according to the emphasis. **Vitabu vikubwa vingi** draws attention to the number rather than to the size, whereas **vitabu vingi vikubwa** lays more emphasis on the size. But here we will study the usual order in unemphasised speech, when two adjectives follow the noun.

1. If one is a numeral, it comes last :

Watoto wadogo wawili.	Two little children.
Watoto wangu wawili.	My two children.

2. If one is a demonstrative (*this, that*, etc.), it comes last, unless the other adjective is a numeral:

Watoto wadogo hawa.	These little children.
Watoto hawa wawili.	These two children.

3. If one is a possessive adjective, it comes first:

Watoto wangu wadogo.	My two children.
Watoto wangu wawili.	My two children.

4. If both adjectives are of the same kind, i.e. both descriptive, they usually follow without any connective:

Watoto wadogo wazuri.   Nice little children.

If a connective is required, as when the adjectives come at the end of a sentence, **tena,** moreover, is usual:

Watoto hawa ni wadogo,	These children are small and
tena wazuri.	pretty.

NOTE: The old usage, which is still the best literary usage, connects the adjectives by **na**, but changes the second into an *abstract noun*; e.g. **Shamba kubwa na uzuri,** A fine large cornfield (lit. A large field with fineness). You will find this construction in the Swahili Bible and elsewhere, but many of the young people of the present generation do not know it. **Na** does not rightly connect two adjectives, e.g. **shamba kubwa na zuri,** although it is becoming customary to use it thus; **tena** is preferable.

It is unlikely that an African speaker would use more than two adjectives together. He would not say, for instance, **Watoto wangu wadogo wawili;** he would break the phrase up and say, **Watoto wangu wawili—wale wadogo.**

Comparison

There are no special forms in Swahili for showing *more* or *most*. Sometimes comparison is just left to be inferred, as when one says:

Yupi mrefu, Ali au Juma?   Which (is) tall, Ali or Juma?

Usually a word like **kupita,** to pass; **kushinda,** to conquer; **kuzidi,** to increase; is used, or, most often, **kuliko** (lit. *where there is*):

Ali ni mrefu kuliko Juma. Ali is taller than Juma.

Machungwa haya ni mazuri kushinda yale mengine. These oranges are better than those others.

Njia hii ni ndefu kupita njia tuliyoifuata tulipokuja. This road is longer than the road we followed when we came.

Kuliko could have been used in any of these sentences.

To denote *most* one says *more than all*, or uses the relative.

Ali ni mrefu kuliko watoto wote. Ali is the tallest of (taller than) all the children.

Njia hii ni ndefu kuliko zote. This road is the longest of (longer than) all.

Hii ndiyo njia iliyo ndefu. This is the road which is long.

Huyu ndiye mtu aliye mwema. This is the man who is good.

Hasa, especially, can be used for emphasis:

Njia zote ni mbaya, lakini hii ni mbaya hasa. All the roads are bad, but this is specially bad.

Mtu aliye mwema hasa ndiye huyu. The man who is especially good is this one.

Ways of Forming Adjectives

A good many Swahili adjectives are made by the use of **-a**, of, or **-enye**, having:

mtu wa haki	a righteous man
maji ya moto	hot water
fedha ya kutosha	enough money
maneno ya furaha	joyful words
chumba chenye giza	a dark room
miti yenye nguvu	strong poles
wenye mali	wealthy people
mwenye afya	a healthy man

Sometimes the **-a** is omitted, and the two nouns come together:

mbwa mwitu	a wild dog	viazi ulaya	potatoes
mwaka jana	last year	mwana kondoo	a lamb

Many English adjectives are best translated by the relative form of the verb:

mwaka uliopita	last year
mwezi ujao	next month
nchi isiyo na maji	a waterless land
meza iliyovunjika	the broken table

Vocabulary

NOTE: If you are not yet very sure of the changes caused by the N prefix it may help you to know that the first five adjectives in this list take the prefix n with nouns of the N class; the next five take m; the twelve following take no prefix; **-refu** becomes **ndefu**, and **-vivu** and **-wivu** are used chiefly of persons. For adjectives beginning with a vowel, see Lesson 11. The last adjectives are of Arabic derivation and do not change.

-gumu, hard	**-ema,** good
-dogo, small	**-epesi,** light, quick
-zima, whole	**-ekundu,** red
-zito, heavy	**-eupe,** white
-zuri, nice	**-eusi,** black
-baya, bad	**-erevu,** cunning
-bichi, raw, unripe	**-ingi,** much, many
-bivu, ripe	**-ingine,** other
-bovu, rotten	
-pya, new	*Unchangeable*
-chungu, bitter	
-chache, few	**bora,** excellent
-fupi, short	**safi,** clean
-kavu, dry	**sahihi,** correct
-kubwa, large	**hodari,** brave
-kuu, great, chief	**ghali,** expensive
-kali, sharp, fierce	**rahisi,** cheap, easy
-pana, wide	**imara,** strong
-nene, fat	**hafifu,** poor, weak
-nono, fat (animals)	**laini,** smooth, soft
-tamu, sweet	**haba,** few
-tupu, bare, empty	**tele,** abundant
-refu, long	**tajiri,** rich
-vivu, idle	**maskini,** poor
-wivu, jealous	**kamili,** complete
-embamba, narrow	

NOTES:

1. Although the distinction should not be pressed too much, **-zuri** is generally used to denote external niceness or prettiness, and **-ema,** intrinsic goodness: **chakula kizuri,** food nice to eat; **chakula chema,** food good for health; etc.

2. **-kuu** does not usually refer to size, for which **-kubwa** is used: **mji mkubwa,** a big town; **mji mkuu,** the chief town.

3. **-nene** is used for persons, and **-nono** for animals.

4. Note the following phrases in which **-zima** is used:

mtu mzima	a full-grown man	**U mzima?**	Are you well?
kitu kizima	a whole number	**Ni mzima.**	I am well.

Exercise 26

Write in Swahili: a sharp knife; many pieces; light loads; short tails; a few blind men; cunning thieves; an idle wife; wide country; new work; a red hen; a long pencil; a white tooth; pure milk; many words; slender trees; black ink; red tongues; empty words; raw meat; rotten fruit(s); abundant water; brave soldiers; hard questions. Food is cheap these days but clothes are dear. These poles are very weak; bring strong poles, long and thick. London is the chief town of England; it is the largest town in the world.

LESSON 28

NUMBERS

IN the early chapters of this book we learnt the first five numbers and the prefixes which they take with the different noun classes. Continuing up to 10 we get: **sita, saba, -nane, tisa** *or* **kenda, kumi,** but, of these, only **-nane,** 8, is variable: **sita, saba,** and **tisa** are Arabic words and do not change.

After 10, Arabic words are used for 20, 30, 40, etc., as shown in the table below, and the intervening numbers take the form of 10-and-1, 10-and-2, etc. When used as adjectives, the Arabic numbers do not change, but the variable numbers—1, 2, 3, 4, 5 and 8—should be made to agree with the noun they qualify:

fifteen books	**vitabu kumi na *vi*tano**
twelve people	**watu kumi na *wa*wili**
twenty-three eggs	**mayai ishirini na *ma*tatu**

Nowadays even the best African writers are very careless about this, but it is still the ruling of Standard Swahili.

There are Arabic names for the numbers 11 to 19, but they are not in general use, and probably the only two you will come across are **edashara**, 11, and **thenashara**, 12.

After **mia**, 100, the numbers are counted by hundreds, **mia mbili, mia tatu,** etc., up to **elfu**, 1000. Then **elfu mbili, elfu tatu,** etc.

In counting and arithmetic the numbers do not take any prefixes, except of course in problems dealing with concrete things. In counting, **mosi, pili,** are sometimes heard for **moja, mbili.**

In naming large numbers, using thousands, it is usual to put the qualifying number before **elfu** instead of after it, e.g. to say **mbili elfu**, 2000, and not **elfu mbili.** Otherwise confusion may occur. We say, for instance:

| 300,001 | **mia tatu elfu na moja** |
| 1,301 | **elfu mia tatu na moja** |

Milioni is used in numbers for million.

The Numbers

1	moja	14	kumi na nne
2	mbili	15	kumi na tano
3	tatu	16	kumi na sita
4	nne	17	kumi na saba
5	tano	18	kumi na nane
6	sita	19	kumi na tisa (kenda)
7	saba	20	ishirini
8	nane	22	ishirini na mbili
9	tisa (kenda)	30	thelathini
10	kumi	33	thelathini na tatu
11	kumi na moja	40	arobaini
12	kumi na mbili	44	arobaini na nne
13	kumi na tatu	50	hamsini

55	hamsini na tano	99	tisini na tisa
60	sitini	100	mia
66	sitini na sita	101	mia na moja
70	sabini	110	mia na kumi
77	sabini na saba	200	mia mbili
80	themanini	250	mia mbili na hamsini
88	themanini na nane	999	mia tisa tisini na tisa
90	tisini	1000	elfu

How Many?

To ask How many? we use **-ngapi** with the adjective prefixes: **Vitabu vingapi? Nyumba ngapi? Watu wangapi?** etc.

How Often?

Once, twice, three times, etc., is shown by the use of **mara**, an **N** class noun meaning *time*: **mara moja,** once; **mara mbili,** twice; **mara tatu,** three times; **mara mia,** a hundred times. To ask How often? we say **Mara ngapi?** How many times.

Note that, as **mara tatu** means three times, " **sita mara tatu** " means " 6, three times ", just the reverse of the English " six times three ", although the result is the same. Anyone who has to teach arithmetic should make a special note of this, for the ignoring of this fact in the earlier stages is the cause of much of the haziness with which African children regard arithmetic.

Order

The numbers denoting order, usually called *ordinal* numbers, are made with **-a**, of: **kitabu cha tatu,** the third book; **siku ya tano,** the fifth day; **mwezi wa saba,** the seventh month; etc. *The first* is **-a kwanza;** *the second,* **-a pili;** and *the last,* **-a mwisho.**

Fractions

The fractions in common use are **nusu,** one-half; **robo,** one-quarter; **kasa robo,** three-quarters; and **theluthi,** a third. Note that **kasa robo** means less-a-quarter, and therefore *one and three-quarters* is **mbili kasa robo,** i.e. two, less a quarter.

D

We express a fifth, a tenth, etc., by the word **sehemu,** part: **sehemu ya tano,** a fifth; **sehemu ya kumi,** a tenth.

Other fractions are made with **kwa,** naming the denominator, i.e. the bottom figures, first: $\frac{3}{8}$, **nane kwa tatu;** $\frac{7}{10}$ **kumi kwa saba.** But these expressions are understood only by those who have learnt some arithmetic, and are not always used accurately even by them.

Exercise 27

Write in English; then put back into Swahili: Ana ruhusa ya siku ngapi? Ruhusa yake ni siku ishirini na nane. Mjini mwetu mna maduka kumi na manne. Nina ng'ombe kumi na mmoja na mbuzi thelathini na watatu. Mzungu ana makarani sita na wasimamizi (overseers) kumi na wawili. Vidole kumi vya mikono na kumi vya miguu ni ishirini. Mji huu una wenyeji mia mbili na hamsini, Wahindi hamsini na watano, Waarabu (Arabs) kumi na sita, na Wazungu wanane. Siku ya kwanza alileta mayai kumi na matano; siku ya pili, kumi na sita; na siku ya tatu, kumi; kesho itakuwa siku ya mwisho. Watoto wasomao hapa ni wangapi? Ni tisini na watano. Umeuza ndizi ngapi na machungwa mangapi? Ndizi arobaini na machungwa ishirini na saba.

LESSON 29

TIME

THE Swahili day (**siku**) begins at sunset, and consists of a night (**usiku**) followed by day-time (**mchana**). " Tonight " (**usiku wa leo**) means to an African the past night, not the night to come.

The day is divided into twenty-four hours. The first hour after sunset is **saa moja** (7 p.m.); then follow **saa mbili, saa tatu,** etc., up to **saa sita ya usiku** (midnight); then **saa saba, saa nane,** etc., up to **saa kumi na mbili** (6 a.m.). Then the counting begins again with the first hour after sunrise until **saa kumi na mbili ya jioni** (6 p.m.). Swahili time is therefore six hours different from English time. If we tell an African to come at nine o'clock, he will come at three in the afternoon—perhaps! For even now there are few clocks about, and punctuality means very little to people in the villages.

The various parts of the day are described as:

usiku	night	**mchana**	daytime
usiku wa manane	midnight	**adhuhuri**	midday
usiku kucha	all night	**alasiri**	afternoon
alfajiri	before dawn	**jioni**	evening
asubuhi	morning	**mchana kutwa**	all day

The Clock

A clock set to African time will be six hours different from English reckoning. *Half-past* is expressed by **u** * **nusu**; *quarter-past* by **u robo**; and *quarter-to* by **kasa robo**. A minute is **dakika** (**N** class); to express minutes after the hour, we say **na dakika,** and, before the hour, **kasa dakika**:

saa tatu u nusu	9.30 English time
saa tatu u robo	9.15
saa nne kasa robo	9.45
saa tatu na dakika tano	9.5
saa nne kasa dakika mbili	9.58

Saa edashara is sometimes used instead of **saa kumi na moja,** and **saa thenashara** instead of **saa kumi na mbili.**

To ask the time, we say **Saa ngapi?**

Days of the Week

Swahili has adopted two Arabic names: **Ijumaa,** Friday, the Mohammedan holy day, and **Alhamisi,** Thursday, its eve. The Arabs themselves call Saturday the seventh day, and Sunday, the first; hence the name for Thursday, **Alhamisi,** the fifth. But Swahili begins numbering the days from the Friday:

Ijumaa	Friday	**Jumanne**	Tuesday
Jumamosi	Saturday	**Jumatano**	Wednesday
Jumapili	Sunday	**Alhamisi**	Thursday
Jumatatu	Monday		

A week is **juma,** now a **MA** class word with a plural **majuma.** But **wiki,** from the English *week*, is now very common, and

* **U.** Arabic *and*.

it will probably become more so, for **wiki iliyopita,** last week, is much easier to say than **juma lililopita.**

The Year

The solar year, with the months as we know them, is now in general use in East Africa. The standardised spelling of the names is as follows:

Januari	**Julai**
Februari	**Agosti**
Machi	**Septemba**
Aprili	**Oktoba**
Mei	**Novemba**
Juni	**Desemba**

But the Mohammedan year of twelve lunar months is still in use among Africans themselves. As with the days of the week, only a few of the Arabic names are known, and in Swahili the year is based on **Ramadhani,** the month of fasting, and the following months are counted **Mfunguo * mosi, Mfunguo pili, Mfunguo tatu,** etc., until **Rajabu** and **Shaabani,** the months preceding Ramadhani. The Moslem year is some days shorter than the solar year, and the months bear no relation to the English months.

In writing dates, the counting numbers are used. One does not say " The first of January ", but " January one ".

Mei kumi na sita.　　The sixteenth of May.
Mwezi ishirini na tatu.　The twenty-third of the month.

Mosi and **pili** are very common for *one* and *two* in dates.

Exercise 28

Write in Swahili: He arrived yesterday evening at half-past five. He will go today about (**yapata**) two o'clock. What time is it now? Ten minutes to ten. In the morning when we wake up it is very cold, but at midday the sun is very hot (**kali**). Sunday is the first day of the week. A year has twelve months, fifty-two weeks and three hundred and sixty-five days. There is a market here every Tuesday; people bring maize, rice, flour, fruit, fish, and many other things. They leave their homes before daybreak and arrive early in the morning (**asubuhi sana**).

* From **fungua,** unfasten; i.e. non-fasting month.

LESSON 30

ADVERBS

In this chapter are gathered together words which, whatever their origin, do the work of adverbs, i.e. describe the action of a verb, telling us how, when, where, etc.

(I) Place and Time

chini	below	mara kwa mara	from time to time
juu	above		
mbele	in front	mara moja	once
nyuma	behind	bado	still, not yet
ndani	inside	bado kidogo	presently
nje	outside	baadaye, halafu	afterwards
katikati	in the middle	zamani	aforetime
mbali	far off	zamani za kale	long ago
karibu	near	leo	today
pamoja	together	jana	yesterday
peke yake	by oneself	juzi	day before yesterday
sasa	now		
sasa hivi	just now	kesho	tomorrow
siku hizi	nowadays	kesho kutwa	day after tomorrow
sikuzote	always		
pengine	sometimes	mapema	early
mara nyingi	often		

Notes:

1. **peke yake** is used for both *by itself* and *by themselves* in speaking of plants or things. But with animals and persons **peke yao** is used for the plural.

2. Although **zamani** as a rule refers to the past, the word itself means a time or an epoch, and we can say **zamani hizi**, in these days; **zamani zilizopita**, in times past, etc.

Juzi or **juzijuzi** is often used indefinitely for *a few days ago, not long ago*, etc.

3. It has been agreed to write **sikuzote** as one word when meaning *always*, and as two when meaning *all the days*:

Siku zote alizokaa hapa.	All the days he stayed here.
Ana matata sikuzote.	He is always troublesome.

Examples

Kuna tumbili nje, wanacheza katika miti, wakipanda juu na kushuka chini. There are monkeys outside; they are playing in the trees, climbing up and coming down.

" **Je, chakula tayari?** " " **Bado kidogo, bwana, viazi bado; lakini vitakuwa tayari sasa hivi.**" " Well, is the food ready? " " Not quite, sir, the potatoes are not yet (done); but they will be ready almost at once."

(2) Manner

upesi	quickly	**tena**	again
polepole	slowly, quietly	**labda**	perhaps
sawasawa	equally	**bure**	in vain
mbalimbali	differently	**tu**	only
kweli	truly	**zaidi**	more
hakika	certainly	**kidogo**	a little
halisi	exactly	**sana**	very
hasa	especially	**mno**	very
kabisa	entirely	**pia**	all, also
kamwe	not at all	**ovyo**	anyhow, carelessly
hata kidogo	not at all	**ghafula**	suddenly

NOTES:

1. **Kamwe** and **hata kidogo** are used only in negative sentences; **kabisa** can be used in both affirmative and negative sentences, and in the latter is equivalent to *not at all*:

Hakusema kamwe; Hakusema hata kidogo; Hakusema kabisa. He did not speak at all.

2. **Sana, mno,** and often **kabisa** are intensifiers and can be translated in various ways: **kimbia sana,** run fast; **ngoja sana,** wait a long time; **shika sana,** hold tight. **Mno** often conveys the meaning of *too* much: **kaa mno,** stay too long. **Pia** is often used with *all* as an intensifier, **Watu wote pia,** the whole lot of them. It has also the meaning of *in addition*, **Alisema pia,** He said also.

3. **Kidogo** lessens the force of the word it qualifies:

Anajua kidogo, He knows a little; **Yuko mbali kidogo,** He is a little way off; **Kazi yake nzuri kidogo,** His work is fair.

Examples

Usiseme upesi, sema polepole tu, nipate kusikia vema. Do not speak quickly; just speak slowly, so that I may hear well.

Sijui kama atakuja kweli; labda hatakuja, amesema tu, na sisi tunangoja bure. I don't know if he will really come; perhaps he will not come, he just said (he would), and we are waiting in vain.

(3) Interrogatives

Some adverbs are used for asking questions—when? where? how? why?: **Alifika lini?** When did he arrive? **Yuko wapi?** Where is he? **Nimjibu namna gani?** How shall I answer him? We have already come across these.

The usual word for *Why?* is **Kwa nini?** or, sometimes **Kwani?** Both words, but especially **kwani?** can be followed by the infinitive:

Kwa nini chakula kimechelewa? Why is the food late?
Kwani kuniuliza? Why ask me?

When inquiring about something unexpected, or which should not be, **mbona?** is often used:

Mbona ninyi watoto mnagombana? Why are you children quarrelling?

Note that **mbona** can never be used by itself, but **kwa nini** can be:

"Bwana, leo hakuna nyama." "Kwa nini?" "Sir, there is no meat today." "Why?"

Ya nini? is sometimes used when inquiring about purpose:

Ya nini kusema hivi? Why (did you) say this?

Exercise 29

Write in Swahili: The clerk is writing very quickly. He began this work the day before yesterday. Tell him again. Do not go too quickly. This knife is no use at all. I have told him from time to time, but I have spoken in vain; I shall not speak again. Put this hen inside by herself. The milk you have brought is very little; bring some more. These things are entirely different; they are not alike at all. The children set out early; now they are on (in) the way; they will arrive in a few minutes.

LESSON 31

THE FORMATION OF ADVERBS

The VI Prefix

WE have already seen that adjective stems given the **vi** prefix become adverbs: **vizuri, v(y)ema, vibaya, vigumu,** etc. And that the same thing happens with the demonstrative adjectives *this* and *that*. The most frequently used forms are **hivi,** thus: **vivi hivi,** just like this; **vile vile,** in the same way; **hivyo,** in the way spoken of; **vivyo hivyo,** just in the way spoken of:

Alisema hivi.	He spoke thus.
Hivyo ulivyosikia.	Thus as you have heard.
Wakasema vile vile.	And they all said the same.
Kila siku husema vivi hivi.	Every day they say the same thing.
Nawe ufanye vivyo hivyo.	And you, do just the same.

The KI Prefix

This prefix used with nouns or noun stems denotes " in the manner of ". The following examples show its use:

Simameni kiaskari.	Stand like soldiers.
Amevaa kizungu.	He is dressed in European fashion.
Kupendana kidugu.	To love as brethren.
Kuwekwa kiwatu.	To be treated (placed) as people.

NOTE: The last phrase comes from an article by an African on the colour bar. He feels that, because of their colour, Africans are often treated as if they were not people to be respected, and he says that much bitterness would be avoided if they were treated as human beings. Notice that the **ki** here is prefixed to the whole word **watu** in order to avoid confusion with **kitu,** a thing.

The U Prefix

This prefix is used to form abstract nouns, and probably the few adverbs beginning with **U** are really abstract nouns: **Nenda upesi,** Go quickly; **Simama wima,** Stand upright. But the prefix is noted here, as it is used to form the adverb from **-pya,** new; this adverb is not **vipya,** as we should expect, but **upya :**

Wameijenga upya. They have built it anew.

Place Prefixes

A great many adverbs are formed with the place syllables, **pa, ku** and **mu,** most of which we have already given. Some of the most commonly used are:

hapa	here	**papa hapa**	just here	**huku**	here
pale	there	**pale pale**	just there	**kule**	there
huko	yonder	**huko na huko**	here and there	**huko nyuma**	meanwhile
po pote	anywhere	**kotekote**	everywhere		

Suffixes

We have already seen how the suffix **-ni** added to a noun gives the noun an adverbial sense: **nyumbani,** in the house; **mezani,** on the table; etc.

The syllable **je,** *how,* can be suffixed to a verb; **Walijuaje?** How did they know? **Umepataje?** How did you get it?

How, in Swahili, frequently takes the place of the English *What?* **Walisemaje?** What did they say? **Tufanyeje?** What shall we do? **Nimjibuje?** What shall I answer him?

The suffix **-pi** can take the place of **wapi?** in such questions as **Unakwendapi?** Where are you going? **Amekwendapi?** Where has he gone?

Note that when the suffix is added the stress moves on to the next syllable:

amekwénda?   Amekwendápi?   Tufánye?   Tufanyéje?

Exercise 30

Read and translate into English; then put back into Swahili: Watoto, njoni! Simameni sawasawa; nataka kuwapa habari za kesho. Nasema hivi: Kesho tuta-kwenda mjini na ngoma (*band*) yetu. Lakini juzi tulipo-kwenda naliona watoto wengine wakienda ovyo na kuta-zama huko na huko. Kwenda hivyo haifai kabisa. Msitazame ko kote, tazameni mbele tu; nendeni kiaskari kabisa.

Wewe, Ali, unafanyaje? Mimi ninatoa mashauri, na wewe huko nyuma unaongea. Njoo, usimame hapa; kaa papa hapa hata (*until*) nimekwisha kusema.

Ninyi, watoto, mmejua duka la nyama, sivyo? Tuta-kwenda kule dukani, na kusimama pale pale tukiimba nyimbo mbili. Nyimbo hizo zikiisha, tutafika sokoni na kuimba nyimbo nyingine vile vile. Ndipo tutarudi hapa shuleni.

LESSON 32

PREPOSITIONS

WE have many prepositions in English—*to, for, in, about,* etc.—used before a noun or pronoun to show in what relation it stands to some preceding word. Swahili has a special form of the verb which takes the place of many English prepositions, and most of the others are formed with the particle **-a.**

Ya

Adverbs followed by **ya** do the work of prepositions:

Simama mbele.	Stand *in front*.
Simama mbele ya nyumba.	Stand *in front of* the house.

Here are some prepositions formed from the adverbs we know, and a few new ones:

chini ya mti	under the tree
juu ya mlima	on the hill
nje ya mji	outside the village

ndani ya sanduku	in the box
nyuma ya nyumba	behind the house
mbele ya (za) watu	before the people
katikati ya shamba	in the middle of the field
zaidi ya kumi	more than ten
kati ya Ali na Juma	between Ali and Juma
baada ya chakula	after food
kabla ya saa nane	before two o'clock
baina ya vitu hivi	between these things
miongoni mwa watu	among the people

NOTES:

1. Most of these adverbs were originally nouns, and the **ya** is the preposition *of* in its impersonal form. **Mbele** is an old word meaning *the breasts*, i.e. the front part of the body, and is still followed sometimes by *of* agreeing with the plural form.

2. **Karibu,** an adverb taken from the Arabic, is followed by **na**; so is **pamoja**. **Mbali** takes either **na** or **ya**:

Simama karibu na moto.	Stand near the fire.
Usiende mbali na nyumba.	Don't go far from the house.
Kaa pamoja na watoto.	Stay with the children.

3. *Before* and *behind*. There is considerable vagueness in the use of **mbele** and **nyuma** in referring to something in front of one. If someone says " **Nimejenga mbele ya mlima** ", he may mean in front of it as it is facing you, i.e. on the near side; or in front of the hill, on its far side. If you are going towards the hill, he probably means on the far side, but you can never be sure.

It is better to use **mbele ya** and **nyuma ya** of position, and **kabla ya** and **baada ya** of time; **kati ya** of position or time in between, and **baina ya** of distinction between. These distinctions cannot be pressed too far, but they are useful and give both clearness and variety to Swahili writing:

Mwalimu alisimama mbele ya watoto. The teacher stood in front of the children.

Kabla ya kuanza mafundisho nataka kusema hivi. Before beginning the lesson I want to say this.

Nyuma ya kibanda kuna takataka nyingi. Behind the hut there is much rubbish.

Baada ya shule mtakwenda kuziondoa. After school you will go and clear it away.

Mgeni atakuja kati ya saa saba na saa nane. Our visitor will come between one and two o'clock.

Pambanua baina ya vitu vifaavyo kwa mbolea na vitu visivyofaa. Distinguish between things which are useful for manure and things which are not.

Note that, although **mbele** and **nyuma** can be used of time, **kabla** and **baada** can never be used of position.

4. **Miongoni** keeps the place prefix, taking **mwa** instead of **ya**. **Miongoni mwa watoto mmoja alisimama.** From among the children one stood up. **Miongoni, ndani** and **chini** were all originally adverbial nouns: **mwongo**, a group of (ten) things; **nda**, the womb, and **nchi**, ground.

Katika

We have had this word before, and noticed that its use was rather wider than that of the English *in*. It is really a preposition of the same form as **kati ya**, but with an old **ka** concord, **kati ka**. But its origin is now ignored and it is a preposition in its own right. It is used of coming *out* of something as well as of going *in* or being *in*, and, as we saw, the in-ness can refer to something like a table, a plate or a bed. The following examples will illustrate its use:

Mtoe mbuzi katika nyumba, umtie katika kibanda chake. Take the goat out of the house and put it in its shed.

Viweke katika meza. Put them on the table.

Watoto wanaandika katika karatasi. The children are writing on paper.

Haifai kulima katika mlima. It is not good to cultivate on a hill-side.

Ondoka katika kiti. Get off the chair.

Nalikuwa katika kusema. I was in the middle of speaking.

Katika watoto hawa si wengi wanaojua kusoma. Among these children there are not many who can read.

Note that, where the **katika** denotes place, and is followed by a noun, the adverbial form of the noun could be used instead:

Mtoe mbuzi nyumbani; Viweke mezani; Ondoka kitini; etc.

Prepositions followed by Pronouns

After **katika,** the full form of the personal pronoun is used: **katika sisi,** among us.

After **na,** the shortened forms used with the verb TO HAVE are used:

mbali *nami*	far from me	**mbali** *nasi*	far from us
pamoja *nawe*	with you	**pamoja** *nanyi*	with you
karibu *naye*	near him	**karibu** *nao*	near them

When speaking of plants or things **nacho, navyo, nao, nayo,** etc., are used, i.e. the **o** of reference agreeing with the particular noun class. The forms are shown in full in the last line of the Table of Concords on pages 154–155.

With **ya** the pronoun takes the same form as the possessive adjectives:

mbele *yangu*	in front of me	**katikati** *yetu*	among us
juu *yako*	above you	**kabla** *yenu*	before you
nyuma *yake*	behind him	**chini** *yao*	under them

When referring to plants or things, **-ake** is used instead of **-ao**:

Hapa pana miti mingi, tutakaa chini yake. There are many trees here, we will sit down under them.

Exercise 31

Read, translate; then put back into Swahili: Shamba la mwalimu ni zuri kabisa. Katikati yake amepanda michungwa. Mingapi? Sijui, lakini zaidi ya kumi. Ndani kabisa ya shamba? Ndani kabisa, kati ya kibanda chake na miembe yake, karibu na migomba. Tangu alipoipanda ni mwezi mzima, na yote ni mizuri, tena mikubwa. Watoto wake wadogo hupenda sana kucheza chini ya miti. Kama mvua ikipiga, huingia ndani ya kibanda. Shamba lao si mbali na nyumba yao, watoto wadogo waweza kwenda huko peke yao.

* **juu yangu, juu yako,** etc., may mean " It's on me ", " It's my business ".

LESSON 33

KWA AND NA

Kwa

IT is probable that the origin of this preposition is **-a** with the concord of place, but now, like **katika,** it is a preposition in its own right, and a very important one. Here are some of the ways in which it is used:

(a) *Place.*

Amekwenda kwa mwalimu. He has gone to the teacher.

Umetoka kwa nani? From whom have you come?

Nimetoka Korogwe kwa Ali. I have come from Korogwe, from Ali.

Wageni watalala kwa nani? With whom will the strangers sleep?

Watalala kwa Jumbe.* They will sleep at the Chief's.

Naenda Mombasa kwa mtoto wangu. I go to Mombasa to my child.

NOTE: **kwa** is not used with names of places. Proper names, as will be seen in the sentences above, take no preposition to show *to* or *from,* and, where no proper name is used, direction is shown by adding the suffix **-ni:**

Anakwenda msituni kuwinda. He is going to the forest to hunt.

Wanawake wamekwenda mtoni. The women have gone to the river.

Shamba and **shule** are generally used like proper names, without the **-ni** suffix:

Amekwenda shamba.   He has gone to his field.

Watoto wamekwenda shule. The children have gone to school.

(b) *Instrument.*

Watoto wanaandika kwa wino. The children are writing with ink.

.* **kuumba,** to create; **kiumbe,** a creature; **jumbe,** the chief creature.

Kata nyama kwa kisu.   Cut the meat with a knife.

Utaweza kukinunua kwa shilingi mbili.   You will be able to buy it for two shillings.

Shamba hili limelimwa na Jumbe kwa jembe la ng'ombe.   This field has been ploughed by the Chief with an ox-plough.

Note that, after a passive verb, the *doer* is introduced by **na** and the *thing he uses* by **kwa**.

(c) *Manner.*

Nimekipata kwa shida tu.   I have got it only with trouble.

Mwamkie mzee kwa heshima.   Greet the old man with respect.

Wameondoka kwa haraka.   They have gone off in a hurry.

Nitarudi kwa njia nyingine.   I shall go back by another way.

Utakwenda kwa miguu? La, nitakwenda kwa gari. Will you go on foot?   No, I shall go by train.

(d) *Purpose.*

Maziwa yafaa sana kwa chakula.   Milk is very useful as a food.

Nimekuja kwa dawa.   I have come for medicine.

Saa yafaa sana kwa kujua wakati wa kwenda kazini. A clock is very useful for knowing the time to go to work.

(e) *Connection.*

Tutaonana uso kwa uso.   We shall see each other face to face.

Wote walikuwapo, wazee kwa watoto, wanaume kwa wanawake.   All were there, old people and children, men and women.

Chakula kilikuwa wali kwa nyama.   The food was rice with meat.

Kumi kwa moja; one-tenth ; **mia kwa tano,** five per cent.

Futi ishirini kwa futi kumi na tano.   Twenty feet by fifteen.

Moja kwa moja. Straight on, continuously. (*Dist.* **moja moja,** one by one.)

Kwa followed by a personal pronoun takes the same forms as **ya**: kwangu, kwako, kwake, kwetu, kwenu, kwao.

Njoni kwangu.	Come to me.
Naomba kwako.	I ask from you.
Ulifika kwake?	Did you get to him?

These forms are often equivalent to our word " home ", but, Africans not being individualists, the words are usually used in the plural:

Nakwenda kwetu.	I am going home.
Kwenu ni mbali?	Is your home far off?
Tuende kwao.	Let us go to his home.

We may notice here, although it has nothing to do with this lesson, the common phrases:

Wamekwenda zao.	They have gone their way.
Amekwenda zake.	He has gone his way.
Naenda zangu.	I am going now.

Cha kwangu, etc., is sometimes used for **changu,** etc., probably to show that the thing spoken of is not regarded as the speaker's private property:

Kalamu hii ya nani? Ni ya kwangu. Whose pen is this? It is mine.

Na

Na can be translated in many ways, *and*, *by*, *with*, etc., so that, by English grammar, it would appear to be sometimes a preposition and sometimes a conjunction. But the word itself just expresses *association*. Here are some of its uses:

(a) *and*.

Lete chai na maziwa.	Bring tea and milk.
Lete na maji pia.	And bring water too.
Nipeni na mimi.	Give me some too.
Nataka tuseme, mimi nawe.*	I want us to talk together, you and I.

* In Swahili " I " precedes " you ".

(b) *with.*

Yupo pamoja nasi.	He is with us.
Atakwenda nawe.	He will go with you.
Vitu alivyokuja navyo.	The things which he came with.
Usiwe na matata.	Don't be troublesome.
Sipatani na mtu huyu.	I don't get on with this man.

(c) *by.*

Unaitwa na baba yako.	You are being called by your father.

(d) *let.*

Na aje.	Let him come.
Watu wote na wajue.	Let all the people know.

(This **na** merely strengthens the force of the subjunctive.)

Vocabulary

kama, like
tangu, tokea, from (time)
(ku)toka, from (place)
hata, until (time)
mpaka, up to (place or time)
bila ⎫
pasipo ⎭ without
kwa sababu ya, because of

kwa ajili ya, for the sake of
kwa habari ya, concerning
badala ya ⎫
mahali pa ⎭ instead of
kwa sababu gani? for what reason?
kwa heri,* good-bye
wanangu, my children
mjomba, mother's brother

NOTE:

Nitangoja penye mwembe.	I will wait at the mango tree.
Ninakwenda kwenye kazi.	I am going to work.
Andika kwa Kiingereza.	Write in English.

Exercise 32

Translate: " Ali, go to Bwagamoyo, to your uncle, and ask him to give me his sickle (**mundu**). Hamisi will go with you. I will wait here at the coconut trees; I want to cut the grass under the trees." The children went to their uncle and greeted him with respect, and said, " We have

* To more than one person = **Kwa herini.**

been told by our father to come to you; he begs you to give him your sickle. He wants to cut the grass near our coconut trees. He says his knife is no good for cutting it. If you consent to give us your sickle, we will go back with it now. Father is awaiting us by the coconuts. Thank you, uncle, we are going now; good-bye." " Good-bye, my children."

LESSON 34

THE PREPOSITIONAL FORM OF THE VERB

JUST as a verb can be made into its passive form by inserting **w** before the final **a**, so, by inserting **i** or **e**, we can make it into a prepositional form, conveying the meaning of *to*, *for*, *on account of*, etc. It will be remembered that **i** follows **a**, **i** or **u**, and **e** follows **e** or **o**.

andika	write	**andikia**	write to
soma	read	**somea**	read to
enda	go	**endea**	go to
fika	arrive	**fikia**	reach
leta	bring	**letea**	bring to
weka	put	**wekea**	put by for
pata	get	**patia**	get for
omba	beg	**ombea**	intercede for
simama	stand	**simamia**	stand over, oversee
anguka	fall	**angukia**	fall on, before

A few words ending in **emka** or **emsha** appear to be exceptions to the rule about **e** and **i**: for **chemka,** boil; **chemsha,** make to boil; **telemka,** go down; **telemsha,** let down; make their prepositional forms in **ia**. But this is because the words were originally **chemuka, telemuka,** etc., and the vowel that governs the inserted letter is this **u**.

Verbs of foreign origin not ending in **a** change the last letter into **ia** or **ea**:

rudi, rudia; jibu, jibia; samehe, samehea; etc.

In verbs ending in two vowels, the dropped **l** reappears before the **ia** or **ea,** making pronunciation easier:

> **faa, falia; zaa, zalia; lia, lilia; ingia, ingilia; chukua, chukulia; ua, ulia; lea, lelea; toa, tolea;** etc.

But **sahau** makes **sahaulia; dharau, dharaulia;** etc.

A verb which has an object in its simple form will have two objects in its prepositional form. The real object is the one which, in the English, comes after the preposition *to, for,* etc., and the word which was the object in the simple form follows after:

Aliandika *barua.*	He wrote *a letter*.
Ali*ni*andikia barua.	He wrote-to *me* a letter.
Nitaleta *chakula.*	I will bring *food*.
Nita*ku*letea chakula.	I will bring-to *you* food.
*M*patie *mtoto* kalamu.	Get-for *the child* a pen.

It should be noticed that some verbs already have the prepositional idea in their simple form:

ficha	hide	*or*	hide from
fuata	follow		follow after
faa	be useful		be useful to
kosa	sin		sin against
ngoja	wait		wait for
cheka	laugh		laugh at

In such cases, the prepositional form, when used, has a slightly different meaning, e.g.

> **fuatia,** follow after, with the intention of catching up; **kosea,** make a mistake, as child in arithmetic; **ngojea,** wait for, with an idea of duration, patience, etc.

Several verbs which we have learnt as simple forms are really prepositional forms which have acquired a special meaning:

amkia	greet	*from*	**amka**	wake
palia	hoe weeds		**paa**	scrape
tumia	use		**tuma**	send on errand

It is impossible to note here all the different shades of meaning caused by the prepositional form, but the following are important:

hama   move from   **hamia**   move to

  Watu wamehama hapa, wamehamia Bwagamoyo. The people have left here, they have moved to Bwagamoyo.

kimbia   run from   **kimbilia** run to

  Mtoto amekimbia; amemkimbilia baba yake. The child has run away; he has run to his father.

nuka   smell bad   **nukia**   smell nice

  Vitu hivi vinavyooza vinanuka sana; lakini majani ya mti huu yanukia vizuri. These rotting things smell badly; but the leaves of this tree smell sweet.

geuka   turn round   **geukia**   turn to face

  Geukeni, watoto, mnigeukie. Turn round, children, turn to face me.

tenda (mtu)   treat badly   **tendea (mtu)** treat well

  Amenitenda mabaya, lakini amemtendea mema ndugu yangu. He has treated me badly, but he has been good to my brother.

The prepositional forms of the monosyllabic verbs we have learnt are:

la	eat	**lia**	**cha**	dawn	**chea**
nywa	drink	**nywea**	**chwa**	set (sun)	**chwea**
fa	die	**fia**	**wa**	be	**wia**
ja	come	**jia**	**pa**	give	**(pea)**

Pa, meaning *give to*, does not need a prepositional form, but the prepositional stem is used in the form *give one another*: **peana mikono,** shake hands; **peana salamu,** exchange greetings, etc.

There are two other monosyllabic verbs: **nya,** fall as rain, used also of passing excrement; and **cha,** fear with reverence, used especially of fearing God.* Both these make their prepositional form in **ea, nyea, chea.**

The passive of **fia,** die to, is often used in the sense of *be*

---

* In the Mombasa dialect **cha** is used for **ogopa,** with no special idea of reverence.

bereaved : **Tumefiwa,** We have had a death here. **Nimefiwa na ndugu yangu.** I have lost my brother.

NOTE : It is tempting to think that **cha,** referring to sunrise, and **chwa,** to sunset, are related verbs, **chwa** being the passive or conversive of **cha.** But all the evidence is against this.

If the verbs are traced through other Bantu languages it will be seen that the **ch** in each verb has a different origin. The sound giving rise to the **ch** in **chwa** has developed into **s** or **sh** in most Bantu languages, and into **ch** or **t** in Swahili; this accounts for the two forms **kuchwa** and **kutwa,** both in use in Swahili.

Moreover, while **chwa** refers to the setting or going down of the sun, **cha** refers to darkness getting light and is used impersonally, *It* has dawned. The reverse of **cha,** get light, is, in many Bantu languages, **ila,** get dark. Probably this root remains in the word **giza,** darkness.

Exercise 33

Translate: Put food by for us. His wife has borne (to) him a child. I want you to sell me some flour. Do not sin against your brother. Look for some water for me. This food will be sufficient for us. Go back to your mother; give her this money that she may buy food for us. The lion sprang on the child. Pray for me to God. Do not laugh at old people. Tomorrow I shall move to Mombasa. You have made a mistake here. Who will carry my basket for me? Many people have come to me. He has lost his child (by death).

LESSON 35

MORE ABOUT THE PREPOSITIONAL FORM

THE prepositional form has two special uses :

1. To convey the idea of complete separation. In this case it is used with **mbali,** far away. Notice the following constructions with **tupa,** throw; **acha,** leave; **kata,** cut; and **ondoa,** take away:

> **Kitupilie mbali.** Throw it right away.
> **Yaachilie mbali mawazo haya.** Let these thoughts quite alone.

Tulikatie mbali tawi hili. Let us cut this branch right off.

Ziondolee mbali nguo hizi; sizitaki tena. Take these clothes right away; I don't want them again.

2. To show the purpose of something. In this case it is preceded by **cha, ya,** etc., or by **kwa:**

Kisu cha kukatia nyama.	A knife to cut meat with.
Moto wa kupikia chakula.	A fire to cook food on.
Fedha ya kununulia nguo.	Money to buy clothes with.
Masikio ya kusikilia.	Ears to hear with.
Unga wa kupikia mkate.	Flour to make bread with.
Kibao kifaacho kwa kuwekea vyombo.	A useful board for putting utensils on.
Mahali pa kuzalia mbu.	A place for mosquitoes to breed in.

It used to be said that this form should only be used with the idea of instrumentality. But nowadays this limitation does not seem to be in force, and it is customary to say:

Nyumba ya kulalia.	A house to sleep in.
Chumba cha kulia chakula.	A room for eating food in.

Notice, however, that though you can say **Vyombo vya kulia chakula; kijiko cha kulia chakula; mahali pa kulia chakula;** etc., you *cannot* say: **Chakula cha kulia: nyama ya kulia:** etc. The food itself is what you eat; you do not eat it *with, in,* etc. You must say, **Nyama ya kula,** etc., just as the word **chakula** itself means " (kitu) cha kula ".

In forming the passive of the prepositional form we must remember what has been said about its object; that the object of the prepositional form is *not the same* as that of the simple form.

Take the verb **soma:**

Alisoma *kitabu*.	He read *a book*.
Ali*ni*somea kitabu.	He read-to *me* a book.

In the passive the object becomes the subject:

***Kitabu* kilisomwa naye.**	*The book* was read by him.
***Mimi* nilisomewa kitabu.**	*I* was read-to the book.

We need, of course, to put the sentence into better English, such as, I had the book read to me, keeping *I* as the subject.

Here is another example:

Simple form:

Nimenunua *sukari*.	I have bought *sugar*.
***Sukari* imenunuliwa.**	*Sugar* has been bought.

Prepositional form:

Nime*wa*nunulia sukari.	I have bought-for *them* sugar.
***Wa*menunuliwa sukari.**	*They* have been bought-for sugar; i.e. They have had sugar bought for them.

From these examples you will be able to understand the construction of:

Tumeibiwa.	We have been stolen-from.
Mama yangu anajengewa nyumba.	My mother is being built-for a house.
Mfalme huombewa kanisani.	The king is prayed-for in church.
Nimejiwa na wageni.	I have been come-to by visitors.
Unatafutiwa mahali pa kulala.	You are being looked-for a place to sleep.

The English translation would be: We have been robbed; My mother is having a house built for her; I have visitors; You are being found a place to sleep. Notice that the English *find* must be translated in Swahili by *look for* until the search is ended: **Ninatafuta mahali.** I am looking for a place. **Nimeona mahali.** I have found a place.

Vocabulary

oga, bathe	**shona,** sew
nawa, wash hands	**suka,** plait
osha, wash things	**fuma,** weave
fua, wash clothes	**finyanga,** make pots
safisha, cleanse	**fagia,** sweep
sabuni, soap	**sindano,** needle
salimu, greet	**salamu,** greetings

Exercise 34

Write in Swahili: a needle to sew with; soap to wash clothes with; a place to wash the cups; hot water for bathing; cold water for washing our hands; polish for cleaning shoes; clay (**udongo**) for making pots with. I want you to plait me a mat. The women are having their hair (**nywele**) plaited. He says he will weave some cloth for me. I am having a dress made (sewn). Cut me some grass to sweep with. Greet the teacher and his children for me.

LESSON 36

CONJUNCTIONS

CONJUNCTIONS join words or sentences. Much of the work done by English conjunctions is done in Swahili by the verb itself:

and	Take the book *and* read. **Shika kitabu usome.**
	He took the book *and* read. **Alishika kitabu akasoma.**
if	*If* he comes, I will tell him. **Akija nitamwambia.**
	(**Kama**, *if*, though not necessary, is often added.)
unless	I shall not do this work *unless* I am told. **Sitafanya kazi hii nisipoambiwa.**
so that	I will come back early *so that* I may see you. **Nitarudi mapema nipate kukuona.**
	(**ili**, *so that*, is frequently used as well).
where	I do not know *where* he went. **Sijui alikokwenda.**
when	I will give him the book *when* he comes. **Nitampa kitabu atakapokuja.**
as	Do *as* you are told. **Fanya unavyoambiwa.**

Conjunctions in common use are:

(a) **NA**. Its uses have been fully shown in Lesson 33.
(b) **AU, AMA**. *Or.*

Nipe chai au maji.   Give me tea or water.
Ndivyo ama sivyo?   Is it so or not so?

When repeated, it is equivalent to either—or:

Ama ni wewe ama ni ndugu yako.   Either it is you or
  it is your brother.

One often finds today **ama . . . au,** but it would seem
better to use the one form in both places, **au . . . au** or
ama . . . ama.

(c) **WALA.**   This takes the place of **na** or **au** in negative
sentences, unless the things are closely connected:

Sikumwona wala sikusikia habari zake.   I did not see
  him, nor did I hear about him.
Sitaki chai wala kahawa.   I don't want tea or coffee.
Sikuwaona, wala yeye wala ndugu yake.   I did not see
  either him or his brother.
Watoto wadogo hawaandiki kwa wino na kalamu.
  The little children do not write with pen and ink.

(d) **LAKINI, BALI.**   *But.*   **Bali** has a stronger force
than **lakini,** denoting " on the contrary ":

Alikuja, lakini sikumwona.   He came, but I did not
  see him.
Maana yake sivyo unavyodhani, bali ni hivi.   Its
  meaning is not as you think, but it is this.

The form **walakini** is also in use.

(e) **ILA.**   *Except, but.*   In its general meaning of " except " it is equivalent to **isipokuwa,** *unless it be*:

Watu wote wamefika, ila mwalimu tu.   Everyone has
  come except the teacher.
Amani haiji ila kwa ncha ya upanga.   Peace does not
  come except by the point of the sword.

Ila following **si** expresses *not only . . . but also*:

Si wagonjwa tu waliokuja, ila watu wazima pia.   It is
  not only sick people who came, but healthy people
  as well.
Si habari ya mashamba tu, ila pia ya makundi yetu.
  It concerns not only our fields, but our flocks as well.

(f) **KAMA, IKIWA.**   *If.*   These can be used with any
tense to express *if*:

Kama hukumwona, haidhuru.   If you did not see him,
  never mind.

Ikiwa amekuja, mpe ile fedha. If he has come, give him the money.

(g) **INGAWA, IJAPO, IWAPO.** These are all impersonal forms of the verb TO BE used as conjunctions:

ingawa, *although.* **Ingawa ni vigumu, nitajaribu.** Although it is hard, I will try.

ijapo, *even if.* **Ijapo nitakufa, sitakubali.** Even if I die, I shall not consent.

iwapo, *if it be.* **Iwapo hujui, uliza.** If you don't know, ask.

(h) **ILI, KUSUDI.** *In order that.*

Nimekuuliza kusudi (ili) nipate hakika. I have asked you in order to be certain.

(i) **KWA SABABU, KWA MAANA, KWA KUWA.** *Because.* **Sababu** means *reason*, **maana** means *meaning*, **kuwa** means *being*; but all are more or less equivalent to *because*:

Sikuja kwa sababu sikupata habari. I did not come because I did not hear about it.

Maana is often used without the **kwa**:

Sikumwuliza, maana sikumwona. I did not ask him because I did not see him.

(j) **KWA HIYO.** *Therefore.*

Sikupata habari, kwa hiyo sikuja. I did not hear about it, therefore I did not come.

NOTE: **Kwa hivyo** is frequently used, but the correct form is **kwa hiyo,** or, **kwa sababu hiyo,** i.e. for this reason.

(k) **(YA) KWAMBA, (YA) KUWA, KAMA.** (He said) *that.* These words are used to introduce what someone said; the **ya** of the first two is frequently omitted:

Nimekwisha kukuambia ya kwamba sina nafasi sasa. I have already told you that I have no time now.

Asema kama amekwenda mara mbili asimwone. He says that he has been twice without finding him.

Barua yake yasema kuwa ni mgonjwa. His letter says that he is ill.

Note that in Swahili reported speech is not put into the past tense, as in English. The tense which the speaker used is kept: **Alisema kama atakuja.** He said that he *will* come. It is interesting to note that the word **kwamba** means *to say*: it is the simple form of the verb from which we get the prepositional form **ambia,** say to.

Conjunctions are much used in English as connectives, introducing new sentences and paragraphs—" Well ", " And so ", " Now ", etc. By far the commonest connective in Swahili is **Basi.**

Basi	Well, Now, So, etc.	**Kisha, Ndipo**	Then
Hata	So, Until	**Ikawa**	It so happened
Pia	Also		
Tena	Moreover	**Zaidi ya hayo**	Moreover
		Pamoja na hayo	

Note that " Now " is often used as a connective in English without any idea of time: " Now, near the tree there lived a woman ". Do not make the common mistake of translating this by **Sasa;** the right word is **Basi.**

Exercise 35

Write in Swahili: He came in the morning but he did not stay long. There was no one there but ourselves alone. This thing (**neno**) is not true; on the contrary it is a complete lie. He said he would go. When he comes, ask him to come here. She is crying because her mother is ill. Although the food was not enough, yet it was well cooked. These people have neither cows nor goats. I have no money here, therefore I cannot buy. I give you this money so that you can find me a fowl.

LESSON 37

THE RECIPROCAL FORM OF THE VERB

THIS form shows an action done mutually or with one another; it always ends in **ana.** If the verb stem ends in **a,** the reciprocal form is made by adding **na**; if the verb ends in **i**, **u** or **i**, the **na** is added to **ia** or **ea**.

jua	know	**juana**	know one another
fuata	follow	**fuatana**	follow one another
penda	love	**pendana**	love one another
rudi	return	**rudiana**	return to each other
jibu	answer	**jibiana**	answer one another
samehe	forgive	**sameheana**	forgive one another

Sometimes the reciprocal form requires the use of another verb in English:

ona	see	**onana**	meet
pata	get	**patana**	agree
kosa	do wrong	**kosana**	quarrel
piga	hit	**pigana**	fight

If the prepositional form is needed to convey the right meaning in the case of one person, it must be used also in the reciprocal form. For instance, *write to someone* is not **andika**, but **andikia**; therefore *to write to one another* must be **andikiana**. Similarly, *read to one another*, **someana**.

Many of the verbs we have learnt are of the prepositional form:

amkia	greet	**amkiana**	greet one another
ambia	say to	**ambiana**	tell one another
saidia	help	**saidiana**	help one another
kimbilia	run to	**kimbiliana**	run to each other
zoea	get used to	**zoeana**	get used to one another

Note that the reciprocal form of **pa**, give to, is **peana**:

> **Walipeana ahadi.** They made promises to one another.

WITH after a reciprocal verb is shown by **na**:

> Go along with your brother. **Fuatana na ndugu yako.**
> I do not get on with this person. **Sipatani na mtu huyu.**
> On the way I met (with) two men. **Njiani nilikutana na watu wawili.**

In some cases the reciprocal **na** is added to the **IKA** form of the verb, which, as we saw in Lesson 22, expresses state or possible state. In these cases it adds little to the meaning. Where, for instance, in a neighbouring Bantu language, people say **oneka,** be seen, in Swahili the verb is **onekana.** Some of the commonest verbs of this kind are:

patikana	be obtainable	**wezekana**	be possible
onekana	be visible	**kosekana**	be wanting
julikana	be knowable		

NOTE: The reader may have been puzzled by the varied meanings given to the verb **kosa.** Its root meaning seems to be *miss*, and its possible meanings, as given in the Standard Swahili Dictionary, are: make a mistake about, blunder, err, do wrong to, fail to get, miss a mark, be deficient, lack, suffer loss. In the vocabularies of a small book it is not possible to give all the possible meanings of every word.

Vocabulary

gawa,	divide	**kuta,**	come across, meet
gusa,	touch	**shika,**	take hold of
gomba,	oppose another	**peleka,**	send, take
fukuza,	drive away	**unga,**	join
ita,	call	**vuta,**	pull
itika,	answer call	**ndoa,**	marriage

Exercise 36

Write in Swahili: The clerk and his wife do not agree. They are always quarrelling. Last month they had a fight. The husband drove away his wife and she went back to her father. Afterwards they returned to each other. But they do not love each other. Perhaps they will separate. It behoves a man and his wife to forgive each other and help each other, because they have been joined together in marriage.

LESSON 38

SOME NOTES ON CONJUNCTIONS

HERE are a few more things which it may be useful to know.

Two or three. If this means " a few ", the conjunction is

omitted in Swahili: Two or three people, **Watu wawili watatu.**

That is why. **Ndiyo sababu, Ndiyo maana.**

Whether . . . or. In addition to constructions with **kama** or **ikiwa** given in Lesson 36, note the following:

> **Kwamba una kidogo au kwamba una wingi, uwe radhi.**
> Whether you have little or much, be content.
> **Ukipenda usipende.** Whether you like it or not.
> **Jogoo likiwika lisiwike, kutakucha.*** Whether the
> cock crows or not, it will dawn.

While. Usually the relative of time is sufficient; but when stress is laid on the two things happening together, **wakati** or **pindi** can be used:

> **Wakati alipokuwa akisema.** While he was speaking.
> **Wabaya waanguke katika nyavu zao wenyewe, pindi
> mimi ninapopita salama.** Let the wicked fall into
> their own nets while I pass by safely.

When *while* or *when* carries the sense of " seeing that ", **hali** is sometimes used:

> **Alisema lori ni yake hali sivyo.** He said the lorry was
> his when it was not.
> **Usifanye hivi, hali umejua imekatazwa.** Do not do
> this, when you know it is forbidden.

Some writers of rather slovenly English use *while* as equivalent to *and*: e.g. " The frontispiece is in colour while the other pictures are in black and white." Do not use a relative of time in such a case; **na** is sufficient.

As if. **Kana kwamba** or **Kama kwamba.** **Kama** and **kana** are two different conjunctions in Arabic; hence the two forms. It has been suggested that Standard Swahili should keep to the second form, but the first is still the most used and probably the one to be preferred:

> **Alicheza pamoja na simba kana kwamba ni wana-
> mbuzi.** He played with lions as if they were kids.
> **Wamepotea kana kwamba hawakuwapo.** They are
> lost as if they had never been.

* See page 147.

Kwani. This word is used in two ways, first as an interrogative, *What for? Why?* and secondly as a conjunction, *For, because.* The first is its proper meaning, from **Kwa nini?** For what? But it is very common in its second meaning which is probably equivalent to the old English use of *For-why*, because.

Kwani kumwogopa mbwa? Why fear the dog?

Usimwogope, kwani hana matata. Do not be afraid of him, for he is not fierce.

Ila. The chief uses of this conjunction were given in Lesson 36; note also this idiomatic use:

> **Juma zima halijapita ila wamekwenda wote.** Before a week had passed they had all gone.
> **Hajawahi kumweleza ila bwana wao akaingia.** Before he had managed to explain to him their master came in.

Kama. This is a word of so many uses that it will be useful to collect them together here.

(a) *like.*

> **Ni ndizi nzuri kama zile za jana.** They are good bananas like those of yesterday.
> **Rangi yake nyekundu kama damu.** Its colour was red like blood.
> **Ni nzuri kama nini!** How beautiful it is!

(b) *as.*

> **Kama upendavyo.** As you like.
> **Fanya kama hivi.** Do it in this way.

(c) *about.*

> **Urefu wake ni kama futi kumi.** Its length is about ten feet.

Yapata, it gets, can also be used:

> **Yapata miaka kumi.** About ten years.

(d) *if.*

> **Kama nyama haipatikani, nunua samaki.** If meat is unobtainable, buy fish.

(e) *whether.*

> **Sijui kama watakuja.** I do not know whether they will come.

(f) *as though.*

Si kama (kwamba) aliona mwenyewe. It is not as if he had seen it himself.

(g) *that.*

Alisema kama ndivyo hivyo. He said that this is how it was.

Notice the idiomatic use of **kama** in the following sentences:

Mavuno ni mengi kama si mengi. The harvest is fair.
Anapenda kama hapendi. He half wants it.

Exercise 37

Ni mamoja kwangu. It's all the same to me.
Amerukwa na akili. He has lost his senses.

Write in English; then put back into Swahili: Ukija usije ni mamoja kwangu; fanya upendavyo mwenyewe. Si watoto tu waliofika kwenye michezo (games), ila wazee wao pia. Sijawahi kusema ila amekwenda zake. Hana ila mke mmoja tu. Watu waliopo ni kama arobaini; sijui kama wengine watakuja. Labda watakuja, hali wanajua kuna michezo. Huko mjini kuna mashauri, ndiyo sababu watu wengine hawakuja; si kama hawataki. Alisema kana kwamba amerukwa na akili.

LESSON 39

THE CAUSATIVE FORM OF THE VERB

WE have now considered the passive, stative, prepositional and reciprocal forms. Let us take another most useful form, the CAUSATIVE. We have had one or two examples of this already: **chemsha,** to bring to the boil; **telemsha,** to lower; **safisha,** to make clean; the root idea is to cause an action to be done.

Most verbs make the causative by changing the final vowel into **isha** or **esha:**

rudi	go back	**rudisha**	send (give) back
weza	be able to	**wezesha**	enable
enda	go	**endesha**	drive

A few take **iza** or **eza**:

fanya	do	**fanyiza**	cause to do
penda	love	**pendeza**	please
uma	hurt	**umiza**	give pain to

It is supposed that the old Bantu causative was made with a **y**, pronounced in such a way as to cause changes in the preceding letter. Its usual effect was to change an **l** into **z** in Swahili, e.g. **lala**, lie down; **laza**, lay down; and if we remember that two vowels usually come together because an intermediate **l** has dropped out, we can understand why most verbs ending in **two vowels** make their causative by inserting **z**:

ingia	enter	**ingiza**	put inside
kimbia	run away	**kimbiza**	drive away
sikia	hear	**sikiza**	make to hear
jaa	get full	**jaza**	fill
kataa	refuse	**kataza**	forbid
zoea	get used to	**zoeza**	accustom
pungua	get less	**punguza**	make less
oa	marry	**oza**	make to marry

But the causative of **zaa** is **zalisha**; **jua**, **julisha**; **kaa**, **kalisha**; **tua**, **tuliza**; and **sahau**, **sahaulisha**.

Under the influence of this causative **y**, **ka** usually changes to **sha**:

ruka	jump, fly	**rusha**	make fly, fling
anguka	fall	**angusha**	throw down
amka	wake up	**amsha**	wake someone
chemka	bubble up	**chemsha**	bring to the boil

But **fika** makes its causative **fikisha**; **cheka**, **chekesha**; **toka**, **tokeza**; **geuka**, **geuza**.

Some verbs ending in **na** make their causatives in the old way:

pona	get well	**ponya**	cure
ona	see	**onya**	warn
kana	deny	**kanya**	rebuke

E

Some of these verbs have a double causative. **Pona** makes also **ponyesha,** used in the same way as **ponya;** **ona** makes **onyesha,** show, its simple causative being used mostly in the sense of warning.

Most reciprocal verbs ending in **ana** make their causative in **isha: pigana,** fight, **piganisha,** make to fight. But **gawana,** divide among oneselves, makes **gawanya.**

A few apparent irregularities are caused by the causative **y** :

lewa	get drunk	**levya**	make drunk
ogopa	fear	**ogofya**	frighten
takata	become clean	**takasa**	cleanse
pita	pass	**pisha**	allow to pass
pata	get	{ **pasha**	cause to get
		{ **pasa**	behove

Pasha is used chiefly in the phrases **pasha moto,** heat up food; **pasha habari,** give someone news. **Pitisha** is more common than **pisha,** the latter being used in the sense of " make room for ", **Mpishe,** Let him pass.

Causative verbs are often made from adjectives and sometimes from nouns:

safi	clean	**safisha**	cleanse
rahisi	easy	**rahisisha**	make easy
sawa	equal	**sawazisha**	make equal
imara	firm	**imarisha**	make firm
tayari	ready	**tayarisha**	make ready
sahihi	correct	**sahihisha**	correct mistakes
fupi	short	**fupisha**	shorten
tajiri	rich	**tajirisha**	make rich
bidii	effort	**(ji)bidiisha**	urge oneself on

It will be seen that the causation is of many kinds. **Pisha,** for instance, just means to stand aside and let someone pass; **angusha,** as well as meaning throw down, can be used of dropping accidentally; **zalisha** is little more than helping a woman in childbirth; **kopesha,** lend, is only acquiescence in borrowing. In some cases a different word needs to be used in the English; *make to see,* for instance, is either *show* or *warn; make to return* is *send back* or *give back,* etc.

In Swahili, moreover, the causative form is used also for the intensive where there is no idea of causality; e.g.

Fuatisha hesabu.	Copy (exactly) the sums.
Kidonda kinawasha.	The sore is (very) painful.
Ng'ombe wanalisha.	The cows are grazing.
Nyamaza !	Be (quite) quiet.

The various derived forms obtained by changing the ending of the verb can be combined: **unga,** join; **ungana,** join together; **unganisha,** cause to join together; etc.

Notice that, from **sikia,** hear, we get **sikiza** or **sikiliza,** make to hear, i.e. *listen*; and from this a reciprocal form, **sikizana** or **sikilizana,** understand one another, get on together.

Funda (little used) makes **fundisha** or **funza,** teach, and **jifunza,** learn, i.e. teach yourself. From these verbs we get **fundi,** a skilled workman; **mwanafunzi,** a learner; **mafundisho,** teaching; etc.

Vocabulary

sali, pray	**choka,** get tired
kopa, borrow	**nyoka,*** become straight
poa, get cool	**shuka,** come down
sogea, move along	**vuka,** cross over
tembea, walk	**kauka,** get dry
enea, spread	**waka,** burn
elea, be intelligible	**zunguka,** go round
tua, set down	**kumbuka,** remember
chukia, hate	**lainika,** get smooth

Note that the causative of **sali** means *lead the prayers*; of **tembea,** *hawk about for sale*; of **elea,** *explain to*; of **tua,** *pacify*; and of **chukia,** *offend*.

Exercise 38

Write the causative forms of the verbs in the Vocabulary. *Translate:* Boil some water. The water is boiling. The medicine has cured him. Show me the way. Your work does not please me. Make the lines quite straight. Lay the child on the bed. Fill the pail (**ndoo**). Give the man his money back. He has had it given back to him. Make the children stand up. Move these boxes into another room. The sun has dried up the water. This teaching is not clear to me. I will explain (it) to you. Show me your

---

* Sometimes written **nyooka.**

book.   When you are teaching do not weary the children.
Light the fire.   It is burning now.   Remind me tomorrow.
Help me across.   This news has spread everywhere; the
children have spread it.   Stretch out your hand.

LESSON 40

MORE ABOUT VERBS

To Do and Undo

OF the derived forms of the verb, the five we have mentioned
are the important ones, and ones that the student should
know how to construct.   There is another ending, **ua**,
which reverses the action of some verbs:

funga	fasten	**fungua**	unfasten
fumba	close	**fumbua**	open
ziba	stop up	**zibua**	unstop
funika	cover	**funua**	uncover
kunja	fold	**kunjua**	unfold
tega	set trap	**tegua**	let off trap
fuma	weave	**fumua**	unravel
bandika	stick on	**bandua**	strip off
tata	tangle	**tatua**	untangle, tear
inama	bend down	**inua**	lift up
vaa	put on clothes	**vua**	take off clothes

It will be noticed that a few of the verbs are not in their
simple forms.   **Funika** and **bandika** have an old **ika**
causative suffix; and **inama** is the verb **ina,** now obsolete,
with a **ma** suffix denoting position (cf. **simama**).

In some cases the **ua** does not reverse the action, but
rather intensifies it:

kama	squeeze	**kamua**	squeeze out
songa	press	**songoa**	wring

Note that after **o** the termination is **oa**.

In the Standard Dictionary and in most modern gram-
mars, this form of the verb is called CONVERSIVE.

Reduplication

The commonest use of the reduplicated verb is to denote continued action :

Mbona unasemasema tu ? Why do you just go on talking ?

Uzi huu unakatikakatika. This thread keeps on breaking.

In many cases reduplication modifies the action. **Sijambo.** I am quite well ; **Sijambojambo,** I am fairly well. **Anajaribujaribu,** He is trying, but not very hard.

The old form of reduplication seems to have been by duplicating the first syllable only, as in **gogota,** tap.

All the Derivative Forms are shown in the Table on page 157, together with three other endings occasionally found.

Verbs of Becoming

We have already seen that some Swahili verbs denote a process of becoming which results in a certain state, and that, to express the completed action, we must use the ME perfect tense. Some of the verbs of this kind we have already learnt are :

jaa	get full	**pona**	get well
lewa	get drunk	**potea**	get lost
choka	get tired	**zoea**	get used to
kauka	get dry	**nyoka**	become straight

Most stative verbs are of this kind :

haribika	get spoilt	**vunjika**	get broken
punguka	get less	**katika**	get cut
chafuka	get into a mess	**onekana**	get found

Some other verbs express a single action resulting in a state or position, and these need great care in their use. Among them are :

kaa	sit down	**amka**	wake up
simama	stand up	**lala**	lie down
piga * magoti	kneel down	**fa**	die

* **piga** is used for a large number of actions : **piga mstari,** draw a line, **piga pasi,** iron clothes ; **piga kelele,** make a noise, etc.

We are so used to saying in English, " He *is* standing up ",
" He *is* lying down", etc., that it is easy to forget and use
the same tense in Swahili. But if we say " A*na*simama ",
" A*na*lala", etc., we denote that he is in the process of
getting to his feet, or on to his bed. Study carefully the
correct forms below:

They are standing up.	**Wamesimama.**
The children are sitting on the ground.	**Watoto wamekaa chini.**
He is awake.	**Ameamka.**
He is dead.	**Amekufa.**
I am lost.	**Nimepotea.**
The men are drunk.	**Watu wamelewa.**
The line is straight.	**Mstari umenyoka.**
The work is finished.	**Kazi imekwisha.**

Verbs of this kind, when used in the past relative, are equivalent to adjectives and should often be translated by an
adjective:

Nipe bilauri iliyojaa maji.	Give me a full glass of water.
Watu waliochoka hulala sana.	Tired people sleep soundly.
Kisima kilichokauka cha-faa nini?	What use is a dry well?
Kondoo aliyepotea ameo-nekana.	The lost sheep has been found.

Some Further Notes

(a) Some verbs take a double prepositional form with a
special meaning: e.g. **shika**, hold; **shikia**, hold for;
shikilia, hold on to. Note the following:

pendelea (*penda*)	be biassed in favour of
endelea (*enda*)	continue
achilia (*acha*)	forgive
chekelea (*cheka*)	smile
ogelea (*oga*)	swim
pigilia (*piga*)	ram mud floors
chelewa (*cha*)	be late
sikiliza (*sikia*)	listen

(b) When a verb has two subjects, of different noun classes, it usually takes the subject prefix **vi** (as for **vitu**) if both are concrete things, or it can be made to agree with the subject nearest to it. If the subjects are abstract, the verb generally agrees with the one nearest to it, or **zi** can be used:

> **Shamba, nyumba na chakula *vi*lipotea.** Field, house and food were lost.
>
> **Maua na bustani yote *i*lipendeza sana.** The flowers and all the garden were delightful.
>
> **Huruma yake na upole wake *u*lisifiwa sana.** His mercy and gentleness were much praised.

Of course, if both belong to the same noun class the subject prefix of that class is used:

> **Maneno yake na matendo yake *ya*likuwa mema.** His words and his deeds were good.
>
> **Wema wake na upole wake *u*liwapendeza watu wote.** His goodness and gentleness pleased everyone.

If one subject is a person and the other a thing, every effort should be made to alter the arrangement of the sentence:

> The people and their customs pleased me greatly.
> **Watu walinipendeza sana, na desturi zao pia.**

Idioms

A few idiomatic ways of speaking are noted below; you may come across them in conversation:

> **Amekwenda kuitwa.** Someone has gone to call him.
>
> **Chakula kimekwenda kuletwa.** Someone has gone for the food.
>
> **Kikapu kimekuja kuchukuliwa.** Someone has come for the basket.
>
> **Nchi imeingia nzige.** Locusts have invaded the country.
>
> **Mji umeingia ndui.** Smallpox has come to the town.
>
> **Ninakwenda kupima nguo.** I am going to be measured for a garment.
>
> **Alimpiga mtoto jiwe la kichwa.** He hit the child on the head with a stone.

**Ukipenda kufuatana nami, vema. La! hupendi,
nitakwenda peke yangu.** If you like to come with me
I shall be pleased. But if not I will go by myself.

Licha ya fedha, hata shamba utapata. Not only money,
but a field as well, you will get.

Wakitenda watoto hayo, sembuse watu wazima! If
they treat children like this, how much more
grown-up people!

Exercise 39

Write in Swahili: Listen, children! Are the clothes
dry? Take off your shoes when you come into the house.
This hole has got stopped up; I am trying to unstop it.
What kind of clothes is he wearing? The book which was
lost, has it been found? Not yet; the children are still
looking for it. This work has gone on (**endelea**) well. Is
the master in? Yes, but he is asleep. Do not wake him.
When he wakes up, give him this letter. Draw (**piga**)
three straight lines. If they can, let them come here; but
if they can't, I will go to them tomorrow. Two books and
six pencils are lost. Not only books and pencils, but even
a chair. Call the cook. Someone has gone to call him.

LESSON 41

AUXILIARY VERBS

ENGLISH makes great use of auxiliary verbs to form verb
tenses: I *am* reading; I *shall* go; I *do* not know: I *have*
heard; etc. In Swahili these forms are expressed by the
verb itself: **Ninasoma; Nitakwenda; Sijui; Nimesikia.**

The verb TO HAVE is never used as an auxiliary in Swahili,
but many compound tenses can be made with the verb TO
BE. The two most commonly used are:

I was reading	**Nilikuwa nikisoma**
I had read	**Nilikuwa nimesoma.**

It is easy to see how these tenses are made: By **nilikuwa,**
I was, I put myself back into the past, and then write the
tense of **soma** as I should have said it at that time.

These two tenses are very common with the relative of time:

| While he was speaking. | **Alipokuwa akisema.** |
| When he had spoken. | **Alipokuwa amesema.** |

In narrative speech, the **KA** tense often takes the place of the **LI** tense in **kuwa:**

Wakawa wakisoma.   And they were reading.

The **KI** tense can be replaced by the **NA** tense:

Alikuwa anaandika.   He was writing.

Remember that with verbs of becoming, we should say:

I was standing.   **Nilikuwa ni*me*simama.**

Here are some more examples:

Watu wote walikuwa wamekwenda sokoni. All the people had gone to the market.

Alipokuwa akilima aliitwa nyumbani. When he was hoeing he was called to the house.

Mnazi ulikuwa ukizaa nazi kubwa sana. The coconut palm was bearing very large nuts.

Watu wawili walikuwa wakisafiri. Two people were travelling.

Watu wote walipokuwa wamelala. When all the people were asleep.

The verb (KW)ISHA, to finish, is much used with the infinitive to form a perfect tense denoting a finished action. The **ku** of the following infinitive is frequently omitted:

Amekwisha kuja. He has already arrived.

Alikuwa amekwisha ondoka. He had already gone.

Mwivi alikuwa amekwisha kimbia. The thief had by then run off.

Alipokwisha kuisoma barua, aliitupa. When he had read the letter he threw it away.

Panya wote wamekwisha kufa. All the rats are dead now.

Nikiisha kununua chakula, nitarudi. When I have finished buying the food I will return.

Twenty years ago we had to learn many tenses formed with the auxiliary verb TO BE, such as: **ningawa nitasoma;**

ajapokuwa amekuja; tukiwa hatusomi. These tenses are still in existence, but for all practical purposes they have been displaced by conjunctions formed from the impersonal forms of the tenses of TO BE :

Ingawa nitasoma.	Although I shall read.
Ijapo(kuwa) amekuja.	Even if he has come.
Ikiwa hatusomi.	If we do not read.

We have already learnt these conjunctions. If in any book we come across them with subject prefixes, we have only to remember that they are tenses of the verb TO BE having just the same meaning.

In connection with this subject of the replacement of tenses by conjunctions, we may note that there is a tense **nisijesoma,** before I read, which was omitted in the earlier lessons as it is replaced nowadays by **kabla sijasoma.**

Exercise 40

Read and translate ; then put back into Swahili: Baba alipokuwa akienda mjini aliona mgeni amesimama njiani. Wakiisha kuamkiana na kupeana habari, baba alisema, " Imekuwaje, bwana, upo hapa peke yako? Umepotea njia ? " Yule mgeni alisema, " Nina shauri na ndugu yangu akaaye Tongwe. Lakini nilipofika kwao nilimkuta hayupo. Alikuwa amekwisha ondoka kwenda Muheza. Nilikuwa sina la kufanya ila kumfuata. Watoto wake walinionyesha njia; wakasema nikiisha fika kwenye minazi niulize tena. Basi, nilikuwa nikingoja hapa nipate kuona mtu wa kumwuliza." Baba akamwambia, " Nami ninakwenda kule kule; tutafuatana pamoja."

LESSON 42

ADJECTIVES AND PRONOUNS

THERE is no need to distinguish between adjectives and pronouns in Swahili, as the words have exactly the same form whether they are used with nouns, as adjectives, or without nouns, as pronouns. The distinction in Swahili is between those which take the *adjective prefixes* and those

which take the *subject prefixes of the verb*. You may need
to refer often to the Table of Concords on pages 154–155
to remind yourself which prefixes a certain word takes.

Adjective Prefixes		*Verb Subject Prefixes*	
-ngapi	how many?	**-enye**	having
-ingi	much, many	**-enyewe**	self
-ingine	other	**-ote**	all
and descriptive adjectives		**-o -ote**	any whatever
and numbers		**-pi?**	which?
		and possessives and demonstratives	

NOTES:

1. With the personal pronouns, **-enyewe** is used as follows:

mimi mwenyewe	I myself	**sisi wenyewe**	we ourselves
wewe mwenyewe	you yourself	**ninyi wenyewe**	you yourselves
yeye mwenyewe	he himself	**wao wenyewe**	they themselves

2. When referring to more than two people, **-ote** with the
personal pronouns takes the forms:

sisi sote	all of us
ninyi nyote	all of you
wao wote	all of them

When referring to two people, **wote** is used unless the
personal pronoun is omitted:

sisi wote, both of us   **nyote wawili,** you two

3. **-o -ote** is often combined with **-ingine** to express *any
other* whatsoever. In this case, the **-o** is attached to the
preceding word, throwing the stress forward:

vitu vinginévyo vyote	any other things whatsoever
watu wenginéo wote	any other people whatsoever
nyumba nyínginézo zote	any other houses whatsoever

-o -ote can be used in this way with other words as well:

aendáko kote	wherever he goes
awáye yote	whoever he be

When used by itself **-o -ote** precedes the verb:

ye yote atakaye	anyone who wishes
cho chote alicho nacho	anything which he has

It is considered correct, at present, to write **-o -ote** as two words. But it seems possible that the word is formed from **-ote** by reduplication of the first syllable (cf. **gogota,** page 125), in which case it would be better written as one word. Its origin is at present obscure.

4. The **o** of reference can be attached to **-ingine** to denote other things of the kind referred to:

vitu vinginevyo	other things of this kind
mazao mengineyo	other crops of this kind
kazi nyinginezo	other similar work

5. **-mojawapo,** any one of certain things. This is probably a compound word derived from such form as **kimoja kiwapo,** one which is here; the **wapo** is now invariable:

kitu kimojawapo	one of the things
sehemu mojawapo	any one part
mmojawapo wa watu hawa	one of these people

Possessives

The possessive pronouns and adjectives are *my, your, his,* etc. They are sometimes attached in a shortened form to words with which they are constantly used. The commonest words are:

(a) *My* companion, companions, child, children: **mwenzangu, wenzangu, mwanangu, wanangu.**

(b) *Your* companion, companions, child, children, wife, husband, brother, brothers: **mwenzako** or **mwenzio, wenzako** or **wenzio, mwanao, wanao, mkeo, mumeo, nduguyo, nduguzo.**

(c) *His* or *her* companion, companions, child, children, wife, husband, father, mother, brother, brothers: **mwenzake** or **mwenziwe, wenzake** or **wenziwe, mwanawe, wanawe, mkewe, mumewe, babaye, mamaye, nduguye, nduguze.**

(d) With *our, your* (plural) and *their,* the only common forms are: **mwenzetu, mwenzenu, mwenzao;**

wenzetu, wenzenu, wenzao; our, your or their companion(s).

Note that **wake,** wives, takes the **N** class concords with possessive adjectives: **wake zetu; wake zake,** sometimes shortened to **wakeze; wake zao,** etc.

We find the contracted forms with a few other words as well, such as **baadaye,** afterwards; **mwishowe,** at last.

The personal pronouns can be used after a possessive adjective for emphasis, or the possessive adjective can be used instead of *of* to denote someone's special property:

Hiki ni kitabu changu *mimi*.	This is my own book.
Kiti *chake* **Jumbe.**	The chair on which the Chief sits.

The object prefix of the verb is used instead of the possessive adjective when speaking of parts of a person's body:

Hamta*ni***ona uso tena.**	You will not see my face again.
Nime*ji***kata mkono.**	I have cut my hand.
Wali*m***funga miguu.**	They bound his legs.
Ali*ni***piga kofi la uso.**	He slapped my face.

Demonstratives

The demonstratives this, that, etc., are often used in a reduplicated form for emphasis:

Shika njia hii hii.	Keep to this same path.
Usiku ule ule akafa.	And that same night he died.
Wakasema maneno yale yale.	They said the same thing.

There are also special forms, especially with reference to something already mentioned; their construction will be seen from the examples given below:

> **Naye akasema maneno** *yayo hayo*. He also said just the same.
>
> **Kila mtu alitoa senti** *zizo hizo*. Each man gave the same number of cents.
>
> **Nami nakupa neno** *lilo hilo*. And I give you just the same advice.

Ni *vivyo hivyo* kwa watu wa siku hizi. It is just the same with regard to people nowadays.

Alikuwa amesimama *papa hapa*. He was standing just here.

Panya wa pili aliingia *mumo humo*. And the second rat went in at the very same place.

Wote wakajibu *vivi hivi*. All answered in the same way.

The Suffix -ni

We have seen that this suffix is sometimes used to denote *you* when more than one person is spoken to: **pendeni,** love (ye); **Nimekuambieni,** I have told you. Other words with which it is used when speaking to more than one person are:

Kwa herini.	Good-bye.
Poleni.	Sorry!
Twendeni (zetu) ⎱	Let us go.
Twende zetuni. ⎰	
Karibuni !	Come in!

Exercise 41

Write in Swahili: How many houses are there in your village? Not many, moreover the houses themselves are no good. All are ready to fall down. We ourselves are used to them, because we belong (are natives) here. We have lived in this same place since our childhood, we and our wives too. This is the chief's house, and these are the houses of his wives. This is his brother's house, and these two are his children's. Which is your house? It is this, and it also is bad. I want to build another, but I have cut my foot. I cannot go far, and near here there are no trees whatever to build with.

LESSON 43

THE FORMATION OF NOUNS

It will have been noticed by now that many verbs and nouns come from the same root. We have had, for instance, the verbs **sikia, imba, oa, pika,** and the nouns

sikio, wimbo, ndoa, mpishi. Probably both verbs and nouns arose originally from some descriptive sound. A mother says to her child taking its first steps, **de ! de !** and says of it, **" Atenda de ! "** Hence arose a verb **deka,** give oneself airs, and its reduplicative, **dedekeza,** spoil a child by too much petting. Words like **de !** are called ideophones, sounds connected with some particular idea. They are not easy to trace in Swahili, as so many Bantu words have been lost and replaced by words of foreign derivation; so all we can do now is to derive a noun from a verb, and this can be done with both Bantu and Arabic words.

The simplest way of forming a noun from a verb is to give the verb stem the prefix of the **WATU** or **KITU** class. It then becomes the name of a person or thing without ceasing to do some of its work as a verb:

mtoa mema	the giver of good	**wapiga ngoma**	drummers
mwuza duka	a shopkeeper	**kifungua kopo**	a tin-opener

If the suffix **-ji** is added it denotes a habitual occupation:

mchungaji	a shepherd	**msemaji**	an orator
mwimbaji	a chorister	**walimaji**	farmers

Another common way of forming the noun is by changing the final **a** of the verb into **i**. There was originally in this **i** the same sound as in the **y** used to make causative verbs, and the same changes take place. We get, for instance:

pika	**mpishi**	a cook
linda	**mlinzi**	a guard
lea	**mlezi**	a nurse
zaa	**mzazi**	parent
lewa	**mlevi**	drunkard
gomba	**mgomvi**	quarrelsome person

Some nouns are formed with a suffix **u**, which also causes sound changes:

oko(l)a	**wokovu**	salvation
haribika	**uharibifu**	destruction
punguka	**upungufu**	diminution
sahau	**usahaulifu**	forgetfulness

The ending **e** generally denotes a person or thing to which the action has been done:

umba	kiumbe	something created, a creature
tuma	mtume	someone sent, a messenger
kata	mkate	something cut, a loaf
shinda	ushinde	being conquered, failure

The commonest ending is **o**, generally denoting a thing or an action:

fungua	ufunguo(f)	a key
ziba	kizibo	a cork
funika	kifuniko	a lid
sikia	sikio(ma)	an ear
imba	wimbo	a song
zaa	mazao	crops
patana	mapatano	agreement

The dropped **l** at the beginning of the verb, which becomes **d** when an **N** class noun is made, accounts for the change from

> **oa,** marry, to ; **ndoa,** marriage ; *and*
> **ota,** dream, to ; **ndoto,** a dream.

Njia, path, is another **N** class noun made from the prepositional form of **ja,** come.

Nouns can be made from any of the derivative forms of the verb, so that, from one verb stem, many nouns can be formed. From **enda,** go, we get **mwendo,** a journey and **mwenzi,** a companion ; from the causative, **endesha,** we get **mwendeshaji,** a driver ; from the prepositional form, **endelea,** go on, we get **maendeleo,** progress ; and from the reduplicated form **enenda,** comes **mwenendo,** behaviour. The dictionary gives eighteen nouns made from **penda,** love.

Arabic nouns are made from verbs by internal vowel changes, though some, such as **msafiri,** a traveller, are made in the Bantu way. All we can say about the changes is that there are usually more **a**'s in the noun than in the verb:

safiri	make a journey	**safari**	a journey
furahi	be glad	**furaha**	joy
amini	believe	**imani**	faith

sali	pray	**sala**	a prayer
abudu	(to) worship	**ibada**	worship
sifu	(to) praise	**sifa**	praise
tubu	repent	**toba**	repentance
bariki	bless	**baraka**	a blessing
saidia	(to) help	**msaada**	help

Exercise 42

Write in Swahili: Give me the key to open the door with.
Find me a cork to stop up the bottle with. The guards
before the gate guarded the king's palace. The travellers
met with many dangers on their long journey. From here
to the town is a distance (going) of about half an hour.
The teacher praised the child's parents because of the good
behaviour of their son. A drunkard is a quarrelsome man.
We must pray with repentance and faith. I asked help
from him, but he refused to help me. Do not be a lover of
money. They rejoiced (with) a very great joy.

NOTE: In the remaining chapters, further explanation is
given of some points which were only briefly considered in the
earlier chapters. Instead of an exercise on the lesson itself,
short passages from various present-day sources are given
for reading and translation.

LESSON 44

THE N AND MA NOUN CLASSES

FROM what has been already said about the various classes
of Swahili nouns, anyone coming across a word like **mashua**
would take it to be a plural noun of the **MA** class, and
would be surprised to be told that it is a singular noun of
the **N** class meaning *boat*. Some explanation of this is
needed.

Arabic nouns when absorbed into Swahili are fitted,
whenever possible, into an appropriate noun class; e.g.
kitabu into the **KITU** class, **mwalimu** into the **WATU**
class, the **ki** and **mw** being counted as the singular prefixes.
Mahali has gone naturally into the place class in place of

the lost **patu,** taking the **pa** concords. Other nouns have had to come into the **N** or **MA** classes. Most are firmly established in one or the other, but there are a few about which there is some difference of opinion.

The general rule is that foreign words, except names of persons and offices, are put into the **N** class, and make no change in the plural. Foreign names of persons and offices, such as **sultani,** sultan; **askofu,** bishop; **bwana,** master; **bibi,** mistress; go into the **MA** class, making their plural by the addition of **ma.** The difficulty arises when the words themselves begin with **ma.**

Ma is a common formative syllable in Arabic, and therefore many nouns taken over by Swahili begin with it. When such nouns denote a concrete thing, needing a singular and plural form, they go into the **N** class; e.g. **mashua yake moja,** his one boat; **mashua zake mbili,** his two boats. Otherwise they are treated as abstract or collective nouns of the **MA** class; e.g. **maradhi,** sickness.

One or two words usually treated as abstract nouns can be treated as **N** class nouns when used in the plural:

maisha mengi	a long life	**maisha nyingi**	many lives
mamlaka ma-	great	**mamlaka zake**	his dominions
kubwa	authority		

The following words are concrete, and belong to the **N** class:

madini	metal	**mara**	time
maili	mile	**mali**	wealth
maiti	dead body	**mashine**	machine
malaika	angel	**maskani**	dwelling-place

Note that **maili** and **mashine** come from the English. Remember that **malaika,** except for the possessive adjectives, takes the prefixes of the **WATU** class: **malaika yangu mlinzi,** my guardian angel. **Maiti** is often used with the concords of the **WATU** class: **maiti amezikwa,** the dead man is buried.

NOTE: We saw that the diversity of letters with which **N** class nouns begin is due partly to the loss of the **N** prefix. When **n** has been dropped before **p, t, k** or **ch,** it leaves these letters with a sharper (aspirated) sound than the usual **p, t, k** or **ch** of Swahili. In many parts of East

Africa the distinction is hardly noticeable; in others the difference between, e.g. **kaa,** sit, and **(n)kaa,** a crab, is quite recognisable. No distinction is made in writing Standard Swahili.

For Reading and Translation

Here are the thoughts of two Africans on Swahili, taken from a correspondence in the Swahili paper *Maendeleo*. There are some explanatory notes at the end.

Kiswahili Kiondoshwe

1. Maneno mengi yatumikayo katika lugha ya Kiswahili yametoka katika lugha za Waarabu, Wazungu na Wahindi. Kiswahili kilipatikana hasa katika sehemu za pwani, nacho ni lugha ya kibiashara. Hakuna watu ambao kabila lao au taifa lao ni la Kiswahili. Ingefaa tuiondoshe lugha hiyo sasa kabla lugha zetu wenyewe hazijaharibiwa.

2. Ubaya wa Kiswahili ni nini? Kitaondoshwa kwa sababu ni mchanganyiko wa maneno ya Kiarabu, Kizungu, Kihindi, na Kibantu? Hii si sababu hata kidogo. Hata Kiingereza ni mchanganyiko wa Kilatini na lugha nyingine za Ulaya. Kiswahili hutuletea faida nyingi. Husaidia Waafrika wasiojua Kiingereza kusikizana na Wazungu. Husaidia Waafrika wa makabila mbalimbali kusikizana. Husaidia Waafrika wanaokijua kusoma magazeti na matangazo ya serikali. Vitabu vilivyopigwa chapa katika Kiswahili ni vingi sana na vyenye maana kabisa katika maendeleo yetu. Kiswahili kitaendelea na kitazidi kusitawishwa mpaka kiwe chema zaidi ya jinsi kilivyo sasa.

NOTES:

lugha	language	**changanya**	to mix
kabila(ma)	tribe	**mchanganyiko**	mixture
taifa(ma)	nation	**tangaza**	to proclaim
pwani	coast	**matangazo**	proclamation
biashara	commerce	**gazeti(ma)**	magazine
serikali	government	**chapa**	print

ondosha causative of **ondoka,** go away
sitawisha causative of **sitawi,** flourish

LESSON 45

CONSECUTIVE TENSES

IN Lesson 17 we saw that the **KA** tense is used when one action follows another, and that its most common use is after the past tense. How it can be used after other tenses is shown in the following examples:

Past. **Nalikosa *ikanipata* nini?** I did wrong, and what happened to me?

Present. **Iwapo mtu mmoja anajenga na mwenzake *akabomoa*, je, faida yao ni nini?** If one man is building and his companion is breaking down, what profit have they?

Future. **Ikiwa mtu atakuja *akakuambia* kama anayo dawa ya ugonjwa huu, usimsadiki.** If a man shall come and say that he has medicine for this disease, do not believe him.

HU *tense.* **Mimi huwapa wanadamu embe zangu *wakala*.** I give men my mangoes and they eat them.

KI *tense.* **Ukimtenda mabaya *akakutoroka*, je?** If you treat him badly and he runs away, what then?

Sometimes the **KA** tense is used with the meaning of *so that*, as in the following examples:

Je, naweza kukupelekea barua *ikafika*? Can I send you a letter so that you get it?

Kibanda kisiwe karibu hata inzi *wakaweza* kutoka na kufika nyumbani. Do not let the hut be so near that flies can come from it to the house.

Linalofaa ni kumwonyesha *akajua*. The best thing is to show him so that he may know.

Notice also the use of the **KA** tense in the common construction for *lest*: **Wasije wakapotea,** Lest they get lost; **Usije ukafa,** Lest you die.

There is also a **KA** form of the *subjunctive* which can follow a verb in the imperative or subjunctive; it differs from the ordinary **KA** tense by ending in *e*. Its use needs care; notice the following points:

In the subjunctive it must not be used if the second verb

is dependent on the first, fulfilling its purpose or intention; in this case the simple subjunctive must be used:

> **Lete chakula** *tupate kula.* Bring food that we may eat.

The verbs must be independent and consecutive:

> **Amwogeshe mtoto** *akamfute* **kwa kitambaa.** Let her wash the child and dry him with a towel.

In the imperative the **ka** seems to be linked with the idea of *going*, so that if one says, for instance, " Kamwite " it is equivalent to saying, " Go and call him ", or " **Kai-tupe** ", " Go and throw it away ". It should therefore be used only when going is implied; it must not be used with a verb denoting coming:

> **Nenda ukatazame.**   Go and see.
> **Katazame.**   Go and see.
> **Njoo utazame.**   Come and see.

It is usual to say that the **KA** tense carries on the tense of the preceding verb; it would be more accurate to say that it carries on the thought in the mind of the speaker. Note how, in the two examples following, the **KA** tense carries on the relative idea of the preceding verb:

> **Wapi yule mtu aliyekuja** *akamnunua* **mbuzi?** Where is that man who came and bought the goat?
> **Tulisikia jinsi alivyoomba** *akapata.* We heard how he asked and got (what he asked for).

But, more often, the relative form does little more than denote time or place, and the following **KA** tense carries on the narrative without having any relative force:

> **Bwana alipoingia, wale watu** *wakasimama wakamwa-mkia.* When the officer entered, the men stood up and greeted him.
> **Alipolikataa shauri letu** *tukanyamaza.* And when he refused our advice we were silent.

As was shown on page 46, the *infinitive* of the verb can follow any tense, and therefore it does much the same work as the **KA** tense, except that it does not allow a change of the subject; it is not only the tense that is carried on, but the subject prefix also. On the other hand, it is free from the limitation of the **KA** tense that the actions should be consecutive:

Moshi unatoka na kupanda juu. The smoke is coming out and rising up.

Mtu huyu unayemwona na kumjua. This man whom you see and know.

Kila mtu auchukue mzigo wake na kuupeleka barabarani. Let each man take up his load and take it to the highroad.

Nitawaambia wavitafute na kukuletea. I will tell them to look for the things and bring them to you.

Alikuta watu wengi wakila chakula na kuongea. He found many people eating and talking.

The two forms can be used together in a sentence:

Hupondwa yakalainishwa na kupepetwa. They are pounded and ground fine and sifted.

For Reading and Translation

From an article by the Kenya Information Office on the choosing of representatives on an African Council.

Uchaguzi Wa Wajumbe

Kila anayetaka kuchaguliwa atakuwa amevaa ukanda wenye rangi mbalimbali. Kutakuwa vile vile na karatasi ngumu zenye rangi mbalimbali sawasawa na rangi za kanda zitakazovaliwa na wale watakaochaguliwa. Basi, kila mpiga kura atachukua karatasi yenye rangi iliyo sawa na rangi ya ukanda wa mjumbe anayetaka kumchagua. Akiisha kuichukua karatasi hiyo ataitia ndani ya sanduku itakayowekwa tayari. Watu wote wakiisha tia karatasi zao, sanduku itafunguliwa, na karatasi zilizomo zitahesabiwa. Basi, mjumbe atakayepata karatasi nyingi ndiye atakayeshinda.

Hivyo uchaguzi utakuwa wa siri, wala hautaleta chuki kati ya mchaguliwa na mchaguzi.

NOTES:

ukanda(k)	belt	**chuki**	ill-feeling
karatasi	paper	**piga kura**	cast lots, vote
rangi	colour	**mjumbe**(wa)	representative
siri	secret	**hesabu**	to count

Notice:

> **chagua,** choose; **mchaguzi,** chooser; **uchaguzi,** choosing;
> **chaguliwa,** be chosen; **mchaguliwa,** the chosen one.

Distinguish between **jumbe,** chief man, and **mjumbe,** messenger.

Note that **sanduku** and **tundu,** given in the book as **MA** class words, are often used, as here, in the **N** class.

LESSON 46

THE AMBA RELATIVE

In Lesson 21 the **AMBA** relative was mentioned as a form which can be used instead of using the relative prefix in the verb. If its use extends, as it probably will, it will continue the simplification of the Swahili verb begun by the use of the impersonal forms referred to on page 130. At present the **amba** relative should not be used for short straightforward sentences, but only where the ordinary relative is difficult to use.

Like the conjunctions derived from the impersonal tenses of TO BE, **amba** began work as a verb. It is, in fact, the relative form of the old verb **amba,** to say, which has lost its subject prefix and become a kind of conjunction or relative pronoun. This means that, like the other conjunctions we have spoken of, it can be used with any tense and is freed from the limitations of the verb form. Some of its uses are shown in the sentences which follow:

(a) This is the child who will not be coming to school tomorrow. **Huyu ni mtoto ambaye kesho hatakuja shule.**

As the one form of the negative relative tense has to do duty for the past, present and future, the use of **amba** makes the statement much clearer.

(b) The thing which he said, and which we shall not forget. **Neno alilolisema ambalo hatutalisahau.**

Here again the idea of the future is better conveyed by **amba,** and its use avoids another relative tense following the first.

(c) I begged for the little hoe which the teacher and his children do not use when hoeing their field. **Naliliomba jembe dogo ambalo mwalimu na watoto wake hawalitumii wanapolima shamba lao.**

If you try to write a sentence like this using the verb with a relative prefix, you will either get the relative separated from the thing it refers to, or you will get a string of words out of place.

(d) John, whose second name is Mark. **Yohana, ambalo jina lake la pili ni Marko.**

This is the sick man of whom my son told you yesterday. **Huyu ni yule mgonjwa ambaye mwanangu alikupa habari zake jana.**

Whenever the relative has a prepositional sense, such as *in which, about whom, whose,* we need the **amba** construction. If you try to translate such sentences without **amba** you will wonder how Swahili ever managed without it. The answer is that idiomatic Swahili would not use a relative at all. The best Swahili speakers would probably say, "John, his other name is Mark" or "This is the sick man; my son told you about him yesterday."

It is, of course, quite wrong to put a relative particle in the verb following **amba,** but the object prefix must be inserted where necessary, as in **hatuta*li*sahau** in (b) above.

It may sometimes be necessary, grammatically, to add a preposition:

This is the book *in* which I saw the picture. **Hiki ni kitabu ambacho *ndani yake* niliiona picha.**

Another way *by* which people get money. **Njia nyingine ambayo *kwayo* watu hupata fedha.**

But, in the second case, the *kwayo* is often omitted.

For Reading and Translation

(From the Swahili monthly paper *Mambo Leo*)

Kutengenezwa na Kupigwa Chapa Gazeti

Gazeti lenu *Mambo Leo* limetimiza miaka ishirini na saba sasa. Wasomaji wengi mara kwa mara huuliza

miendo yake hata likapata kutokea: anayeandika mambo
mnayosoma katika kurasa zake; anayepiga picha; na
mwenye kuchagua yatakayoingia katika gazeti, na kuzuia
yasiyotakiwa.

Huenda msijue, lakini kazi ya kutokeza magazeti ni ngumu
sana na ya kutatanisha. Lazima uwe na watu wanaoweza
kuandika Kiswahili kizuri na kutumainiwa kabisa kwa
kupeleka habari za mambo yanayofanyika sehemu yao ya
Tanganyika. Habari wanazopeleka hazifai kitu ila tuwe
na mashine na wino na karatasi na umeme, na watu walio-
elimika sana, kwa kutengeneza na kupiga chapa magazeti
na kuyaeneza katika nchi.

NOTES:

timia	be complete	**elimika**	be educated
piga chapa	to print	**elimu**	knowledge
piga picha	to draw pictures	**ukurasa(k)**	page
tumaini	to rely on	**umeme**	electricity
tokea	to appear		

tengeneza, prepare, arrange, mend, etc., often, though
   incorrectly, used also for *make*.
hazifai kitu, are worth nothing.
huenda msijue, it may be that you do not know.
   Huenda can be used instead of **labda,** perhaps.

NOTE: **tata,** tangle; **tatua,** untangle, tear; **matata,** trouble-
someness; **tatanisha,** to worry, give trouble.

LESSON 47

PLACE

WE have learnt that most of the forms for *there is, there was,*
etc., are made in Swahili with the verb TO HAVE:

Kuna watu huko sokoni? Hakuna. Are there people
   at the market? There are not.
**Humo tunduni mlikuwa na nyoka? La, hamkuwa
na kitu.** Was there a snake in the hole? No, there
   was nothing in it.

Hapo kale palikuwa na mtu. Long ago there was a man.

Jana hakukuwa na watu sokoni. Yesterday there were no people at the market.

Jioni kutakuwa na ngoma? La, hakutakuwa na ngoma leo. Will there be a dance this evening? No, there will not be one today.

There is also a form of the verb TO BE which is used with a place subject, especially in the past tense:

kulikuwako or, with a relative particle, **kulikokuwako**
palikuwapo   ,,   ,,   **palipokuwapo**
mlikuwamo   ,,   ,,   **mlimokuwamo**

Huko nilikokwenda kulikuwako watu wengi. Where I went there were a lot of people.

Nalisimama pale palipokuwapo rafiki zangu. I stood there where my friends were.

Katika kikapu mlikuwamo machungwa matatu. In the basket were three oranges.

This is the ordinary past tense of the verb TO BE IN A PLACE (cf. **nilikuwapo,** I was there), but with the subject prefixes of place. **Kulikuwako** is sometimes found with the other place particles, **kulikuwapo, kulikuwamo,** there were there, or, there were in there.

We have met the relative present tense of the verb TO BE, **palipo, kuliko, mlimo,** where there is. There are similar forms of the verb TO HAVE, **panapo, kunako, mnamo** which we have not yet considered. These convey better the sense of a place *having something*:

kunako miti   there where there are trees
panapo majani   here where there is grass
mnamo maji   in there where there is water

The **LI** forms are used to denote place or simple connection:

mahali palipo juu   a place on high
huko kuliko kuzuri there where it is nice

Negative forms are also in use:

Twende huko juu kusiko na maji. Let us go higher where there is no water.

Mahali pasipo na watu. A place without people.

The forms **kunako, panapo** and **mnamo** are often used as prepositions, denoting *at, on, about*, etc.

Panapo saa nane.	At two o'clock
Mnamo saa sita.	At midday.
Kunako Jumatano.	On (about) Wednesday.

Ku is used as the subject prefix when speaking of the weather:

Kumepambazuka.	It has dawned.
Kumeanuka.	The weather has cleared up.
Kumekucha.	The sun has risen.
Kumekuchwa.	The sun has set.

The use of these place prefixes is one of the most difficult things in theoretical Swahili, but it is surprising how soon one gets used to the constructions in practice. Do not worry about what is not clear to you now: it will become so later on. There is one more construction to be referred to before closing the chapter:

Humu ndimo mlimoingia panya. This is where the rat went in.

Why a subject prefix of place, when it is obvious it is the *rat* who went in? Look at the idiomatic sentences given on page 127: **Nchi imeingia nzige; Mji umeingia ndui.** The same transposition has taken place between the *place* and the *rat*. All we can say is that it is Swahili idiom.

For Reading and Translation

(From the Union Swahili version of the Bible)

Mtini

Mtu mmoja alikuwa na mtini umepandwa katika shamba lake la mizabibu; akaenda akitafuta matunda juu yake, asipate. Akamwambia mtunzaji wa shamba la mizabibu, " Tazama, miaka mitatu hii naja nikitafuta matunda juu ya mtini huu, nisipate kitu. Uukate, mbona hata nchi unaiharibu? " Akajibu akamwambia, " Bwana, uuache mwaka huu nao, hata niupalilie, niutilie samadi; nao ukizaa matunda baadaye, vema! la, usipozaa, ndipo uukate."

NOTES:

mtini(mi)	fig tree	**tunza**	to care for
mzabibu(mi)	grape vine	**mtunzaji(wa)**	caretaker
samadi	manure	**palilia**	hoe round about

mwaka huu *nao*	this year and it, i.e. this year also
***nao* ukizaa**	and (it) if it bears . . .

Note that in Swahili the introductory words "He said", "He asked", etc., always precede the quoted words. Their position should not be varied as it often is in English. African writers are now experimenting with a varied position, but it is still unnatural in Swahili.

LESSON 48

AFRICAN MANNERS

IN this last lesson a few notes are given on behaviour, for it is not much use knowing how to speak Swahili well unless we know how to speak to people in the right way.

Greetings

The commonest greeting, which can be used everywhere, is **Jambo?** to which the reply is **Jambo.** Sometimes the full form is used, **Hujambo?** (lit. **Huna jambo?** You have nothing the matter?) or, to more than one person, **Hamjambo?** To which one replies **Sijambo,** or, if with others, **Hatujambo.**

An inferior, greeting a superior, says **Shikamoo,** to which the answer is **Marahaba,** Thank you.

An Arab greeting, sometimes used by Moslem Africans, is **Subulkheri,** Good morning, and **Masalkheri,** Good afternoon. Some people know only the morning greeting and use it at any time of the day.

Christians have their own greetings, but they are not likely to use them to others. Probably the commonest is **Salaam,** Peace. The answer is the same.

If one wishes to continue the conversation, one can ask:

U mzima?	Are you well?	Ans.	**Ni mzima.**
Or, **U hali gani?**	What state are you in?	Ans.	**Njema,** *or* **Sijambo.**
Or, **Habari gani?**	What news?	Ans.	**Njema.**

This last way is the commonest, and can be varied in many ways: **Habari za usiku? Habari za siku nyingi? Habari za nyumbani?,** etc. The answer is always **Njema,** whether the news is good or bad. If all is not well, we say **Njema,** and go on to explain what is wrong: **Njema, lakini. . . .**

On parting, at any hour of the day, one says **Kwa heri** or, to more than one person, **Kwa herini.** The answer is the same, or, perhaps, **Kwa heri ya kuonana,** Good-bye until we meet.

When calling at someone's house, stand outside the door and say **Hodi!** You will be answered, **Karibu,** Come in. As you enter and are given a chair, you should say, **Starehe,** Please don't trouble.

A form of condolence which can be used for any trouble, from tripping over something in the path to bereavement by death, is **Pole!** or **Poleni!** The right answer is **Nimekwisha poa** or just **Asante.** If you read the letters in a vernacular magazine, you will often find one, describing some disaster, ending with **Tupeni pole!** Give us " pole ", i.e. Condole with us.

Please is **Tafadhali,** and Thank you, **Asante.** But it is not an African custom to say Thank you, and both these words are taken from the Arabic. Do not think Africans rude if they do not use them.

Good Manners

It is bad manners to take or give anything with the left hand. When anyone wishes to be very polite he uses both hands, but normally one uses the right. In eating, too, Africans always use the right hand.

An African who has a visitor when he is eating is bound to say **Karibu chakula,** Come and eat. Even a tiny child is taught to share its banana with another. Africans are now used to the European practice of not welcoming all and sundry to a meal, but we should remember that our custom is really rude in their eyes.

A man does not ask after another man's wife unless he knows the family well, or has been told she is ill. The usual query is **Hamjambo nyumbani?** Are you all well at home? Be very careful in referring to anyone's wife to speak of her as **mke** and not **mwanamke;** the latter denotes an irregular connection, and its use would be a great insult.

Apart from lack of generosity, two of the worst sins in African eyes are **matusi,** vile language, and **matukano,** abuse, especially when these take the form of reflections on one's mother. Do not say, even to a child, **Huna adabu,** You have no manners; it is a much stronger reproach than one would think, and, being a reflection on the child's upbringing, it is **matukano.** Avoid also the chirping sound we sometimes make with our tongues to express " Oh dear! " A rather similar sound is used by Africans as an insult.

For Reading and Translation

(From a letter in *Maendeleo*)

MALEZI MABAYA

Mara kwa mara tunawaona watoto wengi ambao hawana heshima na adabu nzuri kwa wakubwa wao, au pengine kwa wageni wanaofika katika mji fulani. Nimeona katika miji, hasa Nairobi, Mombasa na Dar es Salaam, mama wengine wenye watoto ambao hawawapeleki shuleni kusoma. Basi, mama hawa wakimwona mgeni, humwambia mtoto, " Mwombe peni ukanunue mkate." Mtoto huondoka na kumwamkia yule mtu shikamoo kubwa, halafu akamwomba peni la mkate. Peni lile mtoto hunyang'anywa na mama akanunua sigareti ama kitu kingine apendacho yeye. Siku nyingine mtoto atamwomba mtu thumuni akamletee mama. Mama, bila kumwuliza alipata wapi, humwambia mwanawe, " Asante sana. Leo umeleta thumuni, kesho ulete shilingi." Basi, njia hii ni ya kumtia bidii mtoto awe mwombaji. Siku moja, akikosa pesa za kumpelekea mama, atafikiri njia za kuiba au kunyang'anya wenzake. Na hivi, kidogo kidogo, atageuka mwizi na mnyang'anyi. Wazazi lazima wachunge desturi zao wasiwafunze watoto desturi zitakazowaharibia maisha.

Notes:

adabu	manners	**nyang'anya**	to snatch
fulani	so-&-so		from
mwombaji	a beggar	**mnyang'anyi**	a thief
wakubwa	elders	**chunga**	to watch over
		fikiri	to consider

Notice the names of non-existing coins: **peni** (penny) here used for a 10-cent piece; **thumuni** (an eighth of a dollar) here used for a half-shilling; and **pesa** (Indian pice) used for money in general. For East African coinage see below.

APPENDIX

Money

LONG ago a silver coin worth about four shillings was the medium for East African trade. Hence a shilling was called a quarter (**robo**) and a sixpence an eighth (**thumuni**). Since then East Africa has known the German rupee, divided into hellers; the Indian rupee divided into pice; and English shillings divided into cents. Many of the old names still remain in use, as we saw in the letter above. The present coinage all over East Africa is:

a shilling	**shilingi**
a half-shilling	**nusu-shilingi,** or **senti hamsini**
a 10-cent piece	**kikumi,** or **senti kumi**
a 5-cent piece	**kitano,** or **senti tano**
a cent	**senti**

All are words of the **N** class, except **kikumi** and **kitano** which belong to the **KITU** class.

Measures

The weights used in Zanzibar in the old days were **wakia**, the weight of one of the old silver dollars, and **ratli**, equal to sixteen **wakia**. These words are now the translation of the British ounce and pound, to which they approximate. British weights and measures are now in use in East Africa, but in the smaller shops in the Tanganyika villages things are still sold, as in German times, by the **kilo**(gramme).

The native measures of length are **mkono**, about half a yard; **wari**, a yard; and **hatua**, a pace. The Tanganyika railway is still measured in **kilometa**, but otherwise the British measures are in use.

The native measures of capacity are the **kibaba**, about a pint, and the **pishi**, equal to four **vibaba**. In some places these have almost disappeared, and in the native markets beans, etc., are sold by the **kopo**, any convenient jam or cigarette tin. Milk and oil are sold by the **chupa**, bottle, and larger amounts by the **debe**(ma), a paraffin or petrol tin holding four gallons. Pint and gallon are little known.

Other words sometimes heard are:

frasila	about 35 lb.
jora	a roll of material about 32 yards.
korija	twenty. Building poles are often sold by the **korija**.

Direction

North	**Kaskazini**	East	**Mashariki**
South	**Kusini**	West	**Magharibi**
Right	**Upande wa kuume**	Left	**Upande wa kushoto**

The other side (of river, lake, etc.) **Ng'ambo.**

The Seasons

The hot season is called **kiangazi**, the time when the sun shines most strongly, or **kaskazi**, the time of the North monsoon. After this come the heavy rains, called the **masika;** then the cool season consisting of **kipupwe** and **demani**, names not much heard up-country, followed by the lesser rains, **vuli.**

One needs to be careful, if one has anything to do with geography, how one chooses words for the seasons. It is right, for instance, to call the English summer **kiangazi**, when the sun shines strongest; but it is wrong to call it **kaskazi**, when the North monsoon blows!

Further Study

The first book the student should get is the *Standard Swahili–English Dictionary*, not only for reference, but also for interest and study. However often the student works through it, he will always find something new and interesting. There is a companion volume, an English–Swahili dictionary, which is also most useful.

For reading, it is best to begin with short stories. There are many little books of folk tales. Original stories should be chosen, not those translated from other languages. Most translations have been too much influenced by the English constructions to be good Swahili.

Monthly Swahili papers, such as *Maendeleo* and *Mambo Leo* are useful.

The Union translation of the Bible, which is the work of Swahili scholars, European and African, can be relied on to be good Swahili, but it is more difficult for a beginner than folk tales told in simple Swahili.

There are good bookshops in the larger towns of East Africa, where the reader can choose for himself the books which seem most useful.

F

TABLE OF CONCORDS

Noun classes	mtu	watu	mti	miti	njia	njia	kitu	vitu
Adjective Prefix	m	wa	m	mi	n	n	ki	vi
-zuri nice	mzuri	wazuri	mzuri	mizuri	nzuri	nzuri	kizuri	vizuri
-ema good	mwema	wema	mwema	myema	njema	njema	chema	vyema
-ingi much, many	mwingi	wengi	mwingi	mingi	nyingi	nyingi	kingi	vingi
-ngapi? how many?		wangapi		mingapi	ngapi	ngapi		vingapi
Verb Prefix	ni- u- a-	tu- m- wa-	u	i	i	zi	ki	vi
of	wa	wa	wa	ya	ya	za	cha	vya
his, its [1]	wake	wake	wake	yake	yake	zake	chake	vyake
all [2]	wote	wote	wote	yote	yote	zote	chote	vyote
this, these	huyu	hawa	huu	hii	hii	hizi	hiki	hivi
that, those [3]	yule	wale	ule	ile	ile	zile	kile	vile
this spoken of	huyo	hao	huo	hiyo	hiyo	hizo	hicho	hivyo
relative prefix	ye	o	o	yo	yo	zo	cho	vyo
this is it (he)	ndiye	ndio	ndio	ndiyo	ndiyo	ndizo	ndicho	ndivyo
and it (he)	naye	nao	nao	nayo	nayo	nazo	nacho	navyo

[1] Similarly -angu -ako -etu -enu -ao.
[2] Similarly -enye, -enyewe, -o-ote, except in sing. of **WATU** class.
[3] Similarly -pi? which? except with **mahali**.

TABLE OF CONCORDS—Continued.

Noun classes	yai	mayai	uzi	nyuzi		mahali		
	(ji)	ma	m	n		pa	ku [4]	mu
Adjective Prefix								
-zuri nice	zuri	mazuri	mzuri	nzuri		pazuri	kuzuri	
-ema good	jema	mema	mwema	njema		pema	kwema	
-ingi many	jingi	mengi	mwingi	nyingi		pengi	kwingi	
-ngapi? how many?		mangapi		ngapi		pangapi	kungapi	

Noun classes	yai	mayai	uzi	nyuzi		mahali		
	li	ya	u	zi		pa	ku	mu
Verb Prefix								
of	la	ya	wa	za		pa	kwa	mwa
his, its [1]	lake	yake	wake	zake		pake	kwake	mwake
all [2]	lote	yote	wote	zote		pote	kote	mwote
this, these	hili	haya	huu	hizi		hapa	huku	humu
that, those [3]	lile	yale	ule	zile		pale	kule	mle
this spoken of	hilo	hayo	huo	hizo		hapo	huko	humo
relative prefix	lo	yo	o	zo		po	ko	mo
this is it (he)	ndilo	ndiyo	ndio	ndizo		ndipo	ndiko	ndimo
and it (he)	nalo	nayo	nao	nazo		napo	nako	namo

[1] Similarly -angu -ako -etu -enu -ao.
[2] Similarly -enye, -enyewe, -o-ote, except in sing. of **WATU** class.
[3] Similarly -pi? which? except with **mahali**.
[4] Similarly infinitives.

VERB TENSES

Subject Prefixes	Present A, NA	Past LI	Future TA
AFFIRMATIVE 1. ni- tu- 2. u- m- 3. a- wa-	**ataka** he wants **atakaye** he who wants **anataka** he is wanting **anayetaka** he who is wanting **hataki** he does not want **asiyetaka** he who does not want	**alitaka** he wanted **aliyetaka** he who wanted **hakutaka** he did not want **asiyetaka** he who did not want	**atataka** he will want **atakayetaka** he who will want **hatataka** he will not want **asiyetaka** he who will not want
	Present Perfect	KI tense	KA tense
NEGATIVE 1. si- hatu- 2. hu- ham- 3. ha- hawa-	**ametaka** he has wanted **hajataka** he has not yet wanted	**akitaka** if he wants **asipotaka** if he does not want	**akataka** and he wanted
	HU tense	Subjunctive	Conditional (Present)
OBJECT PREFIXES 1. ni tu 2. ku wa 3. m wa	**hutaka**[1] he wants (habitually)	**atake** let him want **asitake** let him not want	**angetaka** he would want **asingetaka** } he would not want **hangetaka** }
	Conditional (Past)	Imperative	Infinitive
NON-PERSONAL CLASSES 2. u i 3. i zi 4. ki vi 5. li ya 6. u zi 7. pa, ku, mu 8. ku	**angalitaka** he would have wanted **asingalitaka** } he would not have **hangalitaka** } wanted	**taka** want **takeni** **usitake** do not want **msitake**	**kutaka** to want **kutokutaka** not to want
	Compound Tenses		
	alikuwa akitaka he was wanting **alikuwa hataki** } **hakuwa akitaka** } he was not wanting	**alikuwa ametaka** he had wanted **alikuwa hakutaka** he had not wanted	

[1] All persons.

DERIVATIVE FORMS OF THE VERB

Simple	Passive WA	Stative IKA, EKA	Prepositional IA, EA	Causative ISHA ESHA IZA EZA YA
fumba, close	fumbwa	fumbika, be closed	fumbia, close for	fumbisha, make to close
	Reduplicative		Reciprocal NA	Tenacious TA*
Conversive, UA, OA	fumbafumba, keep on closing		fumbana, close together	fumbata, clutch
fumbua, unclose				

* This form was not given in the Lessons. There is also an ending MA, denoting set in a position (static), e.g. inama, bend down and an ending PA denoting entering upon a state (inceptive), e.g. nenepa, become fat.

KEY TO EXERCISES

Exercise 1 (p. 9)

A big head; a bad pipe; a deep well; a bad sore; good certificates; two shoes; a bed or a chair; knives and books; three small potatoes; one large piece; two long islands; large and small vessels; a good plot of ground; huts and latrines; a basket and some food; five fingers; one hut and four rooms; a long bed and a big chair; four cups and spoons; one small knife; large pieces of iron. One piece will be enough. Three cooking-pots are enough. Was the food enough? Yes, it was. Will three potatoes be enough? Three large potatoes or five small ones. Will the small cups do? Yes, they will do. A small cloth will do.

Exercise 2 (p. 12)

Mkia mrefu; mwavuli mzuri; mto mdogo; mlima mrefu; mswaki mbaya; mizigo mikubwa; mikate mitano; mihindi mizuri; msalaba mdogo; mshahara mkubwa; mikeka na mifuko; michungwa mitatu na miembe minne; minazi na mitende mirefu; mwaka mmoja na miezi mitano; mchele na mtama. Moto una moshi. Mji una migomba na miwa. Miti ina miiba. Kibanda kina milango miwili. Muhogo una mizizi mikubwa. Mwili una mikono na miguu, kichwa, kifua na moyo.

Exercise 3 (p. 14)

Mungu mmoja; watumishi wabaya; walevi wawili; wajane watatu; mjinga mkubwa; watu watano; wagonjwa na waganga; wafalme na watumwa; wanaume na wanawake; mume na mke; wazee na watoto; wenyeji na wageni; mwalimu na wanafunzi. Mpishi ana mchele na mkate. Mtumishi ana mshahara mkubwa. Wanawake wana mtama na muhogo. Mzee ana wake wawili na watoto watano. Mke mmoja anatosha. Mzungu ana mizigo mikubwa. Mwingereza ana msimamizi na watumishi wanne. Mji una Waislamu na Wakristo. Wevi wana visu vikubwa.

Exercise 4 (p. 17)

Asali nzuri; nazi ndogo; saa kubwa; taa mbaya; nguo nzuri; njaa kubwa; meza ndefu; ngoma moja; tende tano; nchi mbili; saa tatu; siku nne; habari nzuri; hatari ndogo; furaha na huzuni; faida na hasara; nyama, samaki, mkate na viazi; mkate na siagi; chai au kahawa; sukari au chumvi; taa kubwa mbili; mbwa wakubwa wawili.

Will the money be sufficient? Yes, it will. Will two coconuts be enough ? Two large coconuts or three small ones. Has the cook any tea ? Yes, he has tea and coffee. A table has four legs. A clock has two hands. The coconut palm has four coconuts. The old man has white hair. The house is cold. The teacher has leave, a month and three days.

Exercise 5 (p. 20)

Machungwa na maembe; maswali na majibu; mananasi matatu; matunda mazuri; magoti mawili; kanisa dogo; makosa mabaya; jambo kubwa; majani marefu; mawe makubwa; masanduku makubwa manne; shimo refu; shoka na majembe mawili; masikio mawili na macho mawili; chakula cha mgeni; vikapu vya mpishi; mwavuli wa bwana; mtumishi wa bibi; mizizi ya miti; wana wa seremala; siku ya huzuni; saa za kazi; soko la machungwa; maduka ya Wahindi; meno ya watoto; majibu ya maswali; mawazo, maneno na matendo; kalamu ya karani.

Exercise 6 (p. 23)

Upishi mzuri; uzi mrefu; ubao mkubwa; wembe mdogo; ugonjwa mbaya; upepo mkubwa; nyavu ndefu; nyua kubwa; udongo mbaya; nyufa ndogo; nyimbo nzuri; kuta nne; mbavu tatu; uso wa mtoto; kuta za nyumba ya mpishi; nyuzi za nyavu. Uji una moto. Nyuso za wanawake zina huzuni. Ulevi una hatari. Unga ulitosha ?

Exercise 7 (p. 26)

The men sat in one place and the women in one place (another). The cook put the milk in a bad place. People are going into church. The children wanted to go to the European's house. There are some animals in the field. Is there water in the well ? There are two children at the door. The women are coming from the market. In the bag there is a piece of meat and two loaves, the guest's food. There is a large snake in the road. Reading and writing are the children's work in school.

Exercise 8 (p. 30)

Mbwa wangu; mbwa zetu; kuku zako; watoto wake; mume wake; kosa letu; mbuzi zetu; nyuso zenu; visu vyako; viatu vyao; mama na watoto wake; Wazungu na watumishi wao; mgomba na ndizi zake; wasimamizi na mbwa zao; farasi zao wazuri; ngamia zetu wabaya; paka wakubwa watatu; samaki wadogo watano; tembo mkubwa mmoja; rafiki zangu wawili; raia wazuri wa mfalme; pepo wabaya na malaika wazuri. Sungura ana miguu minne. Kuna fisi shambani. Mtoni mna mamba. Nzige ni wadudu wabaya. Twiga ni mnyama mrefu. Mbuzi zangu ni wadogo. Mbuzi wa (za) ndugu yangu ni wakubwa.

Exercise 9 (p. 32)

Jumba la mfalme; majoka mawili; kapu la maembe; vipofu wawili; vijito vya maji; majito; majitu mawili. Kipofu anaingia nyumbani. Viwete watatu wanataka kazi. Katika kikapu mna mwiko na vijiko viwili.

Exercise 10 (p. 34)

Viazi vyeupe; chuma cheusi; visiwa vingi; chakula cho chote; mizigo mingine; moto mwingi; mizizi mikubwa; mkate mweupe; watoto wema; watu weusi; ng'ombe mweupe; simba wengi; njaa nyingi; njia ndefu; siku nyingi; chumvi nyeupe; sanduku jembamba; upepo mwingi; neno jema; majani mengi; majani mengi; usingizi mwema; ndevu nyekundu; mahali pengi; mahali pote; mahali po pote; wevi werevu; mkono wote; kikombe cha chai; viatu vyangu vyeupe; mizizi ya miti yote; mwavuli wako mweusi; watoto wenye vitabu; wenyeji wa Unguja; urefu wa ubao wenyewe; maswali ya mwalimu na majibu ya watoto.

Exercise 11 (p. 38)

He is writing. They have arrived. I shall come. They saw. Will you read? He has finished. Are you going back? We know. We have spoken. He will be able to. I want. You will get. They are going in. We have gone. He has come out. We have finished. He will get work. Do you want to see? I am writing a letter. They read the book. They came to the house. Will you get to Zanzibar? We shall go home. I have begun work. Have you heard the news? Do you know the way? We can go and return. He has bought all the eggs. I (am) sell(ing) two fowls. They are working. He has put the money on the table. His work will be good.

Exercise 12 (p. 40)

I shall tell him. We shall ask them (you). He begged us. Have you seen him? Are you asking me? They are asking you. I ask myself. I tell you. Did you get him? We hear you. I answer you. He told him. I have looked at him. I love you. The rain has destroyed his house. The thieves broke the door of the house. All children like fruit. I will put the things into the house. Have the children got the loaves; have you given them out? I am looking for my knife; have you seen it? I am trying to do the sums, I have finished doing three.

Exercise 13 (p. 42)

Kisima hiki; miezi hii; siku ile; mawe yale; ulimwengu huu; mahali pale; vidonda vile; wajinga wale; taa hizi; udongo huu; nyimbo zile; mwaka huu; jicho hili; ugonjwa ule; mahali hapa; humu nyumbani; mle nyumbani; kule shambani.

Chakula hicho; mizigo hiyo; Waingereza hao; huzuni hiyo; makosa hayo; mahali hapo; vitambaa hivyo; milima hiyo; Mzungu huyo; furaha hizo; soko nilo.

Exercise 14 (p. 45)

I do not know. You did not say. He will not come. We are not afraid. Will you not come? They are not selling (do not sell).

Aren't you coming in?   You have not got used (to it) yet.   I shall not go.   He has not come yet.   We have not written yet.   I have not yet asked him.   They have not seen him yet.   You will not get the hoe.   Are not you afraid of me?   We did not like him. He did not tell me.   I did not hinder him.   I have not seen your dog yet.   He does not like our visitor.   We shall not get leave. Haven't you heard the plans yet?   The meat is not done yet.   They did not give any money.   Quarrelling is not good.   His sickness does not get better.   I shall not fail to tell you.   The maize is not yet ripe.   I was not used to seeing drunken people.   That thief is bad, he does not fear God.   These Europeans do not know Swahili. My sore is not healed yet.   The bananas did not go bad; they have ripened nicely.   The children did not talk, they were afraid of the teacher.   His plan will not do.   My wife has not got used to this country.   The food was not very good; it was not cooked enough.

Exercise 15 (p. 50)

Angalia!   Ondokeni!   Ngoja (Ngojeni)!   Asingoje.   Niondoke? Acha kusema.   Nilete chakula?   Nipe kalamu.   Viondoe vikombe. Usiibe.   Wasiimbe hapa.   Usingoje.   Tuangalie.   Usiondoke.   Njoo (hapa).

Leave this place and go to the town.   Wait, don't go just yet. Bring your dog that we may see him.   Let us sing our songs so that the visitors may hear them.   The cook is asking, shall he cook the food?   Tell him to begin to cook the meat, but not to cook the potatoes yet.   Take care of the sick man that he does not get out of bed.   Do you want me to stay at home, or shall I go to work?   The teacher forbade the children to sing or to talk.   Tell the children to take their books and go away, so that the visitors may come in and eat their meal.

Exercise 16 (p. 52)

I saw the village elder building his house, and asked him, " Well, father, have you had a good harvest this year? "   He said, " Sir, we got nothing."   I asked, " Didn't you hoe? "   He said, " As for hoeing, we hoed, and sowed the seed, and it grew.   We hoed the weeds, and guarded (the field) every day so that baboons and pigs should not spoil our maize.   The maize bore, and ripened, and we were just about to reap.   Lo! elephants came at night and broke down the fence round the field, and got in and destroyed the whole field.   We have suffered a heavy loss."   I said to him, " I am very sorry, father, have you no other field? "   He said, " I have a large field of cassava, I shall not lack food.   This morning I went to root up some cassava and pick some oranges, wait, let me give you some oranges."   And he said to his wife, " Bring some oranges here ", and she brought some, and he said to me, " Take some, sir.   Choose the big ones, they are nicely ripe."   So I took five very large oranges and put them in my bag, and said to him, " Father, thank you very much, they will be very useful to me on the way."

Exercise 17 (p. 55)

If you would give money you would get food. If they did not give money they would not get food. If we had given money we should have got food. If we had not given money we should not have got food. If he would plant cassava he would not fear famine. If he had not planted cassava he would have gone hungry (seen hunger). If you would gather your oranges you would be able to sell them in the market. If we had cultivated (a field) this year we should have got a harvest. If the soldiers had not got water they would have returned. If this country got rain many people would build here. If the children had taken care over their work they would not have made (so) many mistakes. If we get meat we shall not buy fish.

Exercise 18 (p. 58)

Quarrelling brings trouble. These days lions roar a great deal. Joy follows grief. It is not good to beat children much. You had better go away now and go home. It is impossible to work today. You should go to school every day. It is not advisable to follow this path, there is water in the way. Never mind, I shall be able to pass. We had better go back quickly. These lamps use a lot of oil. There are no mosquitoes in Nairobi. There are no lions here. There are people here, looking for eggs. Is there water in the well ? No, there is none. If there are only three people, work will be impossible today.

Exercise 19 (p. 62)

Kidonda kisichopona; vyeti vilivyopotea; mkate usiofaa; mitende inayozaa; shida itakayotupata; ndizi zisizoiva; shauri nililosikia; maneno watakayoyasema; wali tunaokula; nyimbo walizo(zi)imba; mahali pasipofaa; mbwa wanayempiga; mama aliyenizaa; mambo tuliyoyazoea; wakati ufaao; siku zijazo; simba waliao usiku; umeme ulioipiga nyumba yangu; mvua inayoiharibu mihindi; upepo uliouvunja mnazi ule; maneno yaliyo-tutia huzuni; wageni walioitazama kazi yetu; kazi yetu waliyoi-tazama; chakula atakachokipika mpishi; uvivu uletao njaa; ugomvi ufuatao ulevi; nyimbo walizoziimba vizuri; mvua isiyo-pungua; wazee tuliowaaga.

Exercise 20 (p. 64)

Nani aliyekupa mayai haya ? Mti huu usipozaa nitaukata. Sijui anapokaa. Hajui atokako wala anakokwenda. Alikuja jana kama alivyosema. Wageni watakapokuja watataka chakula. Ndizi zilipooza, mpishi alizitupa. Fanya kama mwalimu wako alivyokuambia. Tutafanya vizuri tuwezavyo. Sijui mashauri yalivyokwenda. Habari za hapa ni kama ulivyosikia. Nani aliyeijenga nyumba hii ? Tulipowaona wakicheza tulicheka sana. Nitakufuata ko kote (kila mahali) uendako. (U)nisaidie sasa, kama nilivyokusaidia jana. Usisahau kuwapa habari huko unakokwenda. Atakapoamka nitakwenda kumwamkia.

Exercise 21 (p. 68)

Mtoto amezaliwa. Watu wengi waliuawa na simba. Shauri hili halijakubaliwa na wenyeji. Barua yangu imejibiwa vibaya. Ngoma itasikiwa usiku. Jambo hili liliangaliwa sana. Mafuta ya nazi hutumiwa na wapishi. Watoto hawatasamehewa. Tulipewa mbuzi na wazee wa mji. Kama maziwa yangetiwa katika chupa yangeweza kuchukuliwa na mtoto. Mihindi isipoharibiwa na nyani itazaa vizuri. Mihogo imeng'olewa na nguruwe. Njia hii haipitiki. Maneno yake hayasahauliwi. Kazi hii haikufanyika vizuri.

Exercise 22 (p. 72)

He was a good man who made (had) no trouble. The house was not big and the doors were small. The discussions will not be long ones. Don't be a person of many words. If you have no money you should do some work. We sold two cows which were very big. The faults (mistakes) will be many. I have become an old man now. The harvest was not good this year. When the locusts are big they will destroy our maize. If the rain is heavy I shall not be able to leave. I did not buy the fruit which was not good. If he had been my friend he would not have left me in danger.

Exercise 23 (p. 76)

Are you a stranger here? Yes, I am a stranger; my home is at Nairobi. What is your name? My name is Abdala. What tribe are you? I am a Kikuyu. Where are you living now? I live here in the town, it is here that I am working. What is this? It is oil. Whose? My wife's. What kind of oil is it? It is coconut oil which is very good; we do not buy that which is not good. We who are children do not know about this. Those who are ill will not be able to come. This is our church. This is my father, and these are my brothers. The shortest way is this. His words are these, this is what he said to me. It is here that the snake went in.

Exercise 24 (p. 79)

Mbao ziko wapi? Zipo hapa mlangoni. Baba yako yuko wapi? Yumo nyumbani. Maziwa yako wapi? Yamo katika chupa. Vikombe vipo hapa, lakini sahani hazipo. Utakuwapo hapa kesho? Watu waliopo mlangoni wanataka nini? Wasiokuwapo leo watapata fedha yao kesho. Baba anauliza, nani waliomo nyumbani? Vijana waliokuwako mjini wameondoka. Nilipokuwako Uingereza nalimwona mfalme. Nyani wameliharibu shamba letu kabisa; iliyopo sasa ni kupanda tena. Mimi simo; sina nafasi.

Exercise 25 (p. 82)

Hatuna fedha. Hana akili. Kisima hakina maji. Una mayai? Sina. Wana kalamu? Wanazo. Mna taa? Hatuna. Hakuna jibu. Hamna kitu ndani. Hapana nafasi. Masanduku yaliyokuwa na nguo. Vitu vyote alivyo navyo. Mbegu zote nilizokuwa nazo. Kila kuku aliyekuwa naye. Yule aliyekuwa na ndizi. Watu watakaokuwa na majembe. Kalamu nilizokuwa nazo. Vitabu ulivyo navyo. Nchi isiyo(kuwa) na mvua. Mahali pasipo maji.

In olden days there was a man who had some very fine cattle, and there was no one else who had such fine cattle as he. The seeds which he planted that year have now become big trees giving fruits useful to men. Whatever he has is his own. That which I have I give you.

Exercise 26 (p. 87)

Kisu kikali; vipande vingi; mizigo myepesi; mikia mifupi; vipofu wachache; wevi werevu; mke mvivu; nchi pana; kazi mpya; kuku mwekundu; kalamu ndefu; jino jeupe; maziwa safi; maneno mengi; miti myembamba; wino mweusi; ndimi nyekundu; maneno matupu; nyama mbichi; matunda mabovu; maji tele; askari hodari; maswali magumu. Chakula ni rahisi siku hizi, lakini nguo ni ghali. Miti hii ni hafifu sana; leteni miti imara, mirefu na unene (mirefu, tena minene). London ni mji mkuu wa Uingereza; ni mji ulio mkubwa katika ulimwengu.

Exercise 27 (p. 90)

How many days leave has he? His leave is twenty-eight days. In our town there are fourteen shops. I have eleven cows and thirty-three goats. The European has six clerks and twelve overseers. Ten fingers and ten toes are twenty. This town has two hundred and fifty natives, fifty-five Indians, sixteen Arabs, and eight Europeans. The first day he brought fifteen eggs; the second, sixteen; and the third, ten; tomorrow will be the last day. How many children read here? Ninety-five. How many bananas and how many oranges have you sold? Forty bananas and twenty-seven oranges.

Exercise 28 (p. 92)

Alifika jana jioni saa kumi na moja u nusu. Atakwenda leo yapata saa nane. Saa ngapi sasa? Saa nne kasa dakika kumi. Asubuhi tunapoamka kuna baridi sana, lakini adhuhuri jua ni kali sana. Jumapili ni siku ya kwanza ya juma. Mwaka una miezi kumi na miwili, majuma hamsini na mawili, na siku mia tatu sitini na tano. Hapa pana soko kila Jumanne; watu huleta mahindi, mpunga, unga, matunda, samaki, na vitu vingine vingi. Hutoka kwao alfajiri, na kufika asubuhi sana.

Exercise 29 (p. 95)

Karani anaandika upesi sana. Alianza kazi hii juzi. Mwambie tena. Usiende upesi mno. Kisu hiki hakifai hata kidogo. Nimemwambia mara kwa mara, lakini nimesema bure; sitasema tena. Mweke kuku huyu ndani peke yake. Maziwa uliyoleta ni kidogo sana; lete zaidi. Vitu hivi ni mbalimbali kabisa; si sawasawa hata kidogo. Watoto waliondoka mapema; sasa wako njiani; watafika sasa hivi.

Exercise 30 (p. 98)

Children, come here! stand straight. I want to tell you about tomorrow. I say this : Tomorrow we shall go to the town with our band. But the other day when we went, I saw some children walking just anyhow and looking about them. To march like this is very bad. Do not look anywhere, look straight ahead; march just like soldiers do.

You, Ali, what are you doing? I am telling you our plans, and you meanwhile are talking. Come and stand here; remain just here until I have finished speaking.

Now children, you know the butcher's shop, don't you? We shall go to that shop and stand there while we sing two songs. When these songs are finished, we shall go to the market and sing other songs in the same way. Then we shall come back here to school.

Exercise 31 (p. 101)

The teacher's field is very fine. In the middle of it he has planted orange trees. How many? I don't know, but more than ten. Right inside the field? Right inside, between his hut and his mango trees, near the bananas. It is a whole month since he planted them, and all are fine and big. His little children are fond of playing under the trees. If it rains they go into the hut. Their field is not far from their house, the small children are able to go there by themselves.

Exercise 32 (p. 105)

" Ali, nenda Bwagamoyo kwa mjomba wako, umwombe anipe mundu wake. Hamisi atakwenda pamoja nawe. Nitangoja hapa penye minazi; nataka kuyakata majani chini ya miti." Watoto wakaenda kwa mjomba wao, wakamwamkia kwa heshima, waka-sema, " Tumeambiwa na baba tufike kwako; anaomba umpe mundu wako. Anataka kuyakata majani karibu na minazi yetu. Asema kisu chake hakifai kwa kuyakata. Kama ukikubali kutupa mundu wako, tutarudi nao sasa. Baba anatungoja penye minazi. Asante, mjomba, tunakwenda sasa. Kwa heri." " Kwa herini, wanangu."

Exercise 33 (p. 109)

Tuwekee chakula. Mke wake amemzalia mwana. Nataka uniuzie unga. Usimkose ndugu yako. Unitafutie maji. Chakula hiki kitatutosha. Mrudie mama yako; umpe fedha hii atununulie chakula. Simba alimrukia mtoto. Uniombee kwa Mungu. Usiwacheke wazee. Kesho nitahamia Mombasa. Ume-kosea hapa. Nani atanichukulia kikapu changu? Watu wengi wamenijia. Amefiwa na mtoto wake.

Exercise 34 (p. 112)

Sindano ya kushonea; sabuni ya kufulia nguo; mahali pa kuvio-shea vikombe; maji ya moto ya kuogea; maji ya baridi ya kunawia mikono; dawa ya kusafishia viatu; udongo wa kufinyangia vyungu. Nataka unisukie mkeka. Wanawake wanasukiwa nywele. Asema atanifumia nguo. Ninashonewa nguo. Nikatie majani ya kufagilia. Unisalimie mwalimu na watoto wake.

Exercise 35 (p. 115)

Alikuja asubuhi lakini hakukaa sana. Hapakuwa na mtu ila sisi tu. Neno hili si kweli, bali ni uongo kabisa. Alisema kwamba atakwenda. Atakapokuja, mwombe aje hapa. Analia kwa sababu mama yake ni mgonjwa. Ingawa chakula hakikutosha, lakini kilipikwa vizuri. Watu hawa hawana ng'ombe wala mbuzi. Sina fedha hapa, kwa hiyo siwezi kununua. Nakupa fedha hii upate kunitafutia kuku.

Exercise 36 (p. 117)

Karani na mke wake hawapatani. Hugombana sikuzote. Mwezi uliopita walipigana. Mume akamfukuza mke wake, akamrudia baba yake. Baadaye wakarudiana. Lakini hawapendani. Labda wataachana. Yawapasa mtu na mke wake kusameheana na kusaidiana, kwa sababu wameungana katika ndoa.

Exercise 37 (p. 120)

Whether you come or not it's all the same to me; do as you like yourself. It was not only children who came to the games, but their parents as well. I had not time to say anything before he went off. He has only one wife. The people who are present are about forty; I don't know if others will come. Perhaps they will come, since they know there are games. Over there in the village there are discussions going on, that is why some people have not come; it is not that they do not want to. He spoke as if he had lost his senses.

Exercise 38 (p. 123)

Causative Forms : salisha; kopesha; poza; sogeza; tembeza; eneza; eleza; tuliza; chukiza; chosha; nyosha; shusha; vusha; kausha; washa; zungusha; kumbusha; lainisha.

Chemsha maji. Maji yanachemka. Dawa imemponya. Nionyeshe njia. Kazi yako hainipendezi. Nyosha mistari sawasawa. Mlaze mtoto kitandani. Ijaze ndoo. Mrudishie yule mtu fedha yake. Amekwisha kurudishiwa. Wasimamishe watoto. Yahamishe masanduku haya katika chumba kingine. Jua limekausha maji. Mafundisho haya hayanielei. Nitakueleza. Nionyeshe kitabu chako. Unapofundisha, usiwachoshe watoto. Washa moto. Unawaka sasa. Nikumbushe kesho. Nivushe. Habari hii imeenea kila mahali; watoto wameieneza. Nyosha mkono wako.

Exercise 39 (p. 128)

Sikilizeni, watoto! Nguo zimekauka? Vua viatu vyako unapoingia nyumbani. Tundu hili limezibika; ninajaribu kulizibua. Amevaa nguo gani? Kitabu kilichopotea kimeonekana? Bado,

watoto wangali wanakitafuta. Kazi hii imeendelea vema. Bwana
yumo? Yumo, lakini amelala. Usimwamshe. Atakapoamka,
mpe barua hii. Piga mistari mitatu iliyonyoka. Wakiweza, (na)
waje hapa; la! hawawezi, nitakwenda kwao kesho. Vitabu viwili
na kalamu sita vimepotea. Licha ya vitabu na kalamu, hata kiti
pia. Mwite mpishi. Amekwenda kuitwa.

Exercise 40 (p. 130)

When father was going to the village, he saw a stranger standing
in the way. When they had greeted each other and asked each
other the news, father said, " How is it, sir, that you are here by
yourself? Have you lost the way? " The stranger said, " I have
a matter (to discuss) with my brother who lives at Tongwe. But
when I got there I found he was not at home. He had already left
to go to Muheza. There was nothing I could do but follow him.
His children showed me the way; and said that when I came to
the coconut palms I should ask again. So I was waiting here to see
someone to ask." Father said to him, " I too am going to the same
place; we will go together."

Exercise 41 (p. 134)

Kuna (mna) nyumba ngapi katika mji wenu? Si nyingi, tena
nyumba zenyewe hazifai. Zote ni tayari kuanguka. Sisi wenyewe
tumezizoea, kwa sababu tu wenyeji. Tumekaa papa hapa tangu
utoto wetu, sisi na wake zetu pia. Hii ndiyo nyumba ya Jumbe,
na hizi ndizo nyumba za wakeze. Hii ndiyo nyumba ya nduguye,
na hizi mbili za wanawe. Nyumba yako ni ipi? Ni hii, nayo pia
ni mbaya. Nataka kujenga nyingine, lakini nimejikata mguu,
siwezi kwenda mbali, na hapa karibu hapana miti yo yote ya
kujengea.

Exercise 42 (p. 137)

Nipe ufunguo wa kufungulia mlango. Nitafutie kizibo cha
kuzibia chupa. Walinzi mbele ya mlango walililinda jumba la
mfalme. Wasafiri walikutana na hatari nyingi katika safari yao
ndefu. Toka hapa mpaka mjini ni mwendo wakama nusu saa. Mwalimu aliwasifu wazazi wa mtoto kwa sababu ya mwenendo mwema
wa mwana wao. Mlevi ni mgomvi. Yatupasa kusali kwa toba na
imani. Naliomba msaada kwake, lakini alikataa kunisaidia. Usiwe
mpenda fedha. Walifurahi furaha kubwa mno.

Let Swahili Be Done Away With

1. Many words which are used in the Swahili language have come
from the languages of the Arabs, the Europeans and the Indians.
Swahili really belongs to (was got from) the coastal regions, and is
a trade language. There are no people whose tribe or nation is
Swahili. It would be well to get rid of this language now before
our own languages are destroyed.

2. What is the evil of Swahili? Shall it be done away with be-

cause it is a mixture of Arabic, European, Indian and Bantu words ? This is no reason at all. Even English is a mixture of Latin and other European languages. Swahili brings us many advantages. It helps Africans who do not know English to understand and be understood by Europeans (lit. to make each other hear). It helps Africans of different tribes to understand one another. It helps the Africans who know it to read papers and government notices. The books which have been printed in Swahili are very many and very important (having much meaning) in our progress. Swahili will go forward and be increasingly prospered until it is (even) better than it is now.

The Choosing of Representatives

Each man who wants to be chosen will be wearing a belt of a different colour. Similarly, there will be cards (hard paper) of different colours corresponding with the colours of the belts worn by those who are to be elected. So each voter will take a card of the colour which matches the belt of the representative he wishes to elect. When he has taken this card he will put it in a box which will be put ready. When all have finished putting in their cards, the box will be opened and the cards in it will be counted. Then the candidate who has got most cards will win.

In this way the election will be secret, and will not bring bad feeling between a candidate and an elector.

The Editing and Printing of a Paper

Your magazine *Mambo Leo* (Things of Today) has now completed twenty-seven years. Many readers from time to time ask about its stages (goings) until it appears; who writes the things which you read in its pages; who takes the photographs; and who has the choosing of what shall go into the paper, and the keeping back of what is not wanted.

Perhaps you do not know, but the work of publishing papers is very difficult and troublesome. You must have people who are able to write good Swahili, and to be trusted fully to send news of things which happen in their part of Tanganyika. The news which they send is no use unless we have machinery and ink and paper and electricity, and well-trained men, for editing and printing the papers and distributing them through the country.

The Fig-Tree

A man had a fig-tree planted in his vineyard; and went looking for fruit on it and found none. And he said to the keeper of the vineyard, " Look, these three years I come looking for fruit on this fig-tree without getting any. Cut it down, why is it destroying even the ground ? " And he answered and said to him, " Sir, leave it this year also, until I hoe round it and put manure round it, and if after that it bears fruit, good. But if it does not, then cut it down."

Bad Upbringing

From time to time we see many children who have no respect or good manners towards their elders, or sometimes towards strangers who come to a certain town. I have seen in towns, especially Nairobi, Mombasa and Dar es Salaam, some mothers with children whom they do not send to school to read. Well, these mothers, if they see a stranger, say to the child, " Ask him for a penny to buy bread." The child goes out and greets the man with a big shikamoo, and then begs for a penny for bread. That penny is taken from the child by her* mother, and she buys cigarettes or something else she wants herself. Another day the child will ask someone for sixpence and bring it to her mother. The mother, without asking where she got it, says to the child, " Thank you very much. Today you have brought sixpence, tomorrow bring a shilling." Now this is the way to encourage a child to be a beggar. One day, if she lacks coins to take to her mother, she will consider how to steal them or snatch them from her companions. And thus, little by little, she will become a thief and a robber. Parents must watch over their customs lest they teach their children customs which will ruin their lives for them.

---

* Or *his*.

SWAHILI–ENGLISH VOCABULARY

A

-a, of
-a kwanza, first
-a mwisho, last
abudu, to worship
acha, to leave
achilia, to forgive
adabu, manners
adhuhuri, midday
adui, enemy
afya, health
aga, to take leave of
-ake, his, her, its
-ako, your
akili, commonsense
alasiri, afternoon
alfajiri, before dawn
Alhamisi, Thursday
ama, or
ama . . . ama, either . . . or
amba-, who, which
ambia, to say to
amini, to believe
amka, to wake
amkia, to greet
amsha, to wake someone
andika, to write
angalia, to observe, take care
-angu, my
anguka, to fall down
angusha, to throw down
anuka, to clear (sky)
anza, to begin
-ao, their
arobaini, forty
asali, honey
asante, thank you
askari, soldier
askofu(ma), bishop
asubuhi, morning
au, or
au . . . au, either . . . or

B

baada ya, after
baadaye, afterwards
baba, father
badala ya, instead of
bado, still, yet
bado kidogo, presently
baina ya, between
bali, but
bandika, to stick on
bandua, to strip off
barabara, highroad
baraka, blessing
baridi, cold
bariki, to bless
barua, letter
basi, so
bata, duck
-baya, bad
biashara, commerce
bibi, lady, mistress
-bichi, unripe, raw
bidi, to behove
bidii, effort
  jibidiisha, to make an effort
bila, without
bilauri, glass, tumbler
-bivu, ripe
bomoa, to break down
bora, excellent
-bovu, rotten
buibui, spider
bure, in vain
bustani, garden
bwana(ma), master

C

cha, to dawn
cha, to reverence
-chache, few

170

chafuka, to get into a mess
chagua, to choose
chai, tea
chakula(vy), food
changanya, to mix
chapa, print
cheka, to laugh
   chekesha, to amuse
   chekelea, to smile
chelewa, to delay
chemka, to bubble up
chemsha, to boil something
cheo(vy), rank, measure
cheti(vy), certificate, note
cheza, to play, dance
chini, below
chinja, to slaughter
choka, to get tired
   chosha, to make tired
chombo(vy), vessel
choo(vy), latrine, excrement
chui, leopard
chuki, ill-feeling
chukia, to hate
chukiza, to offend
chukua, to carry
chuma, to pick
chuma(vy), iron
chumba(vy), room
chumvi, salt
chunga, to watch over
chungu(vy), cooking-pot
-chungu, bitter
chungwa(ma), orange
chupa, bottle
chura(vy), frog
chwa, to set (sun)

D

dafu(ma), young coconut
dakika, a minute
damu, blood
dawa, medicine
debe(ma), oil tin
demani, cool season
desturi, custom
dharau, to despise
dhuru, to harm
   haidhuru, it doesn't matter
-dogo, small
duka(ma), shop

E

edashara, eleven
-ekundu, red
elea, to be clear to
eleza, to explain (to)
elfu, thousand
elimika, to be educated
elimu, knowledge
-ema, good
-embamba, narrow
embe(ma), mango
enda, to go
   enenda, go.
endelea, to continue
endesha, to drive
enea, to be spread over
eneza, to spread over
-enu, your
-enye, having
-enyewe, self
-epesi, light, quick
-erevu, cunning
-etu, our
-eupe, white
-eusi, black

F

fa, to die
   fiwa, to be bereaved
faa, to be useful
fagia, to sweep
faida, profit
fanya, to do, make
farasi, horse
fedha, money, silver
ficha, to hide (from)
fika, to arrive
fikiri, to consider
finyanga, to make pots
fisi, hyena
frasila, c. 35 lbs.
fua, to wash clothes
fuata, to follow
fuatisha, to copy
fukuza, to drive away
fulani, so & so
fuma, to weave
fumua, to unravel
fumba, to close
fumbua, to open
fundi, craftsman

fundisha, to teach
fundisho(ma), lesson
funga, to fasten, shut
fungua, to unfasten, open
funika, to cover
funua, to uncover
funza, to teach
  jifunza, to learn
-fupi, short
fupisha, to shorten
furahi, to rejoice
furaha, joy
futa, to wipe
futi, foot (measure)

G

ganda(ma), skin, shell
gani?, what kind?
gari(ma), wheeled vehicle
gawa
gawanya } to divide
gazeti(ma), newspaper
geuka, to turn round
ghafula, suddenly
ghali, expensive
giza, darkness
gogota, to tap
gomba, to contradict
gombana, to quarrel
goti(ma), knee
-gumu, hard
gunia(ma), sack
gusa, to touch

H

haba, scarce
habari, news
hadithi, story
hafifu, weak
haki, righteousness
hakika, certainty
halafu, afterwards
hali, state
halisi, exactly
hama, to move from
hamia, to move to
hamsini, fifty
hao, these
hapa, hapo, here
hapana, no

haraka, haste
haribu, to destroy
hasa, especially
hasara, loss
hasha!, certainly not!
hata, until
hata kidogo, not at all
hatari, danger
hatimaye, at last
hatua, stride
hawa, these
haya, hayo, these
heri, good fortune
  kwa heri, good-bye
hesabu, to count
hesabu, number, sums
heshima, respect
hicho, this
hii, this
hiki, this
hili, hilo, this
hivi, hivyo, these
hiyo, this
hizi, hizo, these
hodari, brave
hodi!, May I come in?
hofu, fear
huenda, perhaps
huko, huku, here
humo, humu, in here
huruma, mercy
huu, huo, this
huyo, huyu, this
huzuni, grief

I

iba, to steal
ibada, worship
ijapo, even if
Ijumaa, Friday
ikiwa, if it be
ila, except
ile, that
ili, in order that
imani, faith
imara, firm
imarisha, to strengthen
imba, to sing
inama, to bend down
ingawa, although
ingia, to enter

-ingi, much, many
-ingine, other
inua, to lift up
inzi, fly
isha, to finish
ishirini, twenty
ita, to call
itika, to answer
iva, to ripen, cook through
iwapo, if, supposing

J

ja, to come
jaa, to get full
jambo(mambo), affair, thing
Jambo !, How do you do ?
jana, yesterday
jani(ma), leaf
jaribu, to try
je !, well ! how ?
jembe(ma), hoe
jenga, to build
jibu, to answer
jibu(ma), answer
jicho(macho), eye
jiko(meko), fireplace
jina(ma), name
jino(meno), tooth
jinsi, manner, kind
jioni, evening
jitu(ma), giant
jiwe(mawe), stone
jogoo(ma), cock
joka(ma), serpent
jora, bale of material
jua, to know
    julikana, to get known
jua(ma), sun
juma(ma), week
jumba(ma), palace
jumbe(ma), Chief
juu, above, on
juzi, day before yesterday
juzijuzi, the other day

K

kaa, to sit, stay
kabila(ma), tribe
kabisa, entirely
kabla ya, before

kahawa, coffee
kalamu, pen, pencil
kale, olden time
-kali, sharp, fierce
kama, if, like, that
kama kwamba, as if
kama, to squeeze
    kamua, to squeeze out
kamili, complete
kamwe, not at all
kana, to deny
    kanya, to rebuke
kanisa(ma), church
kapu(ma), large basket
karani(ma), clerk
karatasi, paper
karibu, near
Karibu !, Come in !
kasa, less by
kasa robo, three-quarters
kaskazi, hot season
kaskazini, the north
kata, to cut
kataa, to refuse
kataza, to forbid
kati ya, between
katika, in, out of
katikati, in the middle
kauka, to get dry
-kavu, dry
kazi, work
kelele, noise
kenda, nine
kesho, tomorrow
kesho kutwa, day after tomor-
    row
kiangazi, hot season
Kiarabu, Arabic
kiatu(vi), shoe
kiazi(vi), potato
kibaba(vi), c. 1 pt.
kibanda(vi), hut
kiboko(vi), hippopotamus
kichwa(vi), head
kidogo, a little
kidole(vi), finger, toe
kidonda(vi), a sore
kifaru(vi), rhinoceros
kifua(vi), chest
kifuniko(vi), lid
Kihindi, Indian language
Kiingereza, English

kijana(vi), young man
kijiji(vi), small village
kijiko(vi), spoon
kijito(vi), brook
kikapu(vi), basket
kiko(vi), tobacco pipe
kikombe(vi), cup
kikumi(vi), 10 ct. piece
kila, every
kile, that
kilema(vi), deformed person
kilima(vi), hill
kimbia, to run away
kimbilia, to run to
kimbiza, to drive away
kioo(vi), glass
kipande(vi), piece
kipofu(vi), blind person
kipupwe, cool season
kisha, then
kisima(vi), well
kisiwa(vi), island
kisu(vi), knife
Kiswahili, Swahili language
kitabu(vi), book
kitambaa(vi), cloth
kitanda(vi), bed
kitano(vi), 5 ct. piece
kiti(vi), chair
kitu(vi), thing
kiumbe(vi), creature
kiwanja(vi), plot of ground
kiwete(vi), lame person
kizibo(vi), cork
kiziwi(vi), deaf person
Kizungu, European language
kobe(ma), tortoise
kofi(ma), palm of hand
ko kote, anywhere
kondoo, sheep
kopa, to borrow
kopesha, to lend
kopo(ma), a tin
korija, a score
kosa, to miss, do wrong
    kosana, to quarrel
    kosekana, be missing
kosa(ma), a fault
kotekote, everywhere
kubali, to agree
-kubwa, large
kuku, hen

kule, there
kuliko, more than
kumbuka, to remember
kumbusha, to remind
kumi, ten
kunja, to fold
kunjua, to unfold
kura (piga), to cast lots
kusini, the south
kusudi(ma), intention
kuta, to come across
kutana, to meet
-kuu, great
kwa, with, to, from
k. sababu
k. kuwa }because
k. maana }
k. hiyo, therefore
k. ajili ya, for the sake of
k. nini ?, why ?
kwamba, that
kwani ?, why ?
kwanza, first
kwao, their home
kweli, truth, truly
kwenu, your home
kwetu, our home

L

la, to eat
la !, no !
labda, perhaps
laini, smooth
lainisha, to make smooth
lakini, but
lala, to lie down
laza, to lay down
lazima, necessary(ily)
lea, to bring up child
lemea, to press upon
leo, today
leta, to bring
lewa, to get drunk
lia, to cry, roar
licha, not only
lile, that
lima, to cultivate ground
linda, to guard
lini ? when ?
lisha, to graze
lugha, language

M

maana (N),* meaning
madini (N), metal
maendeleo, progress
mafundisho, teaching
mafuta, oil
magharibi, west
mahali, place
mahindi, maize
maili (N), mile
maisha, life
maiti (N), corpse
majani, grass
maji, water
malaika (N), angel
malezi, upbringing
mali (N), possessions
mama (N), mother
mamba (N), crocodile
mamlaka (N), authority
mamoja, the same
mapatano, agreement
mapema, early
mara (N), time
m. kwa m., from time to time
m. nyingi, often
m. ngapi?, how often
maradhi, sickness
mashariki, the east
mashine (N), machine
mashua (N), boat
masika, the greater rains
maskini, poor
matata, trouble
mate, saliva
matukano, abuse
matusi, insults
mavuno, harvest
mazao, produce
maziwa, milk
mbali, far
mbalimbali, different
mbegu, seed
mbele, in front
mbili, two
mboga, vegetables
mbolea, manure
mbona?, why?
mbu, mosquito

mbuzi, goat
mbwa, dog
mchaguliwa(wa), candidate
mchaguzi(wa), elector
mchana, daytime
m. kutwa, all day
mchanganyiko(mi), mixture
mchawi(wa), sorceror
mchele, husked rice
mchezo(mi), game
mchungaji(wa), herdsman
mchungwa(mi), orange tree
mchwa, termites
mdudu(wa), insect
meza, table
mfalme(wa), king
mfuko(mi), bag
mfupa(mi), bone
mganga(wa), doctor
mgeni(wa), stranger
mgomba(mi), banana plant
mgomvi(wa), quarrelsome man
mgonjwa(wa), sick person
mguu(mi), leg, foot
Mhindi(wa), Indian
mia, hundred
milioni, million
mimi, I, me
miongoni mwa, among
mjane(wa), widow
mji(mi), town, village
mjinga(wa), foolish person
mjomba(wa), mother's brother
mjumbe(wa), messenger
mkate(mi), bread, loaf
mke(wa), wife
mkeka(mi), plaited mat
mkia(mi), tail
mkono(mi), arm, hand
Mkristo(wa), Christian
mkwe(wa), in-law
mlango(mi), door
mle, in that place
mlevi(wa), drunkard
mlima(mi), mountain, hill
mlimaji(wa), farmer
mlinzi(wa), guard
mnazi(mi), coconut palm
mno, very
mnyama(wa), animal

---

* Belongs to N class.

mnyang'anyi(wa), robber
moja, one
m. kwa m., straight on
-mojawapo, any one
moshi, smoke
mosi, one (counting)
moto(mi), fire
moyo(mi), heart
mpaka, up to
mpishi(wa), cook
mpunga, rice
msaada(mi), help
msafiri(wa), traveller
msalaba(mi), a cross
msemaji(wa), orator
mshahara(mi), wages
mshipa(mi), muscle, vein, etc.
msimamizi(wa), overseer
msitu(mi), forest
msomaji(wa), reader
mstari(mi), line
mswaki(mi), toothbrush
mtama, millet
mtende(mi), date palm
mti(mi), tree
mtini(mi), fig-tree
mto(mi), river
mtoto(wa), child
mtu(wa), person
mtume(mi), prophet
mtumishi(wa), servant
mtumwa(wa), slave
mtungaji(wa), editor
muhimu, important
muhindi(mi), maize plant or cob
muhogo(mi), cassava
mume(wa), husband
mundu(mi), sickle
Mungu(mi), God
muwa(mi), sugar-cane
mvi, white hair
mvinyo, wine
mvua, rain
Mwafrika(wa), African
mwaka(mi), year
mwali(wali), maiden
mwalimu(wa), teacher
mwana(wana), child
mwanadamu, human being
mwanafunzi, pupil
mwanakondoo, lamb
mwanamume, man

mwanamke, woman
Mwarabu(wa), Arab
mwavuli(mi), umbrella
mwembe(mi), mango tree
mwendeshaji(wa), driver
mwendo(mi), course, going
mwenendo, behaviour
mwenyeji(w), inhabitant
mwenyewe(w), owner
mwenzi(w), companion
mwezi(mi), month, moon
mwiba(mi), thorn
mwiko(mi), wooden spoon
mwili(mi), body
mwimbaji(wa), chorister
Mwingereza(wa), Englishman
mwisho(mi), end
Mwislamu(wa), Moslem
mwivi(wevi) } thief
mwizi(wezi) }
mwombaji(wa), beggar
mzabibu(mi), grape vine
mzazi(wa), parent
mzee(wa), old person
mzigo(mi), a load
mzizi(mi), root
Mzungu(wa), European

N

na, and, by, with
-na, has, have
naam, yes
nafasi, opportunity
namna, kind
nanasi(ma), pineapple
-nane, eight
nani ?, who ?
nawa, to wash hands
nazi, coconut
nchi, country
ndani, inside
ndege, bird
ndevu, beard
ndipo, then
ndiyo, yes
ndizi, banana
ndoa, marriage
ndoo, pail
ndoto, dream
ndugu, kinsman
ndui, smallpox

nena, to speak
-nene, fat, thick
neno(ma), word
ngamia, camel
ngano, wheat
-ngapi?, how many?
nge, scorpion
ngoja, to wait (for)
ngoma, drum, dance
nguo, cloth(es)
nguruwe, pig
nguvu, strength
ng'ambo, opposite bank
ng'oa, to uproot
ng'ombe, cow
ni, is, are
nini?, what?
ninyi, you
njaa, hunger
nje, outside
njia, way, path
njiwa, pigeon
njoo, come
-nne, four
-nono, fat (animals)
nta, wax
nuka, to smell (badly)
nukia, to smell (nice)
nunua, to buy
nusu, half
nya, to fall as rain
nyama, meat
nyamaza, to be quiet
nyang'anya, to take by force
nyani, baboon
nyati, buffalo
nyoka, to become straight
   nyosha, to stretch out
nyoka, snake
nyote, you all
nyuki, bee
nyuma, behind
nyumba, house
nywa, to drink
nywele, hair
nzige, locust

O

oa, to marry
   olewa, to be married
   oza, to give in marriage

oga, to bathe
ogelea, to swim
ogesha, to bath child
ogopa, to fear
okoa, to save
omba, to ask for
ona, to see
   onekana, to be visible
ondoa, to take away
ondoka, to go away
ongea, to converse
onya, to warn
onyesha, to show
osha, to wash
ota { to grow
    { to dream
-ote, all
-o -ote, any
ovyo, carelessly
oza, to rot

P

pa, to give
paka, cat
pale, there
palia } to hoe weeds
palilia }
pambazuka, to dawn
pamoja, together
-pana, wide
panda, to plant
panda, to go up
panya, rat
pasa, to behove
pasipo, without
pata, to get
patana, to agree
patikana, to be obtainable
peke, alone
peleka, to send, take
penda, to love, like
pendelea, to favour
pendeza, to please
pengine, sometimes
penye, at, by
pepo, evil spirit
pesa, money
pewa, to be given
-pi?, which?
pia, all, also
piga, to hit

p. chapa, to print
p. magoti, to kneel
p. mstari, to draw a line
p. pasi, to iron
p. picha, to photograph
pigana, to fight
pika, to cook
pili, two
pima, to measure
pindi, while
pishi, c. ½ gallon
pita, to pass
poa, to get cool
-pole, gentle
pole !, sorry !
polepole, slowly, quietly
pona, to get well
　ponya, to cure
ponda, to crush
po pote, anywhere
potea, to get lost
punda, donkey
pungua, to get less
punguza, to make less
pwani, coast
-pya, new

R

radhi, content
rafiki, friend
rahisi, easy
rahisisha, to make easy
raia, a subject
rangi, colour
ratli, 1 lb.
-refu, long
robo, a quarter
rudi, to go back
rudisha, to send/give back
ruhusa, permission
ruhusu, to permit
ruka, to fly, jump

S

saa, hour, clock
saba, seven
sababu, reason
sabini, seventy
sabuni, soap
sadiki, to believe

safari, journey
safi, clean
safiri, to travel
safisha, to cleanse
saga, to grind
sahani, plate
sahau, to forget
sahihi, correct
sahihisha, to correct
saidia, to help
sala, prayer
salama, safely
salamu, greetings
sali, to pray
salimu, to greet
samadi, manure
samaki, fish
samehe, to forgive
sana, very
sanduku(ma), box
sasa, now
s. hivi, at once
sauti, sound, voice
sawa, equal, level
sawasawa, just right
sawazisha, to make equal
sehemu, portion
sema, to say, speak
sembuse, still more
senti, cent
seremala(ma), carpenter
serikali, government
shamba, cultivated field
sharti, of necessity
shauri, to advise
shauri(ma), advice
shida, trouble
shika, to take hold of
　shikilia, to hold on to
shikamoo, a greeting
shilingi, shilling
shimo(ma), pit
shinda, to conquer
shoka(ma), axe
shona, to sew
shuka, to go down
shusha, to let down
shule, school
si, not
siafu, red ants
siagi, butter
sifa, praise, character

sifu, to praise
sigareti, cigarette
sihi, to beseech
sikia, to hear
sikiliza, to listen
siki(li)zana, to get on together
sikio(ma), ear
siku, day
sikuzote, always
simama, to stand up
simba, lion
sindano, needle
siri, a secret
sisi, we, us
sisimisi, small ants
sita, six
sitawi, to flourish
sitini, sixty
siyo, no
sogea, to move along
sogeza, to move something
soko(ma), market
soma, to read
songa, to press
songoa, to wring
sote, we all
starehe !, don't trouble !
subulkheri, good morning
suka, to plait
sukari, sugar
sungura, hare
swali(ma), question

T

taa, lamp
tafadhali, please
tafuta, to look for
taifa(ma), nation
taga, to lay eggs
tajiri, wealthy
tajirisha, to make rich
taka, to want
takasa, to cleanse
takata, to be clear
takataka, refuse
-tamu, sweet
tandu, centipede
tano, five
tangaza, to proclaim
tangazo(ma), proclamation
tangu, since

tata, to tangle
tatua, to tear
tatanisha, to perplex
-tatu, three
tauni, plague
tawi(ma), branch
tayari, ready
tayarisha, to make ready
tazama, to look at
tega, to set trap
tegua, to let off trap
tele, abundant
telemka, to go down
telemsha, to let down
tembea, to walk
tembeza, to hawk about
tembo, elephant
tena, again
tenda, to do
tende, dates
tendo(ma), deed
tengeneza, to prepare, put right
thelathini, thirty
theluthi, a third part
themanini, eighty
thumuni, sixpence
thenashara, twelve
tia, to put in
timia, to be complete
timiza, to fulfil
tisa, nine
tisini, ninety
toa, to put forth
tøba, repentance
toka, to go out
tokea, to appear
tokea, toka, from
toroka, to run away
tosha, to suffice
tu, we are
tu, only
tua, to set down
tuliza, to pacify
tubu, to repent
tuma, to send someone
tumaini, to rely on
tumbo(ma), stomach
tumbili, monkey
tumia, to use
tunda(ma), fruit
tundu(ma), hole
tunza, to take care of

tupa, to throw away
-tupu, empty, bare
twiga, giraffe

U

u, you are
ua, to kill
ua(ma), flower
ua(ny), courtyard
ubao(mb), plank
ubavu(mb), rib
ubawa(mb), wing
ubaya, evil
uchaguzi, election
uchawi, witchcraft
udevu(nd), a hair of beard
udogo, smallness
udongo, soil
udugu, kinship
ufa(ny), crack
ufagio(f), broom
ufalme(f), kingdom
ufundi, craftsmanship
ufunguo(f), key
ufuta, oil-seed
ugali, porridge
ugomvi, quarrelling
ugonjwa(ma), sickness
uharibifu, destruction
Uingereza, British Isles
ujane, widowhood
uji, gruel
ujinga, folly
ukali, fierceness
ukanda(k), belt
ukubwa, size
ukurasa(k), page
ukuta(k), wall
Ulaya, Europe
ule, that
ulevi, drunkenness
ulimi(nd), tongue
ulimwengu, world
ulinzi, guarding
uliza, to ask
uma, to bite, hurt
  umiza, to give pain
umba, to create
umeme, lightning
umoja, unity
umri, age
unga, to join

unga, flour
Unguja, Zanzibar
uongo, falsehood
upande(p), side
u. wa kuume, right side
u. wa kushoto, left side
upepo(p), wind
upesi, quickly
upishi, cookery
upole, gentleness
upya, newness
urefu, length, height
usahaulifu, forgetfulness
useremala, carpentry
ushanga, beads
ushinde, defeat
ushindi, victory
usiku, night
u. wa manane, midnight
u. kucha, all night
usingizi, sleep
usitawi, prosperity
uso(ny), face
utajiri, wealth
utamu, sweetness
utii, obedience
utitiri, chicken fleas
utoto, childhood
utu, manhood
uvivu, laziness
uvumba, incense
uwingu(mb), sky
uza, to sell
uzazi, childbirth
uzee, old age
uzi(ny), cord, thread
uzuri, beauty

V

vaa, to put on clothes
vema, well
vibaya, badly
vigumu, difficult
vile(vile), those, thus
vivi hivi   ⎫
vivyo hivyo ⎬ in the same way
  ⎭
-vivu, lazy
vizuri, well
vua, to take off clothes
vuka, to cross over
  vusha, to help over

vuli, the short rains
vuna, to reap
vunja, to break
vuta, to pull

W

wa, to be
wahi, to be in time
waka, to burn (fire)
  washa, to light
wakati(ny), time
wakia, ounce
wala, and not, nor
walakini, however
wale, those
wali, cooked rice
wao, they
wapi?, where?
wari, 1 yd.
wavu(ny), net
waza, to think
wazo(ma), thought
weka, to put (by)
wekundu, redness
wema, goodness
wembe(ny), razor
weupe, whiteness
weusi, blackness
wewe, you
weza, to be able
wezesha, to enable
  wezekana, to be possible
wika, to crow
wiki, week
-wili, two
wima, upright

wimbo(ny), song, hymn
winda, to hunt
wingi, abundance
wino, ink
-wivu, jealous
wivi, wizi, theft
wokovu, salvation

Y

ya, of
y. kuwa } that
y. kwamba }
yai(ma), egg
yale, those
yayo hayo, these same
yeye, he, she
yu, he is

Z

zaa, to bear
zaidi, more
zabibu, grapes
zamani, aforetime
ziba, to stop up
zibua, to unstop
zidi, to increase
zidisha, to multiply
zile, those
-zima, whole
-zito, heavy
zoea, to get used to
zoeza, to accustom to
zuia, to prevent
zunguka, to go round
-zuri, pretty, nice

ENGLISH–SWAHILI VOCABULARY
OF WORDS USED IN THE EXERCISES

A

a, an, *omit*
(to be) able, weza
about, yapata, kama
(news) about, habari za
above, juu, juu ya
abundant/ly, tele
(to) accept, kubali
advantage, faida
advice, shauri(ma)
affair, jambo(mambo)
(to be) afraid, ogopa
after, baada ya
afternoon, alasiri
afterwards, baadaye
again, tena
(to) agree to, kubali
(to) agree with, patana
agreement, mapatano
alike, sawasawa
all, -ote
alone, peke yangu, etc.
also, pia
although, ingawa
always, sikuzote
(to) amuse, chekesha
and, na
and not, wala
angel, malaika
animal, mnyama(wa)
another, -ingine
answer, jibu(ma)
(to) answer, jibu, itika
any, *omit*
any whatever, -o -ote
anywhere, mahali po pote
(to) appear, tokea
Arab, Mwarabu
Arabic, Kiarabu
arm, mkono(mi)
(to) arrive, fika
as, kama

as well, pia
(to) ask, uliza
(to) ask for, omba
(to be) asleep, lala
at, penye
(not) at all, hata kidogo
(to) await, ngoja
(to) awake, amka
axe, shoka(ma)

B

baboon, nyani
bad, -baya
badly, vibaya
bag, mfuko(mi)
banana, ndizi
banana plant, mgomba(mi)
basket, kikapu(vi)
(to) bathe, oga
beads, ushanga
(to) bear, zaa
beard, ndevu
(to) beat, piga
beautiful, -zuri
because, kwa sababu
bed, kitanda(vi)
bee, nyuki
before (time), kabla ya
before (place), mbele ya
(to) beg, omba
(to) begin, anza
behaviour, mwenendo
behind, nyuma, nyuma ya
(to) behove, pasa
(to) believe, amini
below, chini, chini ya
(to) bend down, inama
(it is) better, yafaa
(to get) better, pona
between, kati ya
big, -kubwa

bird, ndege
black, -eusi
blackness, weusi
blessing, baraka
blind person, kipofu(vi)
body, mwili(mi)
(to) boil, chemka, chemsha
bone, mfupa(mi)
book, kitabu(vi)
bottle, chupa
(at the) bottom, chini
box, sanduku(ma)
brave, hodari
bread, mkate(mi)
(to) break, vunja
(to) bring, leta
broom, ufagio(f)
brother, ndugu
buffalo, nyati
(to) build, jenga
(to) burn, waka
but, lakini
butter, siagi
(to) buy, nunua
by, na, kwa
by myself, etc., peke yangu, etc.

C

(to) call, ita
camel, ngamia
(I) can, naweza
(to take) care, angalia
carpenter, seremala(ma)
(to) carry, chukua
cassava, muhogo
cat, paka
cattle, ng'ombe
centipede, tandu
certificate, cheti(vy)
chair, kiti(vi)
cheap, rahisi
chest, kifua
chief, -kuu
Chief, jumbe(ma)
child, mtoto(wa) mwana(wa)
childhood, utoto
(to) choose, chagua
Christian, Mkristo (Wa)
church, kanisa(ma)
clean, safi
(to) clean, safisha

(to be) clear, elea
clerk, karani(ma)
clock, saa
(to) close, fumba
cloth, kitambaa(vi)
clothes, nguo
coast, pwani
coconut, nazi, dafu(ma)
coconut palm, mnazi(mi)
cock, jogoo(ma)
coffee, kahawa
cold, baridi
colour, rangi
Come !, Njoo !
(to) come, (ku)ja
(my) companion, mwenzangu
complete, kamili
(to) consent, kubali
(to) consider, fikiri
(to) continue, endelea
(on the) contrary, bali
cook, mpishi(wa)
(to) cook, pika
cooking, upishi
cord, uzi(ny)
cork, kizibo(vi)
(to) count, hesabu
country, nchi
courtyard, ua(ny)
cow, ng'ombe
crack, ufa(ny)
craftsman, fundi(ma)
creature, kiumbe(vi)
crocodile, mamba
crops, mazao
cross, crucifix, msalaba
(to) cross, vuka
(to) cultivate, lima
cunning, -erevu
cup, kikombe(vi)
(to) cure, ponya
custom, desturi
(to) cut, kata
(to) cry, lia

D

danger, hatari
darkness, giza
date palm, mtende(mi)
dates, tende
daughter, binti

(to) dawn, (ku)cha, pambazuka
day, siku
(before) daybreak, alfajiri
daytime, mchana
deaf person, kiziwi(vi)
(a great) deal, sana
dear (in price), ghali
deed, tendo(ma)
deep, -refu
(to) despise, dharau
(to) destroy, haribu
(to) die, (ku)fa
(to) dig, lima
different, mbalimbali
difficult, vigumu
difficulty, ugumu
discussions, mashauri
disease, ugonjwa(ma)
distance, mwendo
(to) do, fanya, tenda
(it will) do, yatosha, yafaa
doctor, mganga(wa)
dog, mbwa
donkey, punda
door, mlango(mi)
draw (a line, etc.), piga
dream, ndoto
(to) dream, ota
dress, nguo
(to) drink, (ku)nywa
(to) drive away, fukuza, kimbiza
drum, ngoma
(to get) drunk, lewa
drunkard, mlevi
drunkenness, ulevi
dry, -kavu
(to get) dry, kauka

E

each, kila
ear, sikio(ma)
early, mapema
east, mashariki
easy, rahisi
(to) eat, (ku)la
(to be) educated, elimika
effort, bidii
egg, yai(ma)
eight, -nane
either . . . or, au . . au, ama . .
  ama

elders, wazee
elephant, tembo
empty, -tupu
end, mwisho(mi)
(to) end, (kw)isha
enemy, adui
England, Uingereza
English, Kiingereza
Englishman, Mwingereza
(to be) enough, tosha
(to) enter, ingia
entirely, kabisa
especially, hasa
European, Mzungu
even, hata
evening, jioni
every, kila
everywhere, mahali pote
evil, -baya
exactly, halisi
excellency, ubora
excellent, bora
except, ila
(to) explain, eleza
eye, jicho(ma)

F

face, uso(ny)
(to) fail, kosa
faith, imani
(to) fall (down), anguka
famine, njaa
far, mbali
(to) fasten, funga
fat, -nene
father, baba
fault, kosa(ma)
(to show) favouritism, pendelea
fear, hofu
(to) fear, ogopa
fever, homa
few, -chache
field, shamba(ma)
fierce, -kali
fifty, hamsini
(to) fight, pigana
(to) fill, jaza
(to) find, ona
fine, -zuri
finger, kidole(vi)
(to) finish, (kw)isha

fire, moto(mi)
fireplace, jiko(meko)
firm, imara
first, -a kwanza
fish, samaki
five, -tano
flour, unga
flower, ua(ma)
fly, inzi
(to) fly, ruka
(to) fold, kunja
(to) follow, fuata
folly, ujinga
food, chakula
fool, mjinga(wa)
foot, mguu(mi)
(to) forbid, kataza
foreign, -a kigeni
forest, msitu(mi)
(to) forget, sahau
forgetful, -sahaulifu
(to) forgive, samehe
forty, arobaini
forward, mbele
four, -nne
fowl, kuku
Friday, Ijumaa
friend, rafiki
frog, chura(vy)
from, kwa, toka
(in) front, mbele
fruit, matunda
(to get) full, jaa

G

game, mchezo(mi)
garden, bustani
garment, nguo
gate, mlango(mi)
gather (fruit, etc.), chuma
gentle, -pole
(to) get, pata
(to) get better, pona
(to) get less, pungua
(to) get out, ondoka
(to) get used to, zoea
giant, jitu(ma)
giraffe, twiga
(to) give, (ku)pa
(to) give back, rudisha
          G

(to) give out, toa
gladness, furaha
glass, bilauri, kioo
(to) go, (kw)enda
(to) go away, ondoka
(to) go back, rudi
(to) go in, ingia
(to) go on, endelea
(to) go out, toka
goat, mbuzi
God, Mungu
good, -ema, -zuri
good-bye, kwa heri(ni)
grass, majani
great, -kuu
(to) greet, amkia, salimu
greetings, salamu
grief, huzuni
(to) grow, ota
gruel, uji
guard, mlinzi(wa)
(to) guard, linda
guest, mgeni(wa)

H

hair, nywele
half, nusu
half past, u nusu
hand, mkono(mi)
happiness, furaha
hard, -gumu
hare, sungura
harvest, mavuno
haste, haraka
(to) have, kuwa na
having, -enye
he, yeye
he has, etc., ana, etc.
head, kichwa(vi)
(to) heal, pona
health, afya
(to) hear, sikia
heart, moyo(mi)
heaviness, uzito
heavy, -zito
heavy rain, mvua nyingi
help, msaada
(to) help, saidia
hen, kuku
her, yeye, -ake

herdsman, mchungaji(wa)
here, hapa, hapo, huku
(to) hide, ficha
high, juu
hill, mlima(ma), kilima(vi)
him, yeye
(to) hinder, zuia
hippopotamus, kiboko(vi)
his, -ake
(to) hit, piga
hoe, jembe(ma)
(to) hoe, lima, palia
(to take) hold of, shika
hole, tundu
home, kwetu, nyumbani
honey, asali
horse, farasi
hot, -a moto, -kali
hour, saa
house, nyumba
how?, namna gani? -je?
how many?, ngapi?
how often?, mara ngapi
hundred, mia
hunger, njaa
(to) hurt, uma, umiza
husband, mume(wa)
hut, kibanda(vi)
hyena, fisi

I

I, mimi
idle, -vivu
idleness, uvivu
if, kama
ill, -gonjwa
important, -kubwa
in, into, katika
(to) increase, zidi
Indian, Mhindi(wa)
(to) inform, arifu
inhabitant, mwenyeji(we)
ink, wino
insect, mdudu(wa)
inside, ndani, ndani ya
instead of, badala ya
(to) intercede for, ombea
iron, chuma(vy)
is, ni
island, kisiwa(vi)
its, -ake

J

(to) join, unga
journey, safari
joy, furaha
(to) jump, ruka
(to be) just about to, taka

K

key, ufunguo(f)
(to) kill, ua
(what) kind of?, gani? namna gani?
king, mfalme(wa)
kingdom, ufalme
knee, goti(ma)
knife, kisu(vi)
(to) know, jua

L

lady, bibi
lamb, mwanakondoo(wa)
lame person, kiwete(vi)
lamp, taa
land, nchi
language, lugha
large, -kubwa
last, -a mwisho
last month, mwezi uliopita
(at) last, hatimaye, mwishowe
latrine, choo(vy)
(to) laugh, cheka
(to) lay down, laza
laziness, uvivu
lazy, -vivu
leaf, jani(ma)
leave, ruhusa
(to) leave, acha
leave a place, ondoka
(to take) leave of, aga
left, -a kushoto
leg, mguu(mi)
(to) lend, kopesha
length, urefu
leopard, chui
(to get) less, pungua
letter, barua
lid, kifuniko(vi)
lie, uongo
(to) lie down, lala
life, maisha

(to) **lift up**, inua
light, nuru
light in weight, -epesi
(to) **light (fire)**, washa
lightning, umeme
like, kama
(to) **like**, penda
line, mstari(mi)
lion, simba
(to) **listen**, sikiliza
little, -dogo
(a) **little**, kidogo
(to) **live**, kaa
load, mzigo(mi)
loaf, mkate(mi)
locusts, nzige
long, -refu
long ago, zamani
(to) **look**, tazama
(to) **look after**, tunza, angalia
(to) **look for**, tafuta
(to) **look out**, angalia
(to) **lose by death**, fiwa
loss, hasara
(to be) **lost**, potea
(a) **lot**, wingi
(to) **love**, penda

M

machine, mashine
maize, mahindi
maize plant, muhindi(mi)
(to) **make**, fanya
man (person), mtu(wa)
man (male person), mwanamume (wa)
mango, embe(ma)
mango tree, mwembe(mi)
manners, adabu
many, -ingi
market, soko(ma)
marriage, ndoa
(to) **marry**, oa, olewa, oza
master, bwana(ma)
mat, mkeka(mi)
material, kitambaa, nguo
matter, jambo(ma)
(**it doesn't**) **matter**, haidhuru
me, mimi
(a) **meal**, chakula
meaning, maana

(to) **measure**, pima
meat, nyama
medicine, dawa
(to) **meet**, kutana na
(to be in) **a mess**, chafuka
midday, adhuhuri
(in the) **middle**, katikati
milk, maziwa
millet, mtama
(**never**) **mind**, haidhuru
minute, dakika
mistake, kosa(ma)
(to make) **a mistake**, kosea
(to) **mix**, changanya
money, fedha
monkey, tumbili
month, mwezi(mi)
moon, mwezi(mi)
more, zaidi
more than, kuliko
moreover, tena
morning, asubuhi
Moslem, Mwislamu
mosquito, mbu
mother, mama
mountain, mlima(mi)
(to) **move**, hama, hamisha
much, -ingi
my, mine, -angu

N

name, jina(ma)
narrow, -embamba
native, mwenyeji(we)
near, karibu
necessary, lazima
need, haja
needle, sindano
neither . . nor, wala
net, wavu(ny)
new, -pya
newness, upya
news, habari
newspaper, gazeti
nice, -zuri
night, usiku
nine, tisa, kenda
ninety, tisini
no, la, hapana, siyo
noise, kelele
north, kaskazini

not, is not, si
not at all, hata kidogo
now, sasa
number, hesabu

O

(to) observe, angalia
(be) obtainable, patikana
o'clock, saa
of, -a
(to) offer, toa
often, mara nyingi
oil, mafuta
old age, uzee
old person, mzee
on, juu ya
once, mara moja
(at) once, sasa hivi
one, moja
only, tu
(to) open, fungua, fumbua
opportunity, nafasi
or, au
orange, chungwa(ma)
orange tree, mchungwa(mi)
(in) order that, ili
other, -ingine
(you) ought, yakupasa
our, ours, -etu
out, outside, nje
out of, katika
over, juu ya
over there, huko
overseer, msimamizi(wa)
owner, mwenyewe(we)

P

pail, ndoo
palace, jumba(ma)
paper, karatasi
parent, mzazi(wa)
part, sehemu
(to) pass, pita
path, njia
patient, mgonjwa
pen, pencil, kalamu
people, watu
perhaps, labda

permission, ruhusa
person, mtu
(to) pick, chuma
piece, kipande(vi)
pig, nguruwe
pineapple, nanasi(ma)
pineapple plant, mnanasi(mi)
pipe (tobacco), kiko(vi)
pit, shimo(ma)
place, mahali
(to) plait, suka
plan, shauri(ma)
plank, ubao(mb)
plantation, shamba(ma)
plate, sahani
(to) play, cheza
(to) please, pendeza
plot of ground, kiwanja(vi)
pole, mti(mi)
polish, dawa
poor, maskini
porridge, ugali
possession(s), mali
(to be) possible, wezekana
pot (cooking), chungu(vy)
potato, kiazi(vi)
(to make) pots, finyanga
poverty, umaskini
praise, sifa
(to) praise, sifu
(to) pray, sali, omba
prayers, sala
(to) prepare, tengeneza
present, zawadi
(at) present, sasa
(to be) present, (ku)wapo
presently, bado kidogo
pretty, -zuri
(to) prevent, zuia
print, chapa
(to) print, piga chapa
produce, mazao
profit, faida
progress, maendeleo
pupil, mwanafunzi(wa)
pure, safi
purpose, kusudi(ma)
(to) put, weka
(to) put by, weka
(to) put forth, toa
(to) put in, tia
(to) put on (clothes), vaa

Q

(to) **quarrel**, gombana
quarrelling, ugomvi
quarrelsome person, mgomvi(wa)
quarter, robo
question, swali(ma)
quick, quickly, upesi
quietly, polepole
quite, kabisa

R

rain, mvua
rat, panya
rather far, mbali kidogo
raw, -bichi
razor, wembe(ny)
(to) **read**, soma
reading, kusoma
ready, tayari
(to) **reap**, vuna
reason, sababu
red, -ekundu
(to) **refuse**, kataa
(to) **rejoice**, furahi
relative, ndugu
(to) **rely on**, tumaini
(to) **remember**, kumbuka
(to) **remind**, kumbusha
(to) **repent**, tubu
repentance, toba
respect, heshima
(to) **return**, rudi, rudisha
(to) **reverence**, (ku)cha
rib, ubavu(mb)
rice in husk, mpunga
rice, cooked, wali
rice, husked, mchele
rice plant, mpunga(mi)
right, -a kuume
ripe, -bivu
(to) **ripen**, iva
river, mto(mi)
road, njia
(to) **roar**, lia
room, chumba(vy)
root, mzizi(mi)
(to) **rot**, oza
rotten, -bovu
(to) **ruin**, haribu
(to) **run away**, kimbia

S

sack, gunia(ma)
sad, -a huzuni
sadness, huzuni
safely, salama
(for the) **sake of**, kwa ajili ya
salt, chumvi
same, pale pale, ile ile, etc.
(it's all the) **same**, ni mamoja
(to) **save**, okoa
(to) **say**, sema
(to) **say to**, ambia
scorpion, nge
(to) **see**, ona
seed, mbegu
(to) **seek**, tafuta
self, -enyewe, in verbs -ji-
(to) **sell**, uza
(to) **send**, peleka
sense, akili
(to) **separate**, achana
servant, mtumishi
(to) **set out**, ondoka
(to) **set (sun)**, (ku)chwa
seven, saba
seventy, sabini
(to) **sew**, shona
sharp, -kali
sharpness, ukali
sheep, kondoo
shell, ganda(ma)
shoe, kiatu(vi)
shop, duka(ma)
short, -fupi
(to) **show**, onyesha
(to) **shut**, funga
sick man, mgonjwa(wa)
sickness, ugonjwa
silver, fedha
(to) **sin against**, kosa
since, tangu
(to) **sing**, imba
sir, bwana
(to) **sit down**, kaa
six, sita
sixty, sitini
size, ukubwa
skin (of fruit, etc.), ganda(ma)
slave, mtumwa(wa)
sleep, usingizi
slender, -embamba
small, -dogo

smallpox, ndui
smell, nuka, nukia
smoke, moshi
smooth, laini
snake, nyoka
so that, ili
soap, sabuni
soil, udongo
soldier, askari
sometimes, pengine
son, mwana(wa)
song, wimbo(ny)
sorcerer, mchawi(wa)
sore, kidonda(vi)
sorrow, huzuni
(I am) sorry !, pole !
south, kusini
(to) sow, panda
(to) speak, sema
spider, buibui
spirit, pepo
(to) spoil, haribu
spoon (wooden), mwiko(mi)
spoon (European), kijiko(vi)
(to) spread, enea, eneza
(to) spring, ruka
(to) stand up, simama
(to) stay, kaa
(to) steal, iba
still, bado
stomach, tumbo(ma)
stone, jiwe(ma)
(to) stop, acha
(to) stop up, ziba
straight, sawasawa
straight on, moja kwa moja
stranger, mgeni(wa)
stream, kijito(vi), mto(mi)
strength, nguvu
(to) stretch out, nyosha
(to) strike, piga
string, uzi(ny)
strong, imara
subject, raia
suddenly, ghafula
sugar, sukari
sugar-cane, muwa(mi)
(to be) sufficient, tosha
(to be) suitable, faa
sums, hesabu
sun, jua
Sunday, Jumapili

(to) sweep, fagia
sweet, -tamu
sweetness, utamu

T

table, meza
tail, mkia(mi)
(to) take, chukua
(to) take away, ondoa
(to) take care, angalia
(to) take leave of, aga
(to) take off (clothes), vua
(to) talk, ongea
tall, -refu
tea, chai
(to) teach, fundisha
teacher, mwalimu(wa)
teaching, mafundisho
(to) tell, ambia
ten, kumi
thank you, asante
that (adj), yule, kile, etc.
that (conj), kama
the, omit
theft, wizi
their, -ao, -ake
then, kisha, ndipo
there, pale, kule, huko
therefore, kwa hiyo
these, hawa, hivi, etc.
they, them, wao
thick, -nene
thief, mwizi(we), mwivi
thing, kitu(vi), jambo(ma)
(to) think, -ona
third, -a tatu
thirty, thelathini
this, huyu, hiki, etc.
thorn, mwiba(mi)
those, wale, vile, etc.
thought, wazo(ma)
thousand, elfu
three, -tatu
(to) throw (away), tupa
Thursday, Alhamisi
time, nafasi, wakati(ny)
(from) time to time, mara kwa
    mara
(how many) times?, mara ngapi?
(in olden) times, zamani
(what) time?, saa ngapi?

(to get) tired, choka
to, kwa
today, leo
toe, kidole(vi)
together, pamoja
tomorrow, kesho
(day after) tomorrow, kesho kutwa
tongue, ulimi(nd)
too (very), mno
too (also), pia
tooth, jino(me)
toothbrush, mswaki(mi)
tortoise, kobe
town, mji(mi)
traveller, msafiri(wa)
tree, mti(mi)
tribe, kabila(ma)
trouble, matata, shida
true, truly, kweli
(to) try, jaribu
(to) turn round, geuka, geuza
Tuesday, Jumanne
twelve, kumi na mbili, thenashara
twenty, ishirini
twice, mara mbili
two, -wili, mbili

U

umbrella, mwavuli(mi)
uncle, mjomba(wa)
under, chini ya
unity, umoja
unripe, -bichi
(to) unstop, zibua
until, hata
up, juu
up to, mpaka
upon, juu ya
(to) uproot, ng'oa
us, sisi
(to) use, tumia
(to be) used to, zoea
(to be of) use, faa
usually, hu- tense
utterly, kabisa

V

(in) vain, bure
vegetables, mboga

very (much), sana, mno
vessel, chombo(vy)
village, kijiji(vi)
(to be) visible, onekana
visitor, mgeni(wa)
voice, sauti

W

wage(s), mshahara
(to) wait (for), ngoja
(to) wake up, amka
(to) waken someone, amsha
(to) walk, tembea
wall, ukuta(k)
(to) want, taka
(to) warn, onya
(to) wash, osha
(to) wash hands, nawa
(to) wash clothes, fua
watch, saa
(to) watch, angalia
water, maji
wax, nta
way, njia
(a little) way off, mbali kodogo
we, sisi
we all, sisi sote
weak, hafifu
(to) wear, vaa
(to) weary, chosha
(to) weave, fuma
(to) weed, palia
week, juma(ma)
well, vema, vizuri
well?, je?
(are you) well?, hujambo?
(to get) well, pona
well, kisima(vi)
west, magharibi
what?, nini?
what kind?, gani?
what time?, saa ngapi?
whatever, -o -ote
wheat, ngano
when?, lini?
when (relative), -po-
where?, wapi?
where (relative), -po-
wherever, ko kote
which?, -pi?
which (relative), -cho-, vyo-, etc.

white, -eupe
white hair, mvi
who?, nani?
who (relative), -ye-, -o-
whole, -ote, -zima
wholeness, uzima
why?, kwa nini?
(that is) why, ndiyo sababu
wide, -pana
widow, mjane(wa)
wife, mke(wa)
wind, upepo
wing, ubawa(mb)
witchcraft, uchawi
(to) wipe off, futa
with, pamoja na
without, bila, pasipo
woman, mwanamke(wa . . . wa)
wood, mti(mi)
word, neno(ma)
work, kazi
(to) work, fanya kazi

world, ulimwengu
worship, ibada
(to) worship, abudu
(to) write, andika
writing, kuandika

Y

year, mwaka(mi)
yes, ndiyo, naam
yesterday, jana
(day before) yesterday, juzi
yet, bado
you, wewe, ninyi
you all, ninyi nyote
young man, kijana(vi)
your, yours, -ako, -enu

Z

Zanzibar, Unguja

INDEX

TEACH YOURSELF SWAHILI
SUPPLEMENTARY EXERCISES

SUPPLEMENTARY EXERCISES

I

To follow Lesson 4

Give the English and plural of : mke, mkate, mwenyeji, kisiwa, kioo, mwanamume, mwili, mgonjwa, muwa, chungu, mwana, mtume, cheo, mzee, mti, chuma, kijiko, mgomba, moyo, mume.

Give the English and singular of : wafalme, wevi, vyumba, vidonda, miiba, mioto, Wahindi, mihindi, Wazungu, wana-wake, vyeti, minazi, vitambaa, wachawi, mizizi, vitabu, miezi, miaka, wajane, miungu.

Translate : A long—tail, knife, mat, pipe, river; A bad—slave, thing, bed, town, plot of ground; A small—basket, child, shoe, piece, vessel; Four—people, umbrellas, doors, huts, fingers; Two—Indians, maize plants, Englishmen, feet, things.

Je, wageni wana chakula? Wana mizigo? Wanawake wana vikapu vikubwa viwili, kimoja kina mchele, na kimoja kina muhogo na viazi. Na watoto wana miwa mitatu na mikate minne.

Waarabu wana miti mizuri, minazi, michungwa na miembe. Wana mji mkubwa na kisima kirefu. Mwarabu mmoja ana vibanda vitatu. Kimoja kina watu, kimoja kina wanyama, na kimoja kina chakula.

2

To follow Lesson 7

Write in Swahili : folly, danger, beads, seeds, darkness, the world, news, oil, sleep, ink, rain, water, the wind, money, flowers, the sun, sorrow, advice, hunger, work.

Give the English and plural of : nguo, shamba, ukuta, ufalme, mbu, shoka, ulimi, ubao, mnazi, nazi, mwembe, embe, wembe, jicho, jino, siku, chuma, chupa, gunia, uzi.

Translate : One—house, song, egg, day, night; Two—eyes, songs, answers, brooms, wings; Large—courtyards, planks, cracks, fields, tables; Good—soil, vegetables, oranges, milk, dates.

Has the clerk a watch? He has the master's watch, a fine

2

silver watch.   The master has two silver watches, one big and one small.

England, the country of the English, has large towns and fine fields, fields of wheat (*ngano*) and potatoes and vegetables and fruit.

Will the food be enough?   The flour is sufficient, and the meat, and there are enough potatoes.   The cook has two coconuts, they will be enough.

3

To follow Lesson 8

Write in Swahili :   She has—money in the bag, medicine in the bottle, shoes on (her) feet, a sore on (her) finger, beads on (her) arms.   She put—a cloth on the table, clothes in the box, a pot on the fire, beds in the house, bananas in a large basket.

To the Indian's shop;   to the teachers' fields;   to the master's house;   in the child's ear;   in the slave's net;   in the courtyard of the house;   at the church door;   at the father's feet;   by the coconut palms.

There is danger in the way.   There is water in the well. There are people at the door.   There is a snake in the pit. There are houses on the hill.   There are things in the basket. There are strangers by the mango tree.   There is a sick man in the house.   There is good maize in the field.   They wanted to go to the river.   They entered a beautiful place, a place of grass and tall trees and good water.

4

To follow Lesson 10

Write in Swahili :   A—lion, giraffe, elephant, leopard, hyena, buffalo, camel, crocodile, tortoise, scorpion.   Bad spirits, long snakes, great friends, small fowls, two pigs, my father, his brother, our enemies, your friend, your (pl.) dogs, her cat, their horses, my two goats.

Give the augmentative forms (sing. and pl.) of : door, hut, plank, river, knife;   *and the diminutive forms (sing. and pl.) of :* plank, fish, field, bed, tree.

Translate :   Flowers and their seeds;   the cooks and their vegetables;   the fields and their maize;   the coconut palms and their coconuts;   the elephants and their children.   The cat is the great enemy of the rat.   There are bees in the orange trees. There is a scorpion in the hole.   Crocodiles and fish are river animals (animals of in-the-river).   Baboons and monkeys are forest animals. They have long tails The hippo are coming out of the river. My father is writing a letter; he has a pen and a bottle of ink.

5

To follow Lesson 11

Translate : A good—man, tree, seed, book, answer, soil, place, friend; A white—potato, mat, donkey, wall, egg, garment, cock; Black—faces, horses, teeth, clothes, kings, smoke, doors, pipes; Many—mosquitoes, giants, places, diseases, pineapples, matters, hours, thieves; Much—sickness, darkness, profit, reading; Any—food, flour, flower, path, place, stranger, sheep, blind men.

Trees with (having) thorns; a place with water; an old man with white hair; walls with cracks; soil with many stones; centipedes with many legs; a house with many rats; a river with much water; a basket with much flour; a market with much fruit.

The path itself is narrow. The cat herself is black, but (*lakini*) her kittens are white. The fruits themselves are red but their seeds are black. The bag itself is white but its cord is red. The people themselves are good but their children are drunkards. God Himself is good, and all His works are good. All the loads are light. All the umbrellas are black. All the doors are narrow. All the thieves are cunning. All the millet is red.

6

To follow Lesson 13

Translate : I—asked, sat down, wanted, came. We—arrived, heard, saw, finished. Did you—speak, eat, write, get ? You (pl.) answered, went out, knew, could. She—read, loved, died, returned. Did they—begin, enter, stand up, try ? Shall I—stand up, begin, come, eat ? Will you—go, try, be able to, ask ? He will—die, return, write, see. We shall—sit down, speak, hear, arrive. You (pl.) will—know, read, answer, finish. They will—love, want, go in, come out. I—want, love, can, enter. You have—sat down, finished, arrived, asked. Does he—hear, speak, write, come ? We are—eating, reading, beginning, going. Have you—answered, come back, seen, stood ? Are they—dying, coming, trying, reading ?

I—eat, am eating, ate, have eaten, shall eat. He—goes, is going, went, has gone, will go.

We are looking for my donkey. He tries to write. I have put the eggs in my basket. They asked for some money.

You will get the books. Did you break the old man's razor? Have I told you the news? Will they sell the clothes? Do you eat fish? Are you eating fish? Are you buying the planks?

7

To follow Lesson 14

Translate : This—head, number, axe, size, reading; These—coconuts, inhabitants, shells, tongues brothers; That—teacher, honey, question, theft, goat; Those—lamps, glasses, ears, ribs, places; This (already mentioned)—night, little stream, large basket, spider, answer; These (already mentioned)—drums, bodies, cooking pots, places, churches.

He is looking for his friend here. We saw the lion there. The rat will go in here. Have you heard the news of over-there? Two Arabs and three Indians have come to see (look at) our country. There in Zanzibar the Arabs have large plantations of cloves (*mikarafuu*). Here in the pit I saw a large snake. There in the hole there is honey. My child will stay here in the house. I shall go to stand there by the mango tree.

8

To follow Lesson 15

Translate : I do not know. We do not speak. They do not get better. You did not return. You (pl.) did not answer. He did not die. I shall not go. You will not stay. You (pl.) will not try. I have not yet gone. He has not yet bought the house. We have not yet got the money. Don't you know? Are you not afraid? Doesn't he see? Didn't they hear? Did I not look? Did we not tell you? Will you not come in? Will they not be of use? Shall we not be able to? Have you (pl.) not yet sold your goats? Have they not looked for the ink yet?

They—die, are dying, do not die, are not dying, died, did not die, have died, will die, will not die, have not died yet, want to die.

The enemy have entered the town; they are destroying all the houses. Blind men do not see; deaf men do not hear; lame men cannot walk well. The fields want rain; the sun will spoil the maize, it is beginning to die. The cows are not giving milk at present (these days). Are the oranges ripe? They are not ripe yet. Some are beginning to ripen and some are going bad. My house wants doors; the rooms have not yet got doors. The planks have not arrived yet.

9

To follow Lesson 16

Translate : to refuse, to fear, to break, to try, to die; not to do, not to return, not to be able to, not to hinder, not to eat. Come! Stand up! Sing! Wait! Speak! Go ye! Bring ye! Begin ye! Answer ye! Sit ye down! Do not ask. Do not fear. Do not go away. Do (pl.) not look. Do (pl.) not speak. Observe him. Tell me. Look for it (lamp). Buy them (bananas). Don't leave him.

Let the children answer. Don't let the old man hear. Let me look at your book. Shall we tell the teacher? They looked for him everywhere without seeing him. The children asked for food without getting any. We offered (put forth) much money but it was not enough. People are going and returning. Come in and sit down. Give her a book and let her read. Tell the child not to be afraid. Bring some flour and let us put it in the basket. Let us go to the town and buy some fish. Take care of the oranges, don't let them go bad. I want the children to come here so that we can begin our work. Their parents (*wazee*) have forbidden them to do this work. Let us cook some food so that our guests do not go away hungry (*na njaa*). Put the sugar into a box so that the children do not see it.

10

To follow Lesson 19

Translate : If the child cries give it some milk. If we wait here we shall see the lion. If my banana trees bear I will give you some bananas. If the children see the snake they will be afraid. Unless you hide the oranges the children will eat them. If there are not enough planks the carpenters will not be able to work today. If father does not get my letter he will not come. If he does not come today he will not see me.

If the sick man got a good sleep he would soon be better. If you would try hard you would be able to do this work. If the soldiers came back today they would get the thieves. If I knew the place I would go myself. If the dogs had heard the leopard they would have barked (*lia*). If the teacher had come himself he would have been able to choose his books. If we had not guarded our fields the monkeys would have stolen all the maize. If we had not got rain we should not have got a harvest.

The lion roared and the cattle were afraid. The fruit ripened and went bad. The rice grew and bore abundantly. The medicine was effective (*faa*) and the patient recovered.

There are no eggs in the market today. It doesn't matter; it is not good to eat eggs every day; you had better cook vegetables. You will have to go to the field and gather them. Impossible, sir, I have a lot of work. My wife goes there every day; she will bring them.

11

To follow Lesson 21

Translate : The camels who are carrying the sacks of dates; The overseers who are looking after the slaves; My friend who wrote the book which you are reading; The darkness which prevented us from seeing the snake; The meat which will go bad unless we eat it soon; The carpenters who will make tables and chairs; Quarrelling which destroys happiness in a house; Good cows which give us much milk; Indians who do not eat beef (cow meat); Rice fields which are not (big) enough; The pen which the teacher gave me; The bottle which the child broke; The profit which we shall get if we sell our eggs; The path which the Europeans will follow; The work which the craftsmen are doing. The coffee which we bought in the shop; A man who does not know you; A man whom you do not know; The men who have finished work; The work they have finished.

Fallen trees; lost sheep; following wind; useless counsels; insufficient water; He who works wants wage(s). He who fears work will not eat. They who do not hoe will not reap. They who reap rejoice. Who cries today laughs tomorrow. This is a place we are much afraid of. It is here that we saw the lions. This is the hut in which we hid ourselves. When they went away we came out of the hut. And I said to my brother, " (As) I think, they will not come back. We had better go." And he said, " As you like ". When a lion roars who does not fear ?

Write these sentences using the amba *relative :* The shoes which were lost; the toothbrush I am using; Christians who will go to church; The drum the teacher has beaten; The seeds which did not grow; The questions which I cannot answer; A sickness which will not get better; The English language which many people do not know; The place where they are standing.

12

To follow Lesson 22

Write in Swahili : be told, be helped, be greeted, be destroyed, be answered, be bought, be chosen, be born, be uprooted, be forgotten, be sold, be beaten, be given, be killed, be married, be cut, be sought, be asked, be refused, be hindered.

The cassava which was uprooted; the questions which were not answered; the children who will be born; the path which I was shown; a field which is not weeded; things which are being thrown (away); the songs which will be sung; the child who will not be chosen; I who was not given anything; we who were not told.

The medicine will be put into the bottle. His faults have been forgiven. Much money is being given (put forth) by the people. Good children are given sugar. The little children are not to be beaten. Is this the place where the leopard was killed? The plans which were put forth by the old men have not yet been agreed to by the teacher. If she had not consented to be married she would have been beaten by her father. Don't let the books be left here; let them be taken away.

This material is soon spoilt. That string is no use, it breaks (is cut) easily. Unless the work is done today the walls will fall down. The path which we followed is impassable now. These words are not used. His evil deeds cannot be hid; they are known everywhere.

13

To follow Lesson 25

Translate : Many books were good, but one, which was Hemedi's, was not very good. The loaves will not be many, and that in your basket will be a small one. If the sums are many the children who are here today will not be able (to do) them, unless they are very short. If the honey had not been good our profit would have been very small. The flowers would be many if the sun were not so strong (*kali*). May unity be in our land, and strife not be present. Is the water in the path much even (*hata*) now? Yes, there is still much. This is not the man (*yule*) who was ill. The one that was ill is this one. The knife which was in the box is not this one; this is the one which was lost last year. This rice is not good; the good rice is this. I am not the cook; this is the cook; he is ill today and I am helping him. " Children where are you? " " We are here, mother." " Is Juma there? " " He is not here, he is in the village." " Is there much water there where you are? " " No, mother, the water which is here is not much." " Who are with you? " " They are the children of that old man who is ill." " Where did you leave your brother? " " There by the orange tree is where we left him."

14

To follow Lesson 26

Translate : (a) The town which has many inhabitants; the toothbrushes which the children have; the thoughts he has; the certificates which the teacher had; the plan which the clerks had; the eggs which the cook had; the string which we had; roads which will be dangerous; a place which will have water; those who have money; the money which they have; I who have many faults; the many faults that I have. (b) He who has nothing; the food which had no salt; a day which will have no sadness; the medicine which the doctors did not have; reading which had no faults.

Translate the negative sentences (b) *again, using the* amba *relative so that the time of the action may be more clearly shown.*

Translate : What use is a lamp which has no oil? If your friends are in trouble you ought to help them. What! have you no sugar? (No) we have none, we have only milk. Will the old men have things-to-talk-about (*mashauri*) to-morrow? (Yes) they will, but not many. If this country had enough rain it would have good harvests. Those sacks you have, are they in use (have they work)? No, they are (have) not. Next year there will be a shop here. There were not many people at the market. There was no water in the pit. There is no danger here. If there had been danger here I should not have come.

15

To follow Lesson 29

Write these adjectives with njia (*roads*) *:* hard, small, good, bad, new, few, short, chief, wide, long, narrow, white, many, clean, all; *and these with* duka (*shop*) *:* small, whole, bad, new, large, long, narrow, another, any, clean.

Translate : cleanness; excellency; poverty; blackness; idleness; sweetness; sharpness; wholeness; heaviness; new-ness; what news? in what way? hot water; a lamb; are you well? twice; the third week; how many trees? 47; how often? a half; midday; Thursday; what time is it? a quarter past two; all day; all night; five minutes to five; Friday; the last man.

This sweet sugar; that weak pole; these six villages; those clean markets; my new house; your fierce words; his ten fingers; long strong poles; many other things.

The cattle I have are better than those my brother has. All these dogs are fierce, but Ali's is the fiercest of all. All the clothes are pretty, but this is especially pretty. Ten times five is fifty; twice fifty is a hundred; and a quarter of a hundred is twenty-five. Sunday, May 15th, at nine o'clock in the morning.

16

To follow Lesson 31

Translate : Each man by himself; yesterday, today and tomorrow; below and above; inside and out; near and far; now and always; all the people together. Come the day after tomorrow. Look before and behind. He came the day before yesterday.

Speak truly. Go quietly. Return quickly. Do not cry at all. Speak like this. Perhaps they will not want (to). They ate a great deal. Do (it) in the same way. I have none at all. He is asking in vain, he will not get more. Do not give me too much flour; give me just a little. Where is your (pl.) field ? When will you reap ? Look everywhere. They looked here and there. What shall we do ?

Hapo zamani za kale, ulimwengu ulipokuwa mpya, wanyama wote walifanya kazi nyingi kila siku ili uwe mahali pazuri sana. Farasi alifanya kazi nyingi kabisa, na ng'ombe pia, na mbwa na punda na tembo vile vile. Ni ngamia peke yake asiyefanya kazi yo yote. Alikuwa mvivu mno, mchana kutwa alicheza tu. Wanyama wengine hawakupenda uvivu hata kidogo, wakaenda huko alikokaa wakamwuliza polepole, " Rafiki yetu, mbona unacheza sikuzote ? Kwa nini una-tuacha kufanya kazi peke yetu ? '' Yule ngamia hakusema neno lo lote. Wakamwuliza tena na tena wasipate jibu kamwe. Wakasema, '' Tunasema bure, tusimwulize zaidi; kila mara ni vivi hivi, labda akili yake si sawasawa. Tumwa-che akae peke yake.''

17

To follow Lesson 33

Translate : Father, that book which we bought from the Indian for the sake of the child, where is it ? I don't see it. Look inside, I put it in the box. Do not stand near the fire, stand a little way off. I shall come afterwards, perhaps after half an hour. Where is the dog ? She is outside; she is with her puppy (child) outside the house. In front of us, at the bottom of the mountain, we saw elephants. Do not leave me by myself; stay with me. We have come from the teacher; we are going to the village to our relatives. Call the overseer that he may cut down this tree with his axe. We hear with our ears and see with our eyes. They went their

way with gladness.   Your letter was read only with difficulty;
why did you not write with ink?   Just go forward, straight on.
   Goodbye, teacher;   when will you come to our home?
Where is your home, is it far?   It is rather far, but not very.
It is near that village, a little further on.

   Kama ndege aendaye huko na huko mbali na kitundu (*nest*)
chake, ndivyo alivyo mtu aendaye huko na huko mbali na
mahali pake.   Mlee mtoto katika njia impasayo, naye hatai-
acha hata atakapokuwa mzee.   Hata wakati wa kucheka moyo
huwa na huzuni, na mwisho wa furaha ni uzito wa moyo.
Katika kila kazi mna faida, lakini maneno mengi huleta
hasara tu.   Mtu mvivu hataki kulima wakati wa baridi, hivyo
wakati wa mavuno ataomba, hana kitu.   Mtu mvivu husema,
" Simba yuko nje, nitauawa katika njia kuu."   Usimwambie
rafiki yako, " Nenda, urudi halafu, na kesho nitakupa ", nawe
unacho kitu kile karibu.   Ubora wa vijana ni nguvu zao, na
uzuri wa wazee ni kichwa chenye mvi.   Usijisifu kwa ajili
ya kesho, hujui yatakayozaliwa na siku moja.   Sikio lisikialo
na jicho lionalo Bwana ndiye aliyeyafanya yote mawili.   Hayo
ni maneno ya Mfalme Sulemani.

18

To follow Lesson 35

Write in Swahili : Answer for; destroy for; return to;
come to; play with; throw to; lie on; follow after; pass
through; leave to; intercede for; get for; open for; laugh
at; measure for; stand over; give to; put by for; hide from.
   Give the English and the prepositional form of : hama,
kimbia, geuka, cha, dharau, samehe, chemsha, sahau, zaa,
nuka, faa, fua, suka, shona, nawa, tenda, lia, fagia, ng'oa,
kubali.
   Translate : Ametendwa mabaya.   Amehamia Tanga.   Mfua-
tie.   Mwamkie.   Mwondolee mbali.   Mpe fedha ya kununulia
ndizi.   Mafundi wanataka uzi wa kupimia kiwanja cha
nyumba.   Mpishi anaomba sabuni ya kufulia vitambaa vyake.
Mtafutie mgeni kiti cha kukalia.   Njia imenipotea.
   The women are gathering vegetables for us.   His wife has
borne him a son.   The child has been left money by his father.
Do not oppress the poor.   Choose us three good goats.   Open
the door for your mother.   Elephants have ruined our fields
for us.   I have been told this news by the Chief.   These beds
were not slept in yesterday.   The sick man is having food
cooked for him.   The children are having their work examined
(overlooked).   We have been measured out enough flour.
I am being got a bed to lie on.

19

To follow Lesson 38

Translate : I wrote to Ali and Hemedi and said to them, "Come and give me your news." And they came and told me the news of (in) the village. Ali said that he wanted to go to Johannesburg to work. His father and brothers consented, but his mother refused. Although he asked her many times, even ten times, she did not consent. Until at last he said to her, "Well, if you do not like it, I will not go, but why do you refuse?" "Because I am afraid," she said, "I know there is danger there, so I do not want you to go." That is why he did not go.

"People say there is profit there in Johannesburg," I said to him, "but as I see it, there is no profit, but rather loss." "Perhaps," he said, "Well, it's all one to me now, whether I go or not."

Give the English of : patana, peana, juana, ogopana, oana, onana, ombeana, pendana, pigana, gombana; *and the Swahili of :* despise one another; write to each other; return to each other; meet each other; answer one another; say to each other; kill one another; be obtainable; be visible; be possible.

20

To follow Lesson 40

Write in Swahili : Bend (your) head. Lift up (your) hands. Put on your shoes. Close (your) eyes. Open (your) hand. He is drunk. The clothes are dry. The patient is better. That child keeps on falling. The work is getting spoilt. They have found the dead woman. Two tables and eight chairs are finished. My eyes and my teeth are hurting. They brought me a basket full of rice.

Translate, using forms of the verb shown : (*amka*) The sick man is awake. Who wakened him? They greeted one another. The teachers were greeted by the children. (*ona*) The moon is visible. We met yesterday. Warn the child. Show me the letter. (*penda*) She is much loved by her mother. Love one another. Try to please your master. Do not show favouritism to your own children. (*kimbia*) Run away quickly. Drive off the pigs. When we quarrel my wife runs to her mother. (*pata*) Eggs are unobtainable. Why don't you agree with your brother? I reconciled Ali with his wife. Get me some milk. We have had some honey got for us.

21

To follow Lesson 41

Translate : Makarani wote walikuwa wakipatana sana.
Watu hawa walikuwa si ndugu. Palikuwa hapana neno
jingine la kutenda. Nilikuwa nimezoea kusikia maneno
haya. Mwalimu mkuu alikuwa hayupo. Alikuwa amekwenda Ulaya. Shida yake ilikuwa hakujua kusoma. Mji wa
Unguja ulikuwa ndio mji mkuu wa biashara ya utumwa.
Mnafanyaje wanapokuwa wagonjwa ? Viazi vikiwa vime-
pungua tutakula mkate, kama umekwisha pikwa. Vaa nguo
zako. Nimekwisha vaa.

Many people were listening to him. While we were talking
together our master was opening his letters. The Arabs were
taking their slaves to the market to sell. The letter I was
waiting for soon arrived. They were being beaten every day.
When I saw him he was very drunk. The inhabitants of the
town had greatly increased. Our guest had already come.
We have already seen him. At that time I had already got
two children. My daughter had begun to show good progress
(*maendeleo*).

22

To follow Lesson 43

Translate : You yourselves; the sun itself; the stones
themselves; all of us; all of you; you with (having) children;
the whole mango; any place; which months ? a tree with
fruit; another day; much flour; how many cracks ? black
flies; any other words whatever; anything which you want;
wherever we go; whoever sees him; one of the questions;
my child; his brother; her husband; our companions; his
wives; that same day; just the same answer.

How many—places, blind men, monkeys, brooms, answers,
hours, islands, sugarcanes ? Much—iron, fire, darkness,
porridge, reading. Which—room, year, Christian, drum, face,
church, place ? All the—wells, roots, thieves, paths, oil, world,
lame men. Any man whatever; any men whatever.

When we pray it behoves us to believe (in) God, to worship
Him and praise Him. If we repent He will accept our worship,
our prayers and our praises. He, the Giver of all good, will
give us His help and blessing.

The forgetful herdsman let his cattle go into the field and
destroy the crops. The parents rejoiced over their daughter's
marriage. Whom did she marry ? She married a nice young
man, the son of the Chief.

23

To follow Lesson 45

Translate : Where is the water? Here, sir. Bring it. Where is the child? He is in the field, sir. Go and call him. If I call him, and he refuses (to come) what shall I do? Do not play with him or talk to him; but go and call his mother.

When the visitor entered the village and greeted us I said to him, " Wait for me a little so that I (can go and) inform the Chief." And I went and gave the Chief the news that his brother had (has) come.

There was a man and his wife; they had nothing except a sheep and a cock. And one day they got news that their friend was coming to see (look at) them. And the wife said to her husband, " My husband, tomorrow our guest is coming, and we have nothing except this sheep and a cock. And I, to kill my sheep I do not want, and to kill my cock I do not want. What shall we do? " And her husband said to her, " If it is necessary we will kill the sheep." And these words the sheep and the cock heard. So (*hata*) at night the cock began to crow (*kuwika*) with joy, " Ko-ko-ko! Let us kill the sheep! " And the sheep answered, " Allah! Allah! ", meaning " As God wills." When it dawned the wife said, " This guest who is coming is a guest of one day only; what need is there to kill the sheep? We had better kill the cock." The cock was caught and killed, and the one (*yule*) who believed in God was saved.

24

To follow Lesson 46

Translate, using the amba *relative :* This is the paper in which we saw a picture of our town. This paper, which is called Mambo Leo, is prepared in Dar es Salaam. There are many people who have not seen this paper. This is the editor, whose work pleases us very much. He is looking for people who are able to write news of where they live. He is sent many things which are not very useful. He wants to get news from people who are well educated and able to be relied on. The paper is printed by machines which are made to go by electricity. We should like to have a paper which appears every week and not just once a month.

25

To follow Lesson 47

Translate : Are there people here? Today there are not; tomorrow there will be many people because it is market day. Is there water in the well? There is none now; yesterday there was a little, but now it is dried up. Is there fruit in the shops? Not much except bananas. Here at our place there is no danger. In olden times there was a man and his wife. In the morning when the sun rose the man went off. There where he went there was a great river. In the river there were many fish. He looked for a place where there was long grass and hid himself there. Show me the place where the snake was when you saw it. It was just here by this hole. It was in here that it went yesterday. Where was it that the enemy were seen? It was there by the mango trees of the Arabs. Were there no soldiers there? The soldiers were not there. They were there at night but when it dawned they went their way. There in the village two people have died. There is a child come to give us the news. Smallpox has entered the village. Sickness has entered our village too; people die every day.

26

To follow Lesson 48

Translate these conversations : (a) *A child and her teacher.*

Greetings, mother.
Thank you, my child; how are you?
I am well, mother.
What is the news of home?
Good, mother, but my sister Anna is ill.
What is the matter with her?
She has fever (*homa*).
Won't she come to school today?
She will not be able to; she is in bed.
Well, give her my sympathy.
Thank you, mother.

(b) *Visiting in a village.*

Hodi! hodi!
Karibu, bwana, karibu. Habari za siku nyingi?
Njema sana.
Hujambo?
Sijambo, baba; nawe hujambo?
Sijambo, lakini si sana; nina kifua.

Pole.   Tangu lini?
Tangu mwanzo wa mwezi.
Una dawa?
Ninayo.   Nilikwenda dawani nikapata, nayo inanifaa sana.
Vizuri sana.   Nimekuja kukupa habari za mwanao, Karani Petro.
Hajambo?
Hajambo, tena amekuletea fedha kidogo upate kununua nguo.
Asante, bwana; asante sana.   Mwambie asante.
Vema.   Sina budi kwenda sasa, jua linakuchwa na kwetu ni mbali kidogo.   Kwa heri.
Kwa heri, bwana; unisalimie wote.

27

Write in Swahili : The east coast; South Africa; the inhabitants of West Africa; northern lands; across the sea; the right hand; his left leg; the child on the right; half a sack of rice; the rainy season; half a crown; a yard and three-quarters; sixpence; the Sultan of Zanzibar; the Bishop of Mombasa; a foreign language; Arabic.

Translate : In a village shop.

Kitambaa hiki bei gani?
Wari moja shilingi mbili senti ishirini na tano.
Jora nzima, je?
Jora nzima nitakuuzia shilingi sabini na tano.
Ghali sana!   Sitaweza.   Huwezi kupunguza kidogo?
Basi, mama, chukua jora nzima kwa shilingi sabini.
Vema; nitachukua jora moja; nataka kushona nguo za hospitali.   Ni kitambaa kizuri?
Kizuri sana; chafulika vizuri, tena kina maisha marefu.
Vema.
Nini zaidi, bibi?
Nataka madebe mawili mafuta ya taa, chupa nne mafuta ya nazi, na gunia la unga wa mahindi.   Sukari wauzaje?
Frasila moja shilingi kumi na sita.
Nitaweza kupata gunia zima?
Utaweza.   Hata mawili ukitaka.
Moja litatosha.   Andika hesabu; nitaleta fedha kesho vitu vikiisha fika.

KEY

1

Wife, bread, inhabitant, island, glass, man, body, sick person, sugarcane, cooking-pot, son, prophet, rank, old person, tree, iron, spoon, banana plant, heart, husband.

Wake, mikate, wenyeji, visiwa, vioo, wanaume, miili, wagonjwa, miwa, vyungu, wana, mitume, vyeo, wazee, miti, vyuma, vijiko, migomba, mioyo, waume.

Kings, thieves, rooms, sores, thorns, fires, Indians, maize, Europeans, women, notes, coconut palms, cloths, sorcerers, roots, books, months, years, widows, gods.

Mfalme, mwivi, chumba, kidonda, mwiba, moto, Mhindi, muhindi, Mzungu, mwanamke, cheti, mnazi, kitambaa, mchawi, mzizi, kitabu, mwezi, mwaka, mjane, mungu.

Mkia mrefu, kisu kirefu, mkeka mrefu, kiko kirefu, mto mrefu; Mtumwa mbaya, kitu kibaya, kitanda kibaya, mji mbaya, kiwanja kibaya; Kikapu kidogo, mtoto mdogo, kiatu kidogo, kipande kidogo, chombo kidogo; Watu wanne, miavuli minne, milango minne, vibanda vinne, vidole vinne; Wahindi wawili, mihindi miwili, Waingereza wawili, miguu miwili, vitu viwili.

Have the strangers any food? Have they any loads? The women have two large baskets, one has rice, and one has cassava and potatoes. And the children have three sugarcanes and four loaves.

The Arabs have fine trees, coconuts, oranges and mangoes. They have a large village and a deep well. One Arab has three huts. One for (has) people, one for animals, and one for food.

2

Ujinga, hatari, ushanga, mbegu, giza, ulimwengu, habari, mafuta, usingizi, wino, mvua, maji, upepo, fedha, maua, jua, huzuni, (ma)shauri, njaa, kazi.

Cloth, field, wall, kingdom, mosquito, axe, tongue, plank, coconut palm, coconut, mango tree, mango, razor, eye, tooth, day, iron, bottle, sack, thread.

Nguo, mashamba, kuta, falme, mbu, mashoka, ndimi, mbao, minazi, nazi, miembe, maembe, nyembe, macho, meno, siku, vyuma, chupa, magunia, nyuzi.

Nyumba moja, wimbo mmoja, yai moja, siku moja, usiku mmoja; Macho mawili, nyimbo mbili, majibu mawili, fagio mbili, mbawa mbili; Nyua kubwa, mbao kubwa, nyufa kubwa, mashamba makubwa, meza kubwa; Udongo mzuri, mboga nzuri, machungwa mazuri, maziwa mazuri, tende nzuri.

Karani ana saa? Ana saa ya bwana, saa nzuri ya fedha. Bwana ana saa mbili za fedha, moja kubwa na moja ndogo.

Uingereza, nchi ya Waingereza, ina miji mikubwa na mashamba mazuri, mashamba ya ngano na viazi na mboga na matunda.

Chakula kitatosha? Unga unatosha, na nyama, na viazi vinatosha. Mpishi ana nazi mbili, zitatosha.

3

Ana—fedha mfukoni, dawa chupani, viatu miguuni, kidonda kidoleni, ushanga mikononi. Aliweka—kitambaa mezani, nguo sandukuni, chungu motoni, vitanda nyumbani, ndizi katika kikapu kikubwa.

Dukani kwa Mhindi; mashambani kwa wa(a)limu; nyumbani kwa bwana; sikioni mwa mtoto; wavuni mwa mtumwa; uani mwa nyumba; mlangoni pa kanisa; miguuni pa baba; minazini.

Kuna hatari njiani. Mna maji kisimani. Pana watu mlangoni. Mna nyoka shimoni. Kuna nyumba mlimani. Mna vitu kikapuni. Pana wageni mwembeni. Mna mgonjwa nyumbani. Kuna mihindi mizuri shambani. Walitaka kwenda mtoni. Waliingia mahali pazuri, mahali pa majani na miti mirefu na maji mazuri.

4

Simba, twiga, tembo, chui, fisi, nyati, ngamia, mamba, kobe, nge. Pepo wabaya; nyoka warefu; rafiki wakubwa; kuku wadogo; nguruwe wawili; baba yangu; ndugu yake; adui zetu; rafiki yako; mbwa zenu; paka wake; farasi zao; mbuzi zangu wawili.

Lango, malango; banda, mabanda; bao, mabao; jito, majito; jisu, majisu. Kibao, vibao; kisamaki, visamaki; kishamba, vishamba; kijitanda, vijitanda; kijiti, vijiti.

Maua na mbegu zake; wapishi na mboga zao; mashamba na mihindi yake; minazi na nazi zake; tembo na watoto wao. Paka ni adui mkubwa wa panya. Mna (kuna, pana) nyuki michungwani. Mna nge tunduni. Mamba na samaki ni wanyama wa mtoni. Nyani na tumbili ni wanyama wa msituni. Wana mikia mirefu. Viboko wanatoka mtoni. Baba yangu anaandika barua; ana kalamu na chupa ya wino.

5

Mtu mwema, mti mwema, mbegu njema, kitabu chema, jibu jema, udongo mwema, mahali pema, rafiki mwema; Kiazi cheupe, mkeka mweupe, punda mweupe, ukuta mweupe, yai jeupe, nguo nyeupe, jogoo mweupe. Nyuso nyeusi, farasi weusi, meno meusi, nguo nyeusi, wafalme weusi, moshi mweusi, milango myeusi, viko vyeusi; Mbu wengi, majitu mengi (wengi), mahali pengi, magonjwa mengi, mananasi mengi, mambo mengi, saa nyingi, wevi wengi; Ugonjwa mwingi, giza jingi, faida nyingi, kusoma kwingi; Chakula cho chote, unga wo wote, ua lo lote, njia yo yote, mahali po pote, mgeni ye yote, kondoo ye yote, vipofu wo wote.

Miti yenye miiba; mahali penye maji; mzee mwenye mvi; kuta zenye nyufa; udongo wenye mawe mengi; tandu wenye miguu mingi; nyumba yenye panya wengi; mto wenye maji mengi; kikapu chenye unga mwingi; soko lenye matunda mengi.

Njia yenyewe ni nyembamba. Paka mwenyewe ni mweusi lakini watoto wake ni weupe. Matunda yenyewe ni mekundu lakini mbegu zake ni nyeusi. Mfuko wenyewe ni mweupe lakini uzi wake ni mwekundu. Watu wenyewe ni wema lakini watoto wao ni walevi. Mungu mwenyewe ni mwema, na kazi zake zote ni njema. Mizigo yote ni myepesi. Miavuli yote ni myeusi. Milango yote ni myembamba. Wevi wote ni werevu. Mtama wote ni mwekundu.

6

Niliuliza, nilikaa, nilitaka, nilikuja (or naliuliza, etc.); Tulifika, tulisikia, tuliona, tulikwisha; Ulisema? ulikula? uliandika? ulipata? Mlijibu, mlitoka, mlijua, mliweza; Alisoma, alipenda, alikufa, alirudi; Walianza? waliingia? walisimama? walijaribu? Nitasimama? nitaanza? nitakuja? nitakula? Utakwenda? utajaribu? utaweza? utauliza? Atakufa, atarudi, ataandika, ataona; Tutakaa, tutasema, tutasikia, tutafika; Mtajua, mtasoma, mtajibu, mtakwisha; Watapenda, watataka, wataingia, watatoka; Nataka, napenda, naweza, naingia; Umekaa, umekwisha, umefika, umeuliza; Asikia? asema? aandika? aja? Tunakula, tunasoma, tunaanza, tunakwenda; Umejibu? umerudi? umeona? umesimama? Wanakufa? wanakuja? wanajaribu? wanasoma?

Nala, ninakula, nilikula (nalikula), nimekula, nitakula. Aenda, anakwenda, alikwenda, amekwenda, atakwenda.

Tunamtafuta punda wangu. Ajaribu kuandika. Nimeyaweka mayai katika kikapu changu. Waliomba fedha. Utavipata vitabu. Uliuvunja wembe wa mzee? Nimekuambia habari? Wataziuza nguo? Wala samaki? Unakula samaki? Unazinunua mbao?

7

Kichwa hiki, hesabu hii, shoka hili, ukubwa huu, kusoma huku; Nazi hizi, wenyeji hawa, maganda haya, ndimi hizi, ndugu hawa; Mwalimu yule, asali ile, swali lile, wizi ule, mbuzi yule; Taa zile, vioo vile, masikio yale, mbavu zile, mahali pale; Usiku huo, kijito hicho, kapu hilo, buibui huyo, jibu hilo; Ngoma hizo, miili hiyo, vyungu hivyo, mahali hapo, makanisa hayo.

Anamtafuta rafiki yake hapa. Tulimwona simba pale. Panya ataingia humu. Umezisikia habari za huko? Waarabu wawili na Wahindi watatu wamekuja kuitazama nchi yetu. Huko Unguja Waarabu wana mashamba makubwa ya mikarafuu. Humu shimoni niliona nyoka mkubwa. Mle tunduni mna asali. Mtoto wangu atakaa humu nyumbani. Nitakwenda kusimama pale mwembeni.

8

Sijui. Hatusemi. Hawaponi. Hukurudi. Hamkujibu. Hakufa. Sitakwenda. Hutakaa. Hamtajaribu. Sijaenda. Hajainunua nyumba. Hatujaipata fedha. Hujui? Huogopi? Haoni? Hawakusikia? Sikutazama? Hatukukuambia? Hutaingia? Hawatafaa? Hatutaweza? Hamjawauza mbuzi zenu? Hawajautafuta wino bado?

Wafa, wanakufa, hawafi, hawafi, walikufa, hawakufa, wamekufa, watakufa, hawatakufa, hawajafa, wataka kufa.

Adui wameingia mjini; wanaziharibu nyumba zote. Vipofu hawaoni; viziwi hawasikii; viwete hawawezi kwenda vema. Mashamba yanataka mvua; jua litaiharibu mihindi, inaanza kufa. Ng'ombe hawatoi maziwa siku hizi. Machungwa yameiva? Hayajaiva bado. Mengine yanaanza kuiva na mengine yanaoza. Nyumba yangu inataka milango; vyumba havijapata milango. Mbao hazijafika bado.

9

Kukataa, kuogopa, kuvunja, kujaribu, kufa; kuto(ku)fanya, kuto(ku)rudi, kuto(ku)weza, kuto(ku)zuia, kutokula. Njoo! Simama! Imba! Ngoja! Sema! Nendeni! Leteni! Anzeni! Jibuni! Kaeni! Usiulize. Usiogope. Usiondoke. Msitazame. Msiseme. Mwangalie. Niambie. Itafute. Zinunue. Usimwache.

Watoto wajibu. Mzee asisikie. Nikitazame kitabu chako. Tumwambie mwalimu? Walimtafuta kila mahali wasimwone.

Watoto waliomba chakula wasipate. Tulitoa fedha nyingi isitoshe. Watu wanakwenda na kurudi. Ingia ukae. Mpe kitabu asome. Mwambie mtoto asiogope. Lete unga tuutie katika kikapu. Twende mjini tununue samaki. Yaangalie machungwa yasioze. Nataka watoto waje hapa ili tupate kuanza kazi yetu. Wazee wao wamewakataza wasiifanye kazi hii. Tupike chakula ili wageni wetu wasiondoke na njaa. Iweke sukari katika sanduku ili watoto wasiione.

10

(Kama) Mtoto akilia mpe maziwa. Tukingoja hapa tuta-mwona simba. Migomba yangu ikizaa nitakupa ndizi. Watoto wakimwona nyoka wataogopa. Usipoyaficha machungwa watoto watayala. Mbao zisipotosha maseremala hawataweza kufanya kazi leo. Baba asipoipata barua yangu hatakuja. Asipokuja leo hataniona.

(Kama) Mgonjwa angepata usingizi mwema angepona upesi. Ungejaribu sana ungeweza kuifanya kazi hii. Askari wange-rudi leo wangewapata wevi. Ningepajua mahali ningekwenda mwenyewe. Mbwa wangalimsikia chui wangalilia. Mwalimu angalikuja mwenyewe angaliweza kuchagua vitabu vyake. Tusingaliyalinda (Hatungaliyalinda) mashamba yetu tumbili wangaliiiba mihindi yote. Tusingalipata mvua tusingalipata mavuno.

Simba alilia (na) ng'ombe wakaogopa. Matunda yaliiva yakaoza. Mpunga uliota ukazaa sana. Dawa ilifaa (na) mgonjwa akapona.

Hakuna mayai sokoni leo. Haidhuru; si vizuri kula mayai kila siku. Yafaa upike mboga. Itakupasa kwenda shamba(ni) uzichume. Haiwezekani, bwana, nina kazi nyingi. Mke wangu huenda huko kila siku, atazileta yeye.

11

Ngamia wanaoyachukua magunia ya tende; Wasimamizi wanaowaangalia watumwa; Rafiki yangu aliyekiandika kitabu unachokisoma; Giza lililotuzuia tusimwone nyoka; Nyama itakayooza tusipoila upesi; Maseremala watakaofanya meza na viti; Ugomvi uharibuo furaha nyumbani; Ng'ombe wazuri watupao maziwa mengi; Wahindi wasiokula nyama ya ng'ombe; Mashamba ya mpunga yasiyotosha; Kalamu aliyonipa mwalimu; Chupa aliyoivunja mtoto; Faida tutaka-yoipata tukiyauza mayai yetu; Njia watakayoifuata Wa-zungu; Kazi wanayoifanya mafundi; Kahawa tuliyoinunua dukani; Mtu asiyekujua; Mtu usiyemjua; Watu waliokwisha kazi; Kazi waliyoiisha.

Miti iliyoanguka; kondoo waliopotea; upepo ufuatao;

mashauri yasiyofaa; maji yasiyotosha. Afanyaye kazi
ataka mshahara. Aogopaye kazi hatakula. Wasiolima hawa-
tavuna. Wavunao hufurahi. Aliaye leo hucheka kesho.
Hapa ni mahali tunapopaogopa sana. Ni hapa tulipowaona
simba. Hiki ni kibanda tulimojificha. Walipoondoka tuli-
toka kibandani. Nikamwambia ndugu yangu, " Nionavyo
mimi, hawatarudi. Yafaa tuende." Akasema, " Upendavyo." Simba aliapo ni nani asiyeogopa ?
Viatu ambavyo vilipotea; Mswaki ambao ninautumia;
Wakristo ambao watakwenda kanisani; Ngoma ambayo
mwalimu ameipiga; Mbegu ambazo hazikuota; Maswali
ambayo siwezi kuyajibu; Ugonjwa ambao hautapona; Lugha
ya Kiingereza ambayo watu wengi hawaijui; Mahali ambapo
wamesimama.

12

Ambiwa, saidiwa, amkiwa, haribiwa, jibiwa, nunuliwa,
chaguliwa, zaliwa, ng'olewa, sahauliwa, uzwa, pigwa, pewa,
uawa, olewa, katwa, tafutwa, ulizwa, kataliwa, zuiwa.
Muhogo uliong'olewa; maswali yasiyojibiwa; watoto
watakaozaliwa; njia niliyoonyeshwa; shamba lisilopaliwa;
vitu vinavyotupwa; nyimbo zitakazoimbwa; mtoto asiye-
chaguliwa; mimi nisiyepewa kitu; sisi tusioambiwa.
Dawa itatiwa katika chupa. Makosa yake yamesamehewa.
Fedha nyingi inatolewa na watu. Watoto wema hupewa
sukari. Watoto wadogo wasipigwe. Hapa ni mahali ali-
pouawa chui ? Mashauri yaliyotolewa na wazee hayajaku-
baliwa na mwalimu. Kama asingalikubali (hangalikubali)
kuolewa angalipigwa na baba yake. Vitabu visiachwe hapa;
viondolewe.
Kitambaa hiki (nguo hii) huharibika upesi. Uzi ule haufai,
hukatika upesi. Kazi isipofanyika leo kuta zitaanguka.
Njia tuliyoifuata haipitiki sasa. Maneno haya hayatumiki.
Matendo yake mabaya hayafichiki; yajulika kila mahali.

13

Vitabu vingi vilikuwa vizuri, lakini kimoja, kilichokuwa cha
Hemedi, hakikuwa kizuri sana. Mikate haitakuwa mingi, na
ule katika kikapu chako utakuwa mdogo. Kama hesabu
zikiwa nyingi, watoto waliopo leo hawataziweza, zisipokuwa
fupi sana. Asali isingalikuwa (haingalikuwa) nzuri faida yetu
ingalikuwa ndogo tu. Maua yangekuwa mengi kama jua
lisingekuwa kali. Umoja uwepo katika nchi yetu, na ugomvi
usiwepo. Maji njiani ni mengi hata sasa ? Ndiyo, yangali
mengi. Huyu siye yule aliyekuwa mgonjwa. Yule aliyekuwa
mgonjwa ndiye huyu. Kisu kilichokuwamo sandukuni sicho

hiki; hiki ndicho kile kilichopotea mwaka uliopita. Mchele
huu si mzuri; mchele ulio mzuri ndio huu. Mimi siye mpishi;
huyu ndiye mpishi. Yu mgonjwa leo, na mimi ninamsaidia.
"Watoto, mpo wapi?" "Tupo hapa, mama." "Juma
yupo?" "Hayupo, yuko mjini." "Pana maji mengi pale
mlipo?" "La, mama, maji yaliyopo hapa si mengi." "Ni
nani walio pamoja nanyi?" "Ni wana wa yule mzee aliye
mgonjwa." "Mlimwacha ndugu yenu wapi?" "Pale penye
mchungwa ndipo tulipomwacha."

14

(a) Mji ulio na wenyeji wengi; Miswaki waliyo nayo watoto; mawazo aliyo nayo; vyeti alivyokuwa navyo mwalimu;
shauri walilokuwa nalo makarani; mayai aliyokuwa nayo
mpishi; uzi tuliokuwa nao; njia zitakazokuwa na hatari;
mahali patakapokuwa na maji; wale walio na fedha; fedha
waliyo nayo; mimi niliye na makosa mengi; makosa mengi
niliyo nayo. (b) Yeye asiye na kitu; chakula kisichokuwa na
chumvi; siku isiyokuwa na huzuni; dawa wasiyokuwa nayo
waganga; kusoma kusikokuwa na makosa.
Yeye ambaye hana kitu; chakula ambacho hakikuwa na
chumvi; siku ambayo haitakuwa na huzuni; dawa ambayo
hawakuwa nayo waganga; kusoma ambako hakukuwa na
makosa.
Taa isiyo na mafuta yafaa nini? Kama rafiki zako wakiwa
na shida yakupasa kuwasaidia. Je, hamna sukari? Hatuna,
tuna maziwa tu. Wazee watakuwa na mashauri kesho?
Watakuwa nayo, lakini si mengi. Kama nchi hii ingekuwa na
mvua ya kutosha ingekuwa na mavuno mazuri. Magunia
yale uliyo nayo, yana kazi? Hayana. Mwaka ujao patakuwa na duka hapa. Hakukuwa na watu wengi sokoni.
Hamkuwa na maji shimoni. Hapana hatari hapa. Kama
pangalikuwa na hatari hapa nisingalikuja.

15

Njia—ngumu, ndogo, nzuri, mbaya, mpya, chache, fupi,
kuu, pana, ndefu, nyembamba, nyeupe, nyingi, safi, zote;
Duka—dogo, zima, baya, jipya, kubwa, refu, jembamba,
jingine (lingine), lo lote, safi.
Usafi; ubora; umaskini; weusi; uvivu; utamu; ukali;
uzima; uzito; upya; habari gani? namna gani? maji ya
moto; mwana kondoo; U mzima? mara mbili; juma la
tatu; miti mingapi? arobaini na saba; mara ngapi? nusu;
adhuhuri; Alhamisi; saa ngapi? saa nane u robo; mchana
kutwa; usiku kucha; saa kumi na moja kasa dakika tano;
Ijumaa; mtu wa mwisho.

Sukari tamu hii; mti hafifu ule; miji hii sita; masoko safi yale; nyumba yangu mpya; maneno yako makali; vidole vyake kumi; miti mirefu imara; vitu vingine vingi.

Ng'ombe nilio nao mimi ni wazuri (bora) kuliko wale alio nao ndugu yangu. Mbwa hawa wote ni wakali, lakini yule wa Ali ni mkali kuliko wote. Nguo zote ni nzuri, lakini hii ni nzuri hasa. Tano mara kumi ni hamsini; hamsini mara mbili ni mia; na robo ya mia ni ishirini na tano. Jumapili, Mei kumi na tano, saa tatu asubuhi.

16

Kila mtu peke yake; jana, leo na kesho; chini na juu; ndani na nje; karibu na mbali; sasa na sikuzote; watu wote pamoja. Njoo kesho kutwa. Tazama mbele na nyuma. Alikuja juzi.

Sema kweli. Nenda polepole. Rudi upesi. Usilie hata kidogo. Sema hivi. Labda hawatataka. Walikula mno. Fanya vivyo hivyo. Sina hata kidogo. Anaomba bure, hatapata zaidi. Usinipe unga mwingi mno, nipe kidogo tu. Shamba lenu liko wapi? Mtavuna lini? Tazama kotekote. Walitazama huko na huko. Tutafanyaje?

Long ago, when the world was new, all the animals worked hard every day so that it might be a very beautiful place. The horse did an enormous amount of work, and the cow too, and the dog and the ass and the elephant also. It was the camel alone who did no work at all. He was as idle as he could be, all day long he just played. The other animals did not approve of idleness at all, and they went to the place where he lived and asked him gently, " Friend, why are you always playing? Why do you leave us to work by ourselves? " The camel said nothing. They asked him again and again without getting any answer at all. And they said, " We are speaking in vain; don't let us ask him any more; each time it is the same, perhaps his wits are not as they should be. Let us leave him to live by himself."

17

Baba, kitabu kile tulichokinunua kwa Mhindi kwa ajili ya mtoto, kiko wapi? Sikioni. Tazama ndani, nalikiweka ndani ya sanduku. Usisimame karibu na moto, simama mbali kidogo. Nitakuja baadaye, labda baada ya nusu saa. Mbwa yuko wapi? Yuko nje, yuko pamoja na mtoto wake nje ya nyumba. Mbele yetu, chini ya mlima, tuliona tembo. Usiniache peke yangu; kaa pamoja nami. Tumetoka kwa mwalimu; tunakwenda mjini kwa ndugu zetu. Mwite msimamizi aukate mti huu kwa shoka lake. Twasikia kwa

masikio yetu na kuona kwa macho yetu. Walikwenda zao
kwa furaha. Barua yako ilisomeka kwa shida tu; kwa nini
hukuandika kwa wino? Nenda mbele tu, moja kwa moja.

Kwa heri, mwalimu; utakuja kwetu lini? Kwenu ni wapi,
ni mbali? Ni mbali kidogo, lakini si sana; ni karibu na mji
ule, mbele kidogo.

As a bird that wanders far from his nest, so is a man that
wanders far from his place. Bring up a child in the way he
should go, and he will not leave it even when he is old. Even
at a time of laughter the heart is sorrowful, and the end of
mirth is heaviness of heart. In all labour there is profit, but a
multitude of words brings nothing but loss. A slothful man
does not want to plough in the winter, therefore he shall beg
in harvest and have nothing. The slothful man says, "There
is a lion outside, I shall be killed on the highway." Say not to
thy friend, " Go away and come back later, and tomorrow I
will give thee " when thou hast the thing near. The excellency
of young men is their strength, and the beauty of old men is a
head of grey hair. Boast not thyself of tomorrow, for thou
knowest not what a day will bring forth (will be born by a day).
The hearing ear and the seeing eye, the Lord is He who made
them both. These are the words of King Solomon.

18

Jibia; haribia; rudia; jia; chezea; tupia; lalia; fuatia;
pitia; achia; ombea; patia; fungulia; cheka; pimia;
simamia; pa; wekea; ficha.

Move, run away, turn, dawn, despise, forgive, boil, forget,
bear, smell, be useful, wash clothes, plait, sew, wash hands, do,
cry, sweep, uproot, agree.

Hamia, kimbilia, geukia, chea, dharaulia, samehea, chemshia,
sahaulia, zalia, nukia, falia, fulia, sukia, shonea, nawia, tendea,
lilia, fagilia, ng'olea, kubalia.

He has been badly treated. He has moved to Tanga.
Follow him. Greet him. Take him right away. Give him
money to buy bananas with. The craftsmen want rope for
measuring the site of the house. The cook is asking for soap
to wash his cloths with. Find the visitor a chair to sit on. The
road is lost to me, i.e. I have lost the road.

Wanawake wanatuchumia mboga. Mke wake amemzalia
mwana. Mtoto ameachiwa fedha na baba yake. Usiwaonee
maskini. Utuchagulie mbuzi wazuri watatu. Mfungulie mama yako mlango. Tembo wametuharibia mashamba yetu.
Nimeambiwa habari hii na Jumbe. Vitanda hivi havikulaliwa
jana. Mgonjwa anapikiwa chakula. Watoto wanatazamiwa
kazi zao. Tumepimiwa unga wa kutosha. Ninapatiwa
kitanda cha kulalia.

19

Niliwaandikia Ali na Hemedi nikawaambia, " Njoni mnipe habari zenu." Wakaja wakaniambia habari za mjini. Ali alisema ya kwamba alitaka kwenda Johannesburg kufanya kazi. Baba yake na ndugu zake walikubali, ila mama yake alikataa. Ingawa alimwomba mara nyingi, hata mara kumi, hakukubali. Hata mwisho alimwambia, " Basi, iwapo hupendi, sitakwenda, lakini kwa nini unakataa ? " Akasema, " Kwa sababu ninaogopa; najua kuna hatari huko, kwa hiyo sitaki uende." Ndiyo sababu hakuenda.

Nikamwambia, " Watu husema kuna faida huko Johannesburg, lakini, nionavyo mimi, hakuna faida bali hasara." Akasema, " Labda. Basi ni mamoja kwangu sasa nikienda nisiende."

Agree, give one another, know one another, fear one another, marry, see one another, pray for one another, love one another, fight, quarrel; dharauliana, andikiana, rudiana, kutana, jibiana, ambiana, uana, patikana, onekana, wezekana.

20

Inama kichwa. Inua mikono. Vaa viatu vyako. Fumba macho. Fumbua mkono. Amelewa. Nguo zimekauka. Mgonjwa amepona. Mtoto yule anaangukaanguka. Kazi inaharibika. Wamemwona mwanamke aliyekufa. Meza mbili na viti vinane vimekwisha. Macho yangu na meno yangu yanauma. Waliniletea kikapu kilichojaa mchele.

Mgonjwa ameamka. Nani aliyemwamsha ? Waliamkiana. Walimu waliamkiwa na watoto. Mwezi umeonekana. Tulionana jana. Mwonye mtoto. Nionyeshe barua. Anapendwa sana na mama yake. Pendana (mpendane). Jaribu kumpendeza bwana wako. Usiwapendelee watoto wako mwenyewe. Kimbia upesi. Wakimbize nguruwe. Tunapogombana mke wangu humkimbilia mama yake. Mayai hayapatikani. Kwa nini hupatani na ndugu yako ? Nalimpatanisha Ali na mkewe. Nipatie maziwa. Tumepatiwa asali.

21

All the clerks were getting on well together. These people were not related. There was nothing else to do. I had become accustomed to hear these words. The headmaster was absent. He had gone to Europe. Her trouble was she did not know how to read. The town of Zanzibar was the chief town of the slave trade. What do you do when they are ill ? If the potatoes are too few we will eat bread if it has been baked. Put on your clothes. I have already put them on.

Watu wengi walikuwa wakimsikiliza. Tulipokuwa tukiongea bwana wetu alikuwa akizifungua barua zake. Waarabu walikuwa wakiwapeleka watumwa wao sokoni kuuza. Barua niliyokuwa nikiingojea ilifika upesi. Walikuwa wakipigwa kila siku. Nilipomwona alikuwa amelewa sana. Wenyeji wa mji walikuwa wamezidi sana. Mgeni wetu alikuwa amekwisha fika. Tumekwisha (ku)mwona. Wakati ule nilikuwa nimekwisha pata watoto wawili. Binti yangu alikuwa ameanza kuonyesha maendeleo mema.

22

Ninyi wenyewe; jua lenyewe; mawe yenyewe; sisi sote; ninyi nyote; ninyi wenye watoto; embe lote; mahali po pote; miezi ipi? mti wenye matunda; siku nyingine; unga mwingi; nyufa ngapi? nzi weusi; maneno mengineyo yote; kitu cho chote utakacho; po pote tuendapo; ye yote atakayemwona; swali mojawapo; mwanangu; nduguye; mumewe; wenzetu; wakeze; siku ile ile; jibu lilo hilo (lile lile).

Mahali pangapi? vipofu wangapi? tumbili wangapi? fagio ngapi? majibu mangapi? saa ngapi? visiwa vingapi? miwa mingapi? Chuma kingi, moto mwingi, giza jingi, ugali mwingi, kusoma kwingi. Chumba kipi? mwaka upi? Mkristo yupi? ngoma ipi? uso upi? kanisa lipi? mahali papi? Visima vyote, mizizi yote, wevi wote, njia zote, mafuta yote, ulimwengu wote, viwete wote; mtu ye yote; watu wo wote.

Tunaposali yatupasa kumwamini Mungu, kumwabudu na kumsifu. Kama tukitubu atakubali ibada yetu, sala zetu na sifa zetu. Yeye, Mtoa mema yote, atatupa msaada wake na baraka yake.

Mchungaji msahaulifu aliwaacha ng'ombe zake waingie katika shamba na kuharibu mazao. Wazazi waliifurahia ndoa ya binti yao. Aliolewa na nani? Aliolewa na kijana mwema, mwana wa Jumbe.

23

Maji yako wapi? Hapa, bwana. Lete. Mtoto yuko wapi? Yuko shamba, bwana. (Nenda) kamwite. Nikimwita naye anakataa, nifanyeje? Usicheze naye wala kuongea naye: bali uende ukamwite mama yake.

Mgeni alipoingia mjini akatuamkia, nilimwambia, "Ningojee kidogo nikampe Jumbe habari." Nikaenda nikampa Jumbe habari ya kuwa nduguye amefika.

Palikuwa na mtu na mkewe; hawakuwa na kitu ila kondoo

na jogoo. Siku moja wakapata habari kwamba rafiki yao
anakuja kuwatazama. Yule mke akamwambia mumewe,
" Mume wangu, kesho mgeni wetu anakuja, nasi hatuna kitu
ila kondoo huyu na jogoo. Nami kumchinja kondoo wangu
sitaki, na kumchinja jogoo wangu sitaki. Tufanyeje ? "
Mume wake akamwambia, " Kama ni lazima tutamchinja
kondoo." Na maneno hayo kondoo na jogoo wakasikia.
Hata usiku jogoo akaanza kuwika kwa furaha, " Ko-ko-ko !
Tumchinje kondoo ! " Na kondoo akajibu, " Allah ! Allah ! "
maana yake, " Mungu apendavyo ". Kulipopambazuka mke
alisema, " Mgeni huyu anayekuja ni mgeni wa siku moja tu ;
kuna haja gani ya kumchinja kondoo ? Yafaa tumchinje
jogoo." Jogoo akakamatwa akachinjwa, na yule aliyemwa-
mini Mungu akaokoka.

24

Hili ni gazeti ambalo ndani yake (ambamo) tuliona picha ya
mji wetu. Gazeti hili ambalo jina lake ni (huitwa) Mambo
Leo, hutengenezwa Dar es Salaam. Kuna watu wengi ambao
hawajaona gazeti hilo. Huyu ndiye mtengenezaji ambaye
kazi yake inatupendeza sana. Anatafuta watu ambao waweza kuandika habari za kwao. Hupelekewa mambo mengi
ambayo hayafai sana. Ataka kupata habari kwa watu ambao
wameelimika vema na kuweza kutumainiwa. Gazeti hupigwa
chapa kwa mashine ambazo huendeshwa kwa umeme. Tunge-
penda kuwa na gazeti ambalo latokea kila juma wala si mara
moja kwa mwezi tu.

25

Pana watu hapa ? Leo hapana ; kesho patakuwa na watu
wengi kwa sababu ni siku ya soko. Mna maji kisimani ?
Hamna sasa ; jana mlikuwa na kidogo, lakini sasa yamekauka.
Kuna matunda madukani ? Si mengi ila ndizi tu. Hapa petu
hapana hatari. Hapo zamani palikuwa na mtu na mkewe.
Asubuhi kulipokucha yule mtu aliondoka. Huko alikokwenda
kulikuwa na mto mkubwa. Mtoni mlikuwa na samaki wengi.
Alitafuta mahali panapo majani marefu akajificha mle. Nionyeshe mahali alipokuwapo nyoka ulipomwona. Alikuwa
papa hapa penye shimo hili. Ni humu alimoingia jana. Ni
wapi walipoonekana adui ? Ni pale penye miembe ya Waarabu.
Hapakuwa na askari pale ? Askari hawakuwapo. Walikuwapo
usiku, lakini kulipopambazuka walikwenda zao. Huko mjini
kumekufa watu wawili. Kumekuja mtoto kutupa habari. Mji
umeingia ndui. Ugonjwa umeingia katika mji wetu nao, watu
hufa kila siku.

26

Shikamoo, mama.
Marahaba, mwanangu, hujambo?
Sijambo, mama.
Habari za kwenu?
Njema, mama, lakini ndugu yangu Anna hawezi (yu mgonjwa).
Ana nini?
Ana homa.
Haji shule leo?
Hataweza, yuko kitandani.
Basi, mpe pole.
Asante, mama.

Hodi! Hodi!
Come in, sir, come in.   What is the news of many days?
Very good.
Are you well?
I am well, father; and you, are you well?
I am well, but not very; I have a cough.
I am sorry.   Since when?
Since the beginning of the month.
Have you any medicine?
Yes, I went to the dispensary and got some, and it is doing me much good.
I am very glad.   I have come to give you news of your son, Clerk Peter.
Is he well?
He is well, and he has sent you a little money to buy clothes.
Thank you, sir, thank you very much.   Say thank you to him.
All right.   I must go now, the sun is setting, and I live some way away.   Good-bye.
Good-bye, sir; give my greetings to everyone.

27

Pwani ya mashariki; Afrika ya Kusini; wenyeji wa Afrika ya Magharibi; nchi za kaskazini; ng'ambo ya bahari; mkono wa kuume; mguu wake wa kushoto; mtoto wa upande wa kuume; nusu gunia la mchele; masika; shilingi mbili u nusu; Yadi mbili kasa robo; nusu shilingi (senti hamsini, thumuni); Sultani wa Unguja; Askofu wa Mombasa; lugha ya kigeni; Kiarabu.

Katika duka la kijijini.

What is the price of this material?

Two shillings and twenty-five cents a yard.

And for a whole bale?

I will sell you the whole bale for seventy-five shillings.

Too much! I cannot manage it. Cannot you make it less?

Well, mother, take the whole bale for seventy shillings.

All right. I will take a bale; I want to make some hospital clothes. Is it good material?

Very good; it washes well and lasts a long time.

Good.

What else, madam?

I want two tins of paraffin, four bottles of coconut oil, and a sack of maize flour. How do you sell sugar?

Sixteen shillings the frasila.

Can I get a whole sack?

Yes, even two, if you want them.

One will be enough. Write the bill; I will send (bring) the money tomorrow when the things have arrived.

ADVERTISING & PUBLICITY   ALGEBRA   AMATEUR ACTING   AN
BOOK-KEEPING   BRICKWORK   BRINGING UP CHILDREN   BUSI
CHESS   CHINESE   COMMERCIAL ARITHMETIC   COMMERCIAL
COMPOSE MUSIC   CONSTRUCTIONAL DETAILS   CONTRACT BRIDG
SPEEDWORDS   ECONOMIC GEOGRAPHY   ECONOMICS   ELEC
ENGLISH GRAMMAR   LITERARY APPRECIATION   ENGLISH RENA
REVIVAL   VICTORIAN AGE   CONTEMPORARY LITERATURE   ETC
FREELANCE WRITING   FRENCH   FRENCH DICTIONARY   FRENC
LIVING THINGS   GEOLOGY   GEOMETRY   GERMAN   GERMA
GOOD CONTROL OF INSECT PESTS   GOOD CONTROL OF PLANT D
GOOD FARMING BY MACHINE   GOOD FARM WORKMANSHIP   G
GOOD MARKET GARDENING   GOOD MILK FARMING   GOOD PIG
GOOD ENGLISH   GREEK   GREGG SHORTHAND   GUIDEBOOK TO
GREAT   BOLIVAR   BOTHA   CATHERINE THE GREAT   CHATHAM   C
LIBERALISM   HENRY V   JOAN OF ARC   JOHN WYCLIFFE   LENIN   LOU
ROBES

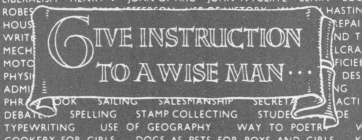

GIVE INSTRUCTION
TO A WISE MAN···

HASTIN
HOUS   REPAI
WRIT   ND T
MECH   LCRA
MOTO   FICIE
PHYSI   DES
ADMI   NG
PHR   OOK   SAILING   SALESMANSHIP   SECRETA   ACTI
DEBAT   SPELLING   STAMP COLLECTING   STUDE   DE
TYPEWRITING   USE OF GEOGRAPHY   WAY TO POETR   V
COOKERY FOR GIRLS   DOGS AS PETS FOR BOYS AND GIRLS   K
PHOTOGRAPHY FOR BOYS AND GIRLS   RADIO FOR BOYS   RIDIN
SOCCER FOR BOYS   STAMP COLLECTING FOR BOYS AND GIRLS
ACTING   ANATOMY   ARABIC   ASTRONOMY   BANKING
CHILDREN   BUSINESS ORGANISATION   CALCULUS   CANASTA
COMMERCIAL ART   COMMERCIAL CORRESPONDENCE   COMM
CONTRACT BRIDGE   COOKING   CRICKET   DRAWING   DR
ECONOMICS   ELECTRICITY   ELECTRICITY IN THE HOUSE   ELC
ENGLISH RENASCENCE   ENGLISH RENASCENCE TO THE ROMAN
LITERATURE   ETCHING   EVERYDAY FRENCH   TO EXPRESS YO
DICTIONARY   FRENCH PHRASE BOOK   GARDENING   GAS IN
GERMAN   GERMAN DICTIONARY   GERMAN GRAMMAR   GERM
CONTROL OF PLANT DISEASES   GOOD FARM ACCOUNTING
GOOD FARM WORKMANSHIP   GOOD FRUIT FARMING   GOOD
GOOD MILK FARMING   GOOD PIG KEEPING   GOOD POULTRY
GREGG SHORTHAND   GUIDEBOOK TO THE BIBLE   HINDUSTAN
CATHERINE THE GREAT   CHATHAM   CLEMENCEAU   CONSTANTINE
ARC   JOHN WYCLIFFE   LENIN   LOUIS XIV   MILTON   PERICLES   PETEF
USE OF HISTORY   WARREN HASTINGS   WOODROW WILSON   HO
HOUSEHOLD ELECTRICITY   HOUSE REPAIRS   ITALIAN   JOIN
MANAGEMENT   MATHEMATICS   HAND TOOLS   ENGINEER
DRAUGHTSMANSHIP   METEOROLOGY   MODELCRAFT   MODERN
MUSIC   NORWEGIAN   PERSONAL EFFICIENCY   PHILOSOPHY
SHORTHAND   PLANNING AND DESIGN   PLUMBING   POLISH